BROMLE

3 0128 0

D0548055

The Cock
Lane Ghost

The Cock Lane Ghost

Murder, Sex and Haunting
in Dr Johnson's London

Paul Chambers

SUTTON PUBLISHING

First published in 2006 by
Sutton Publishing Limited · Phoenix Mill
Thrupp · Stroud · Gloucestershire · GL5 2BU

Copyright © Paul Chambers, 2006

All rights reserved. No part of this publication may be reproduced, stored in a
retrieval system, or transmitted, in any form, or by any means, electronic,
mechanical, photocopying, recording or otherwise, without the prior permission
of the publisher and copyright holder.

Paul Chambers hereby asserts the moral right to be identified as the author of
this work.

British Library Cataloguing in Publication Data
A catalogue record for this book is available from the British Library.

ISBN 0-7509-3869-2

BROMLEY PUBLIC LIBRARIES	
02674678	
Bertrams	06.05.06
133.129421	£14.99
DELANE	

Typeset in 11/14pt Garamond.
Typesetting and origination by
Sutton Publishing Limited.
Printed and bound in England by
J.H. Haynes & Co. Ltd, Sparkford.

Contents

ACKNOWLEDGEMENTS

The researching and writing of this book were by no means a solo process, and my profound thanks go to all those people who were kind enough to offer me their time, advice and knowledge. In particular I would like to thank the staff at the following institutions for allowing me access to their records and for their patience when answering my many questions: Bodleian Library; British Library; British Newspaper Library; Cambridge County Record Office; Cambridge University Library; Family Records Centre (National Archives); Guildhall Library, London; Institute for Historical Research; The National Archives: Historical Manuscripts Commission; The National Archives: Public Record Office; Norfolk Record Office; Royal Historical Society; Society of Genealogists and University College London.

A big thank you must go to my agent, Sugra Zaman of Watson, Little Ltd, for her sterling work on my behalf and to the magnificent staff at Sutton, especially Christopher Feeney and Hilary Walford, whose advice and patience are greatly appreciated. I also offer my particular gratitude to John Baxter and Michael Davies, who volunteered to read the typescript and whose comments and corrections are invaluable. Finally, I must thank my wife, Rachel, for her patience and her ability to fit around the strange hours and habits of an author, and my daughter, Eleanor, my parents and my parents-in-law for their support and encouragement.

PREFACE

Several years ago I found myself in London's Charing Cross Road with half an hour to spare. I decided to spend it browsing one of the second-hand bookshops for which this road is justifiably famous. I made only one purchase, a battered modern edition of Charles Mackay's *Extraordinary Popular Delusions and the Madness of Crowds*, a work that was originally published in 1841. *Extraordinary Popular Delusions* is a compendium of historical episodes where large numbers of people have been taken in by various financial, religious or other scams, usually through their own gullibility. By his own admission Mackay wrote the work to 'collect the most remarkable instances of those moral epidemics which show how easily the masses have been led astray, and how imitative and gregarious men are, even in their infatuations and crimes'.

It was several weeks before I started to read the book and months more before I reached the section entitled 'haunted houses'. It was there that I read Mackay's description of a scandal that had excited all Britain in 1762. A house in a narrow, medieval-looking London street called Cock Lane was at the heart of the scandal.

Prior to this I had not heard of Cock Lane, but, nonetheless, within days I was scouring London's libraries for further information. I quickly discovered that the brief description given in *Extraordinary Popular Delusions* did not do the scandal any justice. Spurred into searching other local and national archives, I gradually gathered the small snippets of information that by themselves meant little but that, when joined together, formed part of a great jigsaw.

As the pieces fell into place, a compelling true story began to emerge that contained many plots and subplots, some of which could have come directly from a detective novel, others perhaps from a gothic horror, a comic farce or a love story. The central characters were no less varied. They were all colourful, forceful and, in most cases, deeply flawed. Some showed naivety, ignorance, cowardice or greed, others were vain, calculating, vengeful and even murderous.

Add to this the volatile nature of eighteenth-century London society, and it is little wonder that in 1762 the Cock Lane affair had the entire country in an uproar. The story's heady mixture of sex, murder and the supernatural eventually dragged in the clergy, members of parliament, royalty, the Lord Mayor and even leading lights of the literary world such as Samuel Johnson and Oliver Goldsmith. Cock Lane created such an outcry that the story entered English folklore and remained entrenched in the public's imagination until the time of the First World War.

It took me several years to research the story to its full extent and I will admit that there were times when it obsessed me. Thanks to the bountiful historical archives that Britain has seen fit to preserve, I have been able to take Mackay's (and others') brief summary of this case and find the necessary evidence to expand it into the gripping and twisted tale that it really is. Furthermore, I believe that I am telling this story in its entirety for the first time in over two centuries and possibly for the first time ever in print. Although the Cock Lane affair might at times seem unbelievable, what follows is in fact a true story.

1

THE DRUNKEN PARISH CLERK

Richard Parsons was more often than not the architect of his own misfortune. He was a habitual drunkard, and his shambling figure was a common sight on the cobbled streets of London's west Smithfield. On most nights Parsons would stagger out of the Wheat Sheaf public house and, fuelled with as much brandy as he could afford that evening, weave his way homeward singing bawdy songs. According to the writer Horace Walpole, Richard Parsons was 'a drunken parish clerk', while Dr Samuel Johnson referred to him as an 'impostor' and a 'fraud'. Dipsomania and an untrustworthy nature were just a selection of the many bad habits exhibited by Richard Parsons. Generally, if there was anything untoward taking place in his neighbourhood, then a penny to a pound Mr Parsons would have a hand in it.[1]

It was a normal Sunday morning in October 1759 when Richard Parsons got up early and, while almost certainly nursing a hangover, dressed himself and walked the short distance between his house and his place of work at St Sepulchre's church. As one of the church's officiating clerks, Parsons was required to attend all the Sunday services, helping to organise the furniture and offering assistance to frail, ill or bewildered parishioners.

St Sepulchre's parish church lies at the heart of the City of London, just a short walk from St Paul's Cathedral. On this particular Sunday, Richard Parsons was fussing about in the pews, preparing for a morning service, when he spied a handsome young couple enter the church. The man and woman were strangers to Parsons and were better dressed than the majority of the parish's impoverished population. Personal wealth was a quality that Parsons found greatly attractive, and, as he guided the couple from the doorway to a vacant pew, he made a point of introducing himself. After the service had finished Parsons approached the couple and engaged them in conversation.[2]

The man, who looked to be no more than 30 years old, introduced himself as William Kent and his companion as his wife, Frances, who preferred to go by the name of Fanny. They explained that they were new to the neighbourhood and needed somewhere to lodge for a few months while some building work was completed on a property they had purchased. They asked Parsons if he knew of a local lodging house that might be able to accommodate them.

To Parsons this was the best possible news. His own house was just around the corner and in it was a spare room that he would let out to lodgers. The thought of having tenants who might actually be able to pay their way was an attractive proposition, and to his relief the young couple agreed to take a look at the room. The trio made the short walk from St Sepulchre's church to the western end of a narrow thoroughfare named Cock Lane where Parsons lived with his wife and two daughters.

The Parsons' house was a tall terraced affair, only a couple of rooms wide but with three floors and a deep cellar. It was rented but had been neglected by both the owner and his tenants and was far from luxurious. A few years later one visitor described it as being 'wretchedly small and miserable'.[3] However, William and Fanny urgently needed accommodation, and, as we shall see, they were also seeking anonymity. A deal was struck, and within a few days William and Fanny Kent were living under the same roof as Richard Parsons and his family.

As the days and weeks passed, so William and Fanny began to learn something of their landlord and of the new neighbourhood into which they had moved. Richard Parsons was a rough-and-ready sort with a minimal amount of education who had spent most of his adult life working at St Sepulchre's church. Aged 44, he was at least the third generation of his family to have lived and worked in the streets around Cock Lane. In time Parsons had become an officiating clerk at the church and was in charge of relatively menial tasks such as stocktaking. It was a thankless job with few prospects, but it was at least gainful and steady employment.[4]

St Sepulchre's church was located near to the infamous Newgate prison, home to some of the capital's most notorious criminals plus anybody awaiting public execution at the famous Tyburn gallows. Newgate prison provided Richard Parsons with one of his more unusual duties in which he had to fulfil the terms of a bequest made to the parish by one Robert Dew. In 1605 Dew gave St Sepulchre's church £50, a hand bell and instructions that, on the night before an execution, a person from the church was to stand outside the prison, as close to the condemned person's cell as possible, ring the hand bell and read out a lengthy and sanctimonious speech beseeching the prisoner to repent.

One can imagine the inebriated figure of Parsons, clanging bell in hand, outside the prison wall mumbling his way through Dew's excruciating rhyming couplets:

> You prisoners that are within,
> Who for wickedness and sin,
> After many mercies shewn to you,
> Are now appointed to die tomorrow . . .

One witness to this scene commented that 'upon these occasions there is generally so much noise that nobody can hear one word the bellman says'.[5]

In 1745, and with his job as officiating clerk secure, Parsons married Elizabeth Ball, a local girl some thirteen years his junior. The couple became the tenants of a house on Cock Lane, where they had two children, Betty born in 1749 and a second daughter Anne, born in 1753.[6]

By rights the Parsons should have been better off than many other London families. Richard's job at the church was permanent and brought in a regular, if not spectacular, wage that would have been more than enough to feed and clothe Elizabeth and the children. However, this stability was illusory. Like so many other families of the day, Parsons's steady job and family planning did not reveal the true story of his finances. Richard Parsons had a drink problem, a legacy of the so-called gin craze that had engulfed London's lower classes.

The gin craze began in the 1720s after the government effectively ended the policing of the sale of liquor by shopkeepers. This 'reform' permitted alcohol (the cheapest form of which was gin) to be sold not just in pubs and taverns but at any and every outlet. By 1740 over 7,000 gin outlets existed in London alone, tots of the stuff even being sold by people pushing wheelbarrows and handcarts through the streets. A few pence could buy enough gin to put the average man into a coma: it was not long before the streets of London were swimming with the incapably drunk.

The artist William Hogarth, ever keen to reveal society's underbelly, captured the horror of the situation in *Gin Lane* (1751), in which paralytic Londoners lie sprawled about the streets unable to work, feed themselves or take care of their children. (Hogarth compares this desolation with *Beer Street*, the cartoon's companion piece, where all is prosperity and good cheer.) At the height of this craze over eleven million gallons of gin were sold on the London streets, much of it drunk by the underclass that inhabited the city's slums. Productivity declined and crime levels rose while death rates soared. London was in the grip of rampant alcoholism, which by the 1750s had begun to tear at society's fabric.

Things became so bad that the government, which was by nature non-interventionist, was forced to act. In 1751 a series of new licensing laws saw a clampdown on the many 'gin shops' and street vendors that had sprung up during the previous decades. The inevitable result was a hike in the cost of spirits. Overnight the thousands of alcoholics created by the gin craze, including Richard Parsons, were forced to pay more for their favourite tipple. By the time of William and Fanny's arrival at Cock Lane, a good percentage of Richard Parsons's wages was disappearing straight into the coffers of various local public houses. He was especially likely to be found at the Wheat Sheaf, located almost next door to his own residence on Cock Lane and run by his friend James Franzen, a man Oliver Goldsmith once described as being a 'weak, ignorant publican'.[7]

Parsons's drink problem put the family on the breadline, but their situation was not unusual, and, despite living in a marriage in which there was a shortage of money and an excess of alcohol, Elizabeth does not seem to have been that unhappy with her lot. After all, debt and alcoholism were facts of life for many eighteenth-century Londoners.

Of Richard and Elizabeth's children, we know very little about their youngest daughter, Anne, aged 6 at the time of the Kents' arrival. However, her elder sister Elizabeth, known to all as Betty, achieved a dubious renown and has even managed to gain an entry in the modern *Dictionary of National Biography*.[8]

Betty Parsons was aged 10 in 1759 and was a streetwise child. She was extrovert and confident with strangers, was mischievous and could, when the occasion required it, be an adept liar. Her schooldays, if they existed at all, are likely to have been short, and, with the four-year gap between her and her younger sister, Betty would have been a relatively self-contained individual. But, despite some bad points, Betty also had a tender side and appears to have craved affection, especially from her father, and would go to some lengths to get it. Betty's willingness to go along with her father's ill-thought-out schemes would later be a cause of her parents' downfall.

During the first few weeks of William and Fanny's residency, Richard and Elizabeth Parsons went out of their way to accommodate their new lodgers. Despite what must have been cramped conditions and the obvious difference in their background, the Parsons and the Kents found that they could get along quite well. Maybe this was because Richard Parsons was, for a while at least, on his best behaviour, or maybe it was because William had not twigged to, or didn't care about, his landlord's heavy drinking and other bad habits. Either way, the two men were at ease with each another, falling readily into conversation. Bit by bit Mr Parsons began to learn about his tenants.

William had told his hosts that he and Fanny were newly-weds from the county of Norfolk who had moved to London so that William could become a trader in stocks and shares. To accomplish this he was in the process of selling up his Norfolk business interests so that he could buy and furnish a house for himself and Fanny.

To this end William had already found a property on Bartlett Court in nearby Clerkenwell, but it was run down and in need of extensive repairs before the couple could move in. Ordinarily that would not have been a great problem, but William confided to Parsons that there was an urgency to the proceedings. The house had to be made habitable by the coming February for Fanny was five months pregnant and William wanted the couple to be properly housed by the time of the birth. Richard Parsons, who had perhaps already become used to the income provided by his lodgers, now knew that he had only a few months before they left. The prospect of losing a well-to-do acquaintance like William Kent was not a pleasing one.[9]

In the short term Parsons had no need to worry. William was finding it hard to extricate himself from his former business interests. This often required him to travel back to Norfolk, where he stayed for several days at a time. Fanny was unhappy about these frequent absences and, as her pregnancy advanced, demanded that William take on a domestic servant to help with her day-to-day chores as well as to keep her company. The Parsons agreed, and in due course a girl named Esther Carlisle was taken on, possibly at the recommendation of Parsons's publican friend James Franzen. Esther had her own lodgings and so would come to Cock Lane daily. She had been lucky to find a position with the Kents, as at that time there were more young girls in London than there were domestic positions for them to fill. The unlucky ones would end up on the streets, where they would be preyed upon by unscrupulous brothel-keepers and others eager to exploit their naivety.

If Esther had been lucky, then so too had William and Fanny Kent. Their new servant turned out to be an intelligent, honest, hard-working girl with a strong personality. Esther was no fool and was quickly mistrustful of the Parsons family, but she got on well with William and Fanny and remained ferociously loyal even after her time with them had finished.

Esther's most striking physical characteristic was her bright red hair, which was so distinctive that within a few days of her arriving in Cock Lane she had picked up the remarkably unoriginal nickname of 'Carrots'. Betty Parsons was especially fond of this name and used it continually. The label stuck and was soon used by everyone in the street. Only Fanny and William continued to use Esther's real first name, while she, as most servants did, referred to them as her 'master' and 'mistress'.[10]

Esther's success meant that by the late autumn of 1759 all appeared to be going smoothly for the young lodgers. Indeed, Richard Parsons and William Kent were getting on well, so much so that Richard decided that the time was right to approach his lodger for the loan of some money. Richard took William to one side and spun him a yarn about being temporarily short of funds. In fact, he complained that, without a loan, he would be unable to feed his family that week. William, surprisingly, agreed to lend his feckless landlord twelve guineas – a hefty sum that would have been enough to feed the entire Parsons family in quite some style for several weeks or more.

An agreement was signed in which Richard promised that he would repay William at the rate of one guinea a month for a year. The fact that William and Fanny would have moved out of his house before the end of the loan's term was not considered to be a problem, as they would be living nearby. When the other residents of Cock Lane got wind of the arrange-ment, they must have had a chuckle at William's naivety: it was well known that Richard Parsons and cash loans were not a good combination.

It was shortly after making this loan that William made a second and much more grievous error: he took Richard into his confidence and told him his deepest secret. Both men would spend the next few years bitterly regretting what was said that day. It was to cost both of them dearly. The secret that William divulged to his landlord concerned the truth behind his and Fanny's arrival in London. There was a lot more to it than William just wanting to become a City businessman. In fact, William and Fanny's history together turned out to be a tragic tale of forbidden love and family jealousy.

By birth William was a native of Norwich, a city on England's windswept eastern coastline.[11] His father, Thomas, was a weaver who, like many in the town, was a manufacturer of worsted, a specialist and expensive cloth that was local to the region.[12] The scale of the worsted business in Norwich was such that almost everyone in Heigham parish, where William's father Thomas Kent was based, was involved in the trade in one form or another including some of Thomas's brothers. By the time of William Kent's birth, in 1729, his father was a freeman of Norwich and a successful local businessman.[13]

William's mother, Elizabeth, was actually Thomas Kent's second wife, his first wife Mary having died before 1717.[14] There was a sizeable age gap between Thomas and Elizabeth, and by the time of William's birth Thomas was 48; a few years later Elizabeth Kent found herself a young widow, her husband having died in his early fifties. Elizabeth chose not to remarry and around the year 1752 she uprooted herself, William (and possibly William's brother Robert and his sister Elizabeth) from Norwich and moved twenty miles away inland to central Norfolk and the rural parish of Mileham. When Elizabeth arrived at Mileham, she was a moderately wealthy woman and able to support herself and her immediate family comfortably.[15]

By 1756 only William, who was then in his late twenties, remained living with his mother. From what we know of William's adult life, he seems to have lacked ambition; he not only lived at home with his mother but was also apt to daydream of get-rich-quick schemes and of one day leaving the rural surroundings of Mileham parish for the excitement of London. His father's money had bought William a good start in life. He was healthy and educated but his mother still controlled the purse strings and so William did not have the financial means to leave the parish and set up on his own. For the time being he was stuck in rural Norfolk.[16]

Samuel Foote's satirical play *The Orators*, which was written as the Cock Lane scandal unfolded and was in part based on it, offers a character sketch of the adult William Kent as he appeared to possibly biased observers. Shadrach Bodkin, the character based on Kent, is portrayed as a good-looking but overly confident young man whose opinion of himself was far too high. When Shadrach Bodkin (that is, William) is asked about his career as a tailor, he replies that his is not just an ordinary career in the textile industry but instead 'a compelling' that racks his whole body. There are hints too that William was a womaniser. When asked whether he has communed with other men's wives, Bodkin replies, 'Yea, and with widows, and with maidens.' This, of course, could all be artistic licence, but, given later events, one can understand why William was widely perceived as being a self-deluded character with an eye for the ladies.

However, back in 1756 William was still a bachelor and was living the high life in Mileham village. He had found himself a job as manager of the local inn, situated on a main road that ran direct to the large port of King's Lynn.[17] His work brought him into close contact with many local people, including those from the parish of Litcham, situated immediately to the east of Mileham along the same trunk road. It is possibly through his job that William came into contact with the Lynes family.

The Lynes were a prominent local family whose ancestors had been lords of a manor in the nearby village of Little Dunham. In the early 1700s Thomas Lynes, a younger son in the family, and his wife, Susan, moved to Litcham, where they bought a sizeable estate on the outskirts of the parish. The couple produced two sons and five daughters, all of whom lived with them on the estate.

By the time that William Kent and his mother had moved to Mileham, Thomas and Susan Lynes were both dead. However, the seven Lynes children continued to live on the family estate, with the welfare of the five daughters being placed in the hands of Thomas and John Lynes, their two sons. By 1756 the eldest daughter, Catherine, had married and left home, while the next youngest, Anne, had left Litcham to go and live on her own in London. This left the three youngest daughters living with their brother John: their names were Susan, Elizabeth and Frances.[18]

During 1756 William Kent and Elizabeth Lynes became friendly with one another, although the exact circumstance of their meeting is not known. The few brief descriptions that we have of Elizabeth and William paint the couple as vivacious and handsome. Both were the younger of several siblings and from wealthy backgrounds, although William's family of Norwich weavers were distinctly *nouveau riche* in comparison to the gentrified pedigree of the Lynes. William and Elizabeth were dreamers and apt to fall in love at the drop of a hat and were in many ways well suited for one another. Their mutual attraction can surely have been of little great surprise to their friends.[19]

The liaison between Elizabeth and William was by no means welcomed in all quarters. Elizabeth's elder brother John, in whose house she still lived, strongly disapproved of the relationship. The landed gentry were notoriously protective of their sisters and daughters, as there was the very real danger that they could be taken advantage of by somebody who was more interested in their potential inheritance than their physical and spiritual well-being.

Marrying into a well-to-do family was the eighteenth-century equivalent of winning the lottery, and potential suitors were thoroughly vetted. Indeed, it was not unusual for wealthy parents to ignore their daughters' feelings altogether and pick their husbands for them. This not only stopped unwanted suitors from claiming a stake of the family inheritance, but it also allowed the parents to marry their daughters into other wealthy families so that they themselves could benefit from the social connections that this would bring. Anyone who has read Jane Austen's *Pride and Prejudice* will be familiar with the anguish that Mrs Bennet had when trying to find suitable husbands for her four daughters.

In the absence of her parents, Elizabeth's two brothers were in charge of her moral welfare, and they proved to be very protective of their sisters. John Lynes (and therefore probably also his brother Thomas) was less than convivial towards the idea of William Kent pursuing Elizabeth. But, before the Lynes could express their disapproval of William and Elizabeth's relationship, their worst fears were confirmed. In mid-February 1757 it was a humble William Kent who came to the Lynes' house in order to break the news that their sister Elizabeth was expecting a child and that he was the father.[20]

2

A BIRTH, SOME DEATHS
AND AN ELOPEMENT

Marriage arrangements, even in the comparatively recent past, were surprisingly haphazard. In Hanoverian England a pregnancy out of wedlock was not an unusual occurrence and was often the event that persuaded two long-standing lovers to tie the knot, sometimes to the relief of their families. However, John Lynes is unlikely to have expressed relief at the news of his sister's unplanned pregnancy, as it meant she would have been forced to marry William Kent. In any other circumstance such a marriage would have been prevented by him.

Although out-of-wedlock pregnancies were an accepted fact of life, marriages were public affairs where anyone could just turn up and watch the proceedings. The sight of an obviously pregnant bride would set tongues wagging and could make life a misery for the child. For this reason, unexpected pregnancies necessitated a speedy wedding before the bride's bump became too prominent.

Only a few years previously William and Elizabeth's situation would not have been a problem, as a wedding could have been organised at very short notice. But in 1753 Lord Hardwicke passed his Clandestine Marriage Act, which required engaged couples to announce their intention to marry in their respective parish churches on the three Sundays preceding the wedding. This law was passed in response to a number of high-profile cases where unscrupulous men had kidnapped wealthy heiresses and married them by force in front of crooked priests, some of whom would perform the ceremony from their prison cell! This public announcement in local churches gave parishioners a chance to object to the wedding, and it is known to have prevented several bigamous marriages from taking place after the pre-existing wife or husband got to hear of a spouse's unlawful intentions.[1]

Lord Hardwicke's act placed an irksome hurdle in the way of William and Elizabeth's urgent need to wed, and it was early March before the ceremony could go ahead. It was customary for the wedding to take place in the bride's church, and so it was that on Tuesday 8 March 1757 William Kent and Elizabeth Lynes walked up the aisle of Litcham parish church, made their vows before the priest and left as man and wife, much to the chagrin of her brothers.[2]

The daydreaming lovers had been thrust into the real world and would now be forced to take responsibility for their own actions, and their first priority was to leave the district. The delays caused by the marriage act meant that by the time of their wedding Elizabeth was already in her third month of pregnancy. The time gap was such that most parishioners would be able to work out from the child's birth date that Elizabeth must have been pregnant prior to the marriage. The couple had to make a tactical withdrawal from the Litcham area before the pregnancy became too advanced and then not return until several months after the child's birth.

William probably hoped that he and Elizabeth could be despatched to London, but someone, possibly John Lynes or perhaps William's mother, had other ideas. Instead of London, William and Elizabeth were to be sent twenty miles south of Litcham to the remote country parish of Stoke Ferry. Here he (or the Lynes) had purchased a concession for the couple to run a country inn.[3] William was at last to become a businessman of sorts, although it was not perhaps exactly what he wanted. Stoke Ferry was a very small village and there are few details about William and Elizabeth's time there, but by all accounts they were happy together and very much in love. William himself described his new life with Elizabeth as a being a time of 'great love, harmony and friendship' and they 'enjoyed all the happiness a married state could bestow'.[4]

Even so, Elizabeth's enforced isolation from Litcham caused her to miss her friends and family. To ease her loneliness it was agreed that Frances Lynes, known to all as Fanny, should travel down from Litcham to be a companion to her elder sister and also help her through the latter stages of her pregnancy. Thus it was that William, Elizabeth and Fanny spent a contented summer together in Stoke Ferry, awaiting the child's birth.

Elizabeth's pregnancy went to full term, and around 15 September 1757 her labour began and the local midwife was summoned. Childbirth in the eighteenth century presented a serious risk to the lives of both mother and baby. Elizabeth would have gone through the childbirth process aided solely by a female midwife who, according to Dr William Smellie, an authority on childbirth, ought to be 'a decent, sensible woman, of a middle age, able to bear fatigue'.[5]

If the literature of the time is to be believed, then at the first sign of labour Elizabeth would have been sent to bed to await the arrival of the midwife. There were no effective anaesthetics, but as the contraction pains got closer together Elizabeth would have been offered glasses of diluted wine in order to dull the pain. When the pain became severe, then the wine would have been abandoned in favour of gin or brandy. During the final stage of labour small amounts of laudanum would be administered. Throughout the labour the midwife would check on the baby's position and progress by occasionally putting her hand into the mother's vagina, a painful process that necessitated the administration of more wine or gin. It is a far cry from today's controlled birth techniques but was nonetheless functional and served the mother and child as well as could be expected.

William was almost certainly not present during the labour and birth, as this was discouraged by midwives. He would probably have waited in another room or gone to a friend's house to await further news. Fanny, on the other hand, may well have attended her sister through the entire process, as the presence of female relatives was thought to be advantageous to the patient.[6]

Despite the wine, gin and laudanum, childbirth remained a painful and traumatic process that demanded a prodigious amount of energy and the loss of a great deal of blood. At the moment of birth the mother could be in a dangerously weakened state and suffering from blood loss or from wounds that could pick up an infection. This was especially true for first-time mothers.

The baby might not fare much better. It too would be exhausted and weakened from its time in the birth canal. The midwives' remedy of pouring wine down the newborn baby's throat or even squirting it up their nostrils is unlikely to have helped matters much. Nor did washing the baby in beer and butter, another recommended course of action.

Elizabeth's labour did not proceed well and the birth became complicated. The baby was eventually delivered alive, but the trauma proved to be too much for the gentle Elizabeth, who died shortly afterwards, probably from loss of blood. William was now the father of a baby boy, but as a consequence had lost his beloved wife. Just six months after his marriage, the young William Kent was a widower.

The following Saturday, William, Fanny and other friends and family gathered at Stoke Ferry parish church to witness the burial of Elizabeth Kent. The sadness of the occasion would scarcely have been lifted by the christening of William and Elizabeth's son, who was also given the name of William.[7]

In the weeks following Elizabeth's death William became desolate and for a while lost interest in his business, sinking instead into a deep depression. To help him through this period of melancholia Fanny remained living with him, looking after the baby and acting as the household's governess.

The trauma of childbirth had left the newborn William in a vulnerable state, and the onset of autumn saw the child become weaker and prone to illness. William and Fanny were forced to watch as the sickly infant struggled to survive, resisting all attempts at medical treatment. It was hopeless, and on 19 November, barely two months after his birth, William Kent junior was lowered into his mother's grave at Stoke Ferry churchyard.[8]

The death of his son was the final straw for William, who determined to quit Stoke Ferry and begin a new life elsewhere. Unfortunately, the concession on his public house still had over a year to run, and, try as he might, he could not extricate himself from the contract, nor did he have the money to buy his way out. For the time being he was stuck in his house at Stoke Ferry, haunted by the memory of his dead wife and child. The only comfort available to him was Fanny, who, after the child's death, had been allowed to remain with William, working as his housekeeper.

Fanny Lynes is described as being very much like her dead sister Elizabeth both physically and in personality, and it was perhaps inevitable that William, who came to rely on her emotionally, would start to develop feelings of affection. Fanny reciprocated, and within a short time William and Fanny found themselves in love. In his defence William later implied that the liaison was an inevitability. 'I always had a great affection for my wife,' he explained, 'and her sister now living with me and she being very much like my wife in temper and person, I conceived a great love for her and she the same for me.' He also said that the relationship had started as a result of the deep conversations that he and Fanny would have in the months following Elizabeth's death.[9]

William and Fanny's affection for one another placed them in an awkward and socially dangerous position. They might well have been in love, but they were not married, and, furthermore, they were living under the same roof. If a single word of their mutual attraction were to find its way into Stoke Ferry, then the swift action of the gossips' tongues would guarantee a scandal. William's public-house business meant that he could not afford to upset his customers, and neither he nor Fanny wanted to be forced to leave the village with his or her honour tarnished.

Then there was the question of Fanny's family. Even before his marriage to Elizabeth, William Kent was not liked by the Lynes brothers. Were they to get wind of news about Fanny's feelings for William, then the consequences would be disastrous for the couple. At the very least Fanny would be whisked back to Litcham and placed out of William's reach forever. Fortunately the couple had some self-control and did not let their relationship progress beyond mutual admiration into something of a more physical nature.

Precisely when William and Fanny fell in love is uncertain, but they took no direct action to address the situation until the autumn of 1758 and then only in response to yet another sad event in William's life. At the beginning of November that year William's mother, Elizabeth, died in Mileham village, and, for the third time within a year, William found himself attending the funeral of a close family member.

The death of Elizabeth Kent also brought with it a solution to some of William's problems, for, just before Christmas 1758, he inherited a sizeable sum of money. The exact amount remains unknown, but it was evidently enough to allow him to buy his freedom from his public-house concession, leaving enough spare to leave Stoke Ferry and start again elsewhere. This was to be his and Fanny's lifeline. Freed from his financial obligations, William could now wed Fanny without having to consult her family. It also meant that the couple were free to abandon Norfolk and follow William's dream of becoming a London businessman. Buoyed up by his change in circumstance, William began to make plans for their marriage and imminent departure from Stoke Ferry.[10]

It is at this point in the story that we first encounter John Augustin Leavy, a gentleman who lived in Greenwich but who had extensive business interests in Norfolk and also a house in the Stoke Ferry area. Leavy's occupation remains a mystery, but it required him to have a good knowledge of England's complex legal system. It was for this reason that just after Christmas 1758 William travelled to Greenwich, then a small village on the outskirts of London, to seek Leavy's advice. William wanted to know whether there was any reason why he and Frances should not be legally wed.[11]

While Leavy made his enquiries, William decided to spend a few days in London looking for suitable accommodation and/or business opportunities. However, any plans he was making were destroyed when Leavy approached him with the results of his enquiry. According to him there was no way that William and Fanny could be legally wed.

It was a distraught William that fled back to Norfolk in order to break the bad news to Fanny. The obstacle to their union was William and Elizabeth's young son, who had lived for only a couple of months before expiring. According to Canon Law, a man may marry his sister-in-law only if the marriage to the sister produced no living children. Because Elizabeth's baby had lived, even though for such a short while, William was now barred from marrying Fanny. William later described Fanny as being 'much chagrined at this disappointment'. One suspects that she (and he) would have been a good deal more upset than this.[12]

After the tears had ceased flowing, William and Fanny sat down to discuss what they should do next. If their love was to survive, then there was only one realistic option: to elope. However, given all that had happened over the previous couple of years, in particular William's falling-out with the Lynes brothers, neither of them wished to aggravate the situation. Having agreed that elopement was out of the question, they took the painful decision that they should part company. William would carry out his plan of going to London, while Fanny would return to her brother John's house in Litcham.

William later wrote to Fanny instructing her to 'forget, if possible, that tender tho' unhappy affection we have for each other'. Secretly he hoped that by throwing himself into a new business venture he could 'ease the passion he had unfortunately indulged' and that Fanny, by being surrounded by family, would be able to do the same.[13]

So it was that in January 1759, and with heavy hearts, William and Frances went their separate ways: she heading north to Litcham; he south to stay in lodgings he had organised on The Strand, London.

In the months after their parting William and Fanny's hope that distance and time would lessen their desire for each other turned out to be in vain. Fanny was particularly upset. She had been uprooted from her sweetheart in Stoke Ferry and then forced to return to her brother's house. Her mood was melancholic, and, although she had promised William not to communicate with him, it was only a matter of weeks before she sent her first letter to his London residence. The letter pleaded with William to abandon his resolve and let her come down and stay with him. William did not reply. He was determined to try and expunge Fanny from his memory, but she was not to give him the chance to do so.

Letter after letter travelled from Norfolk to London, each one begging that she be allowed to leave Litcham to join him in his lodgings. Eventually William could stand the torment no more and relented, agreeing that Fanny could join him but under certain conditions.

The first of these was that, if they wanted to live together in full view of the public, then they would have to pretend that they were man and wife. From the moment of her arrival in London, Miss Fanny Lynes would have to pretend that she was Mrs Fanny Kent. The second condition was more problematic. The bad blood between William and the rest of the Lynes meant that, once she had left Litcham, Fanny would have to cut herself off from the rest of the family, especially her brothers. William could foresee the trouble he was about to cause and wanted to be sure that, once in London, he and Fanny could not be bothered by others. Fanny agreed to these conditions, even though she knew that cutting her family ties would be hard for her to bear.

William next turned to his good friend John Leavy. William confessed all that had happened between him and Fanny and asked Leavy for his advice on how he should get the girl out of Norfolk without detection. Leavy believed that he had the answer. He had shortly to go to Norfolk for a two-week business trip that necessitated his staying in Stoke Ferry. If Fanny could get herself to the large town of Swaffham, halfway between Stoke Ferry and Litcham, then Leavy would personally escort her back to London. William wrote to Fanny suggesting the idea, and she wrote back at once agreeing to the plan. At the end of May, John Leavy set off for Norfolk with the promise that he would return with Fanny in his possession within two weeks. The time would allow William to make all the necessary arrangements for her arrival.[14]

Until that point William had been living in simple lodgings on The Strand. If Fanny was to live with him as his wife, he would have to leave his boarding house. Not only would the couple need more space, but they would also need to find new lodgings where they could act out their pretend marriage from the moment of arrival. The best solution would be for William to buy a house of their own, and this was indeed what he intended to do, but this would take a while and in the meantime they would have to make do with rented accommodation.

All went according to plan. John Leavy got a message to Fanny, instructing her to be in Swaffham town centre early in the morning on 3 June, his final day of business. Leavy travelled up from Stoke Ferry and met Fanny; they then took the Great Yarmouth coach to London, an uncomfortable direct journey that could be covered in one day. At around five o'clock in the evening, and after a bone-shattering journey of many hours, the coach arrived in London, disgorging Fanny and Leavy onto the pavement outside William's lodgings. William meantime had travelled downriver to Greenwich to make use of Leavy's vacant house. Not to be deterred, Leavy and Fanny took a riverboat downstream, and thus it was late in the evening when the two lovers were reunited. They had not seen one another for nearly six months.

William had yet to find suitable accommodation, and so for the time being they remained in Greenwich, either as the guests of Leavy or in temporary lodgings. During this time they adjusted to living together as man and wife. Fanny would now only answer to the name of Mrs Kent.

At the beginning of July William had the idea of cementing their relationship by making a will in which he would name Fanny as the main beneficiary. He was motivated by a genuine desire to make sure that Fanny would be financially secure in the event of his death. Fanny's estate was much smaller than William's, and there was the realistic danger that her family might punish or even disinherit her. Even though William did not need Fanny's money, she nonetheless wanted to reciprocate and decided to make a will in his favour. At the time this act of mutual trust and affection looked perfectly natural, but William and Fanny had unwittingly laid one of the cornerstones of the later Cock Lane scandal.

The drawing-up of the wills was left in the hands of Mr Leavy, who by his own account had 'some legal training'. Thus it was that on 7 July an attorney named Mr Morse, plus Leavy, Robert Pitman, the local schoolmaster, and Catherine Bambridge, his servant, all gathered in Greenwich to bear witness to the making of the two wills.

The contents of William's will are unknown, but the words of Fanny's rather simple will have come down to us. In it she makes a limited provision for her two brothers and three sisters, giving them the sum of half a crown each. She then states that William is to have 'all my real estate whether freehold or copyhold whatsoever and wheresoever which I shall be possessed of or entitled unto in possession reversion or remainder by and under the act deeds will or bequest of my brother Thomas Lynes or any other person . . .'. For good measure she made William her executor, which meant that it would be up to him to make sure that her instructions were carried out. Considering that he was the main beneficiary, this was not exactly a great burden. The clause concerning her brother Thomas would, in time, gain its own significance. A few days after this Fanny and William took their leave of Greenwich and moved to London to live there full-time as Mr and Mrs Kent.[15]

What happened over the next three months is hazy, but it would appear that William had arranged for them to lodge at a property in the Mansion House area of the City, near to the present-day site of Southwark Bridge. It was here that William's naivety about London life began to manifest itself.

First, he lent his landlord an outstandingly large sum of money (£20) and then seemed genuinely surprised when the fellow defaulted on his payments. Unsure as to how to get his money back, William took legal action. As there is no record of a civil action involving William Kent from this time, we must assume that the landlord paid up before the case came to court.

While all this was occurring, some of his fellow lodgers found out about William and Fanny's matrimonial relationship (or the lack of it). If taking legal action against his landlord did not get William and Fanny kicked out of their lodgings, then this revelation certainly did. As Mr Leavy later put it, Fanny and William were asked to vacate their room because 'the people of the house did not altogether approve of their conduct'. However, in truth William and Fanny may not have been the ones who let this secret slip.

Back in Norfolk the Lynes family had not taken their sister's elopement lying down. They were aware that the couple had escaped to London and had been taking stringent steps to locate their whereabouts, including publicising the fact that the couple were living together in sin. William later claimed that he and Fanny could have lived as man and wife without detection 'had not her relations, who by all the ties of honour and generosity were concerned to keep it a secret, taken every opportunity of divulging it to the world, and, from a pretend regard for her reputation, endeavoured to publish her shame'. Thus it may well have been the Lynes family, or an agent of theirs, who alerted William's Mansion House landlord to the true nature of his 'marriage' to Fanny. Either way, the couple were on the street.

It was now October 1759, and, after only a few months together in London, the Norfolk lovers found themselves in urgent need of accommodation. This need was all the more pressing because Fanny was four months pregnant. Like her dead sister, Fanny had become pregnant out of wedlock by William.[16]

By this point William had taken on the lease for a house in Bartlett Court, Clerkenwell, but it was uninhabitable. It was a Sunday, and, not knowing what else to do, William and Fanny went to St Sepulchre's church, perhaps because it was on the way to his brother's house or perhaps because there was a distant family connection to the parish. There they met with Richard Parsons and accepted the offer of lodgings in his Cock Lane house. In many respects Cock Lane is no ordinary London street. In fact, William and Fanny had chosen to live in a road that had quite a historical past behind it.

3

COCK LANE

In 1759 Cock Lane was a steep, rough cobbled street that the journalist Aleph recalls as being 'dingy, narrow and half-lighted'. It was situated close to St Paul's Cathedral on the northern edge of the 'alsatia' or slum district of Blackfriars, an area that was notorious for harbouring thieves, prostitutes, drunkards and the destitute.

By 1754 the Blackfriars slum had achieved such bad press that the Lord Mayor proposed clearing it completely in order to build a new bridge across the Thames. Most Londoners considered the huge expense of the Blackfriars Bridge project to be a bargain just so long as it also rid the city of the sea of human dross living nearby. The author Samuel Johnson certainly thought so and wrote several letters in favour of a particular architect's design and subsequently became enraged when it was not chosen.[1]

Fortunately Cock Lane was protected from the poverty of Blackfriars by the outsized Smithfield meat market located on its eastern entrance. In the eighteenth century Smithfield was the largest cattle, swine and poultry market in Great Britain and was highly prosperous. The turnover of trade at Smithfield was enormous, and inevitably some of the money brought in by visiting farmers and merchants would find its way into the immediate neighbourhood; the shops, public houses and light industry around Smithfield all benefited from the market's prosperity. But, if the money was welcome, then many other aspects of Smithfield were not.

Farmers driving their cattle to Smithfield from Holborn, to the west, would occasionally miss the appropriately named Cow Lane and stray into the much narrower Cock Lane. Sleeping residents would be rudely awoken to the sound of clattering hooves and mooing as herds of defecating cows would become wedged between the tall brick buildings on either side of the road. The sound of cursing residents would follow the cattlemen as they slowly coaxed their cows onward to market. Every August, during the annual Bartholomew Fair, Cock Lane would be filled not with cows but instead with drunken revellers and prostitutes. Maybe it was the sight of such hedonism that, in 1688, caused John Bunyan, who had been visiting the Fair, to collapse and die at the southern end of Cock Lane.[2]

Even when it was not full of stray cattle and the overspill from the Fair, Cock Lane was not exactly a salubrious place. Loose paving stones, mud, overflowing cesspits and the sound of horses' hooves on cobbles all combined to make this road, and many others in London, smelly, noisy and sometimes dangerous places to linger.

Cock Lane has the distinction of being one of the oldest traceable urban streets in Europe, its name having been recorded as far back as AD 1241. Cokkes Lane, as it was then written, was the only London street where prostitution was legally permitted. It is probably from this medieval sex trade that the road gets its semi-offensive appellation. During Christmas 1305 some local residents became so fed up with the brothels in Cock Lane that they entered the house of a William Cook 'and tore away eleven doors and five windows with hammers and chisels'. The Mayor later forced the wreckers to make good the damage they had caused. In 1337 two sisters, Agnes atte Hole and Juliana atte Celer, were prosecuted for being 'prostitutes and harbourers of men of ill fame' at the house of John le Bellere in 'Cokkes Lane'.[3]

As well as a seedy past, Cock Lane's other main historical claim to fame is for being the spot where, in 1666, the Great Fire of London finally burned itself out, singeing St Sepulchre's church but sparing the rest of the parish. Shortly after the fire the Lord Mayor of London erected a golden statue of a fat boy at the Lane's eastern entrance to mark the place where the flames died out. The statue's corpulence was meant to remind Londoners that the fire had been God's revenge on the rampant financial greed of the City. The statue has remained in place ever since, but then again so has the City's reputation for avarice.

By the 1750s Cock Lane was loosely associated with the silk-weaving industry that had centred itself in the neighbouring Bethnal Green district. In particular, the Dolphin Inn had become a well-known weavers' drinking tavern. Aside from the weavers, the residents of Cock Lane were the disparate mix London seems to specialise in throwing together. Some, such as Mr Bowyer, the bookbinder, were part of the recently evolved 'middling sort' (or middle classes). Others, such as Bateman Griffith, a carpenter, and Captain Thomas Wilkinson, a soldier, were more typical of the neighbourhood in that, although they had a trade, they were not well-off. Other residents must have worked in neighbouring Smithfield or in the assortment of taverns, shops and inns that serviced it.[4]

Even though it was of historical note, until the 1760s Cock Lane remained a neglected back road known only to those who had a cause to use it. Richard Parsons and his family would change all that. Their activities would for a time make Cock Lane one of the most famous streets in London. The Parsons' behaviour would stir up the London mob and swamp the local community with thousands of tourists both rich and poor. Cock Lane would fill endless column inches in the newspapers and remain a topic of conversation for the next century and a half.

4

SMALLPOX

William Kent was not a man who learned from his past mistakes; indeed it seems he was particularly apt to want to repeat them. By November 1759 he had managed, for the second time, to get an unmarried woman pregnant and, for the second time, loaned his landlord a considerable amount of money on a flimsy promise of repayment. However, of all the mistakes he had made since being in London, his biggest by far was to tell Richard Parsons about the true state of his relationship to Fanny and that they were in hiding from the Lynes family.

The house in Cock Lane was no palace, especially with the drunken Richard Parsons in residence, but, for a couple who wished to melt into London's back streets, it had thus far proved to be perfect. Private lodgings were much easier to hide in than London's commercial boarding houses, which could be easily checked by the Lynes.

Aside from their wanting to lynch William Kent, by the end of the summer the Lynes family had another good reason for wanting to find their sister Fanny. In August her elder brother Thomas had died after a long illness. His death would come as a shock to the young Fanny, but, as the Lynes had yet to find where she was living, she continued to remain ignorant of events back home in Litcham.[1]

Although only five months pregnant, Fanny was spending long periods of time in the Parsons' cramped house, rarely venturing beyond the front door. She was less than pleased at William's continued business trips to Norfolk, but she used his absences to form a closer connection with the Parsons family, especially Betty, their eldest daughter.[2] Betty was certainly a mischievous child and one who received little attention from her parents, but she also had an affectionate side. Conversely, Fanny was noted for her gentle nature, and as a consequence a friendship of a sort was struck up between the lonely country woman and the impish London girl.

In November William was called away once more, this time to attend a wedding. Naturally, Fanny was left behind in London. Tired of being on her own, she asked Betty Parsons if she would sleep with her that night. Betty, who was then sharing a room with her sister, Anne, agreed at once. Quite what the two of them found to talk about is anybody's guess, but from Fanny's point of view the human company was probably more welcome than the conversation. In fact, Fanny was to get more than she could ever have bargained for.

The two girls went off to sleep naturally enough, but in the middle of the night Fanny was awoken by a strange scratching noise that persisted for some minutes. The scratching appeared to be coming from one of the bedroom walls. Fanny was perplexed but not unduly concerned. The terraced nature of most London houses (including those in Cock Lane) meant that all manner of strange sounds could be heard emanating from neighbouring properties.

The next night William was still absent and again Betty was invited into Fanny's bedroom. Once more Fanny was disturbed by unexpected noises, but this time it was not a scratching noise but a sustained series of knockings that roused her. Like the scratching, the knocking noises also appeared to be coming from the walls, and as the night drew on so they became louder and more violent, ensuring that neither Fanny nor Betty could get a wink of sleep.

The next day Mrs Parsons found herself confronted by her lodger, who was very peeved at having lost a night's sleep. Even so, Richard and Elizabeth Parsons claimed not to have heard the noises and so were at a loss to explain their origin. 'There is an industrious shoemaker living nearby,' said Mr Parsons; 'perhaps that is the cause'. Fanny accepted this explanation and hoped that the noise would soon abate: the hope was to be a vain one.

That night the noises recommenced and were louder and more violent than ever. Fanny, who was still sharing her room with Betty, had become tired and very fed up with the situation. In the early hours her patience snapped. Fanny went downstairs and fetched up Mr and Mrs Parsons so that they could witness the noisy phenomenon for themselves.

'Tell me,' said the unamused Fanny, 'does your industrious shoemaker work on Sundays?'

'No,' replied Mr Parsons. 'Why do you ask?'

'Because today is Sunday and the noise is greater than ever before!'

The Parsons still claimed to be at a loss as to the origin of the noise and could only promise to look further into it. The next morning saw William's return to London, which meant that Betty was again forced to share a room with her sister. The noises did not return that night, and, as far as can be gathered, in the coming weeks they were heard only intermittently and then not in William and Fanny's room: only ever in other parts of the house. News of the noises circulated idly about the neighbourhood. There was the occasional suggestion that the house might be home to a spirit or other ghost, but no real attention was paid to the matter.[3]

By November Fanny had entered her sixth month of pregnancy and her condition was now obvious to all who met her. William engaged the services of a local doctor named Thomas Cooper who came to Cock Lane every couple of weeks to check that all was well with Fanny's pregnancy.

Christmas came and went, and as January progressed so the work on William's house in Bartlett Court continued apace and a completion date of late February was given. Knowing that he would soon be leaving Cock Lane, William pressed Richard Parsons over the repayment of his twelve-guinea loan made the previous October. Parsons had promised to repay it at the rate of one guinea a month, but three months had passed and William had yet to receive a single penny.

William had already sued his first London landlord for defaulting on a loan and was anxious to avoid getting into a similar situation with

Richard Parsons. William's pursuit of his payments was gentle at first and was greeted by Mr Parsons with promises of imminent repayment, but, as the days passed and still no money arrived, so William's patience began to wear thin. The relationship between lodger and landlord, which had begun so well, disintegrated rapidly.

The flashpoint came in the middle of January, when, after he had been frustrated by Mr Parsons a further time, William's humour failed him. An almighty row erupted between the two men, during which William forcefully demanded that his money be paid back in full there and then. Mr Parsons refused and then made a veiled threat to expose the couple for the fornicators that they really were. Apoplectic with rage at this attempt at blackmail, William declared that he was going to sue Parsons and would that day engage the services of a lawyer. Perhaps inevitably, Parsons reacted to this by evicting William and Fanny from his house, throwing their belongings onto the cold and damp cobbles of Cock Lane.

This left William with a serious problem. Finding suitable accommodation in London was tricky at the best of times, but he had a wife whose pregnancy was nearing the end of its eighth month and less than a day in which to find somewhere to house her. The servant Carrots was left to take care of Fanny and the belongings, while William scoured the neighbourhood in a frantic manner looking for lodgings, enquiring at every shop and public house he could find. His search paid off and he was able to secure a single room above a nearby jeweller's shop owned by a Mr Hunt. The room was small and far from ideal, but in the circumstance beggars could not be choosers: it would have to do. Less than an hour after being thrown out of the Parsons' house, William and Fanny, with help from Carrots, gathered up their things and took up residence in their new lodgings.[4]

The new room was small, poorly furnished and generally very unsuitable, but the couple somehow managed to put up with it for several days before a new problem arose. On 25 January Fanny began to complain of a severe backache, which, even though she was only in her eighth month of pregnancy, she took to be the early stages of her labour. William was not so sure and summoned his friend Mr Leavy from Greenwich for a second opinion. By the time Leavy had arrived Fanny was not just suffering from backache but also had an alarmingly high temperature. Leavy took one look and advised that they call the doctor. Dr Cooper came immediately and was less than impressed with William and Fanny's new lodgings, describing them as 'highly inconvenient' for the couple. He took William to one side and told him if he was to treat Fanny successfully then she would need to be moved to somewhere more suitable – and quickly.[5]

William sensed the seriousness of the situation and went to clear the builders from his house at Bartlett Court. Dr Cooper accompanied Fanny on the short coach journey to Bartlett Court, which, by the time they arrived, William had hastily furnished with a bed and a few other essential items. Fanny was by now very poorly indeed, but Dr Cooper could do no more than diagnose a 'virulent eruptive fever'.

Now that Fanny was properly housed, Dr Cooper set about making arrangements for Fanny's treatment. Still unsure what he was dealing with, he recommended that Fanny should be bled (that is, some of her blood should be drained off in order to rid her of any that might be 'bad' – probably the last thing she needed) and that she should be given several types of cordial medicine to help bring down the fever. The next day Dr Cooper returned, bringing with him James Jones, Fanny's apothecary. Overnight Fanny's condition had worsened, and she was now very ill indeed. The most obvious change was a virulent red rash that now covered her face and was beginning to spread down her body. At the sight of this both Dr Cooper and Mr Jones knew exactly what they were dealing with. There could be no doubt about it: Fanny had contracted smallpox.

In the eighteenth century few diseases were more feared than smallpox, a virus that would periodically sweep through urban areas, affecting large numbers of people. Although not necessarily fatal in adults (the chance of a sufferer dying was around one in three), smallpox was a painful and disfiguring disease that, in the 1750s, was claiming the lives of around two or three thousand Londoners a year and leaving thousands of others with skin covered in pock scars that marked where the characteristic pustules had been.

The fear factor associated with smallpox frequently led to those who contracted it being shunned by society. For example, any servant who contracted it could be instantly dismissed without legal recourse (usually employers were responsible for their servants' healthcare should they fall ill), but attempts had been made to deal with the problem. In the early part of the eighteenth century a number of smallpox hospitals were built around London. These served two functions: first, to take in those who had contracted the disease so that they could be given specialist care away from the community and, secondly, to help with the inoculation of those who had yet to contract the disease.

The smallpox inoculation method was discovered in the 1720s, and by the time of William and Fanny's arrival in London the practice was commonplace. To become inoculated a healthy person would have pus from a mildly infected individual introduced into a scratch made on their skin. The healthy person would then contract a mild form of smallpox and become ill, but not dangerously so, for a few days before recovering fully. Having contracted a milder form, the inoculated person would then have some resistance to the more dangerous virulent forms that would occasionally sweep through the city.

This was all very well for native Londoners, who, as well as having been inoculated against smallpox, could also be expected to have exceedingly hardy constitutions produced by repeated encounters with a wide variety of urban diseases. However, smallpox, which thrives in environments where people live close to one another, was a much rarer sight in the villages and farming communities outside the city. This meant that, while many city-dwellers had a natural immunity to smallpox, most country folk did not and so put themselves at risk when coming into the town. This was the case with Fanny.[6]

The bad news did not stop there. The severity of Fanny's eruptive fever and the speed at which the rash was spreading meant that she had contracted a particularly dangerous form of the disease. Dr Cooper was not hopeful of Fanny's chances, but he and Mr Jones began to busy themselves, giving instructions to Carrots and William as to how best to care for her while also prescribing medicinal cordials to help her fight off the virus. Before he left for the evening, Dr Cooper took William to one side, out of earshot of Fanny. 'We shall do all we can to help her,' he said, 'but you must prepare yourself for the worst.'

Over the next two days Fanny's symptoms, while not relenting, did not seem to get much worse, which gave hope to William and Carrots. However, on 30 January, just five days after Dr Cooper had first been called, the rash covering Fanny's body erupted into a sea of large, pallid-looking pustules, which are the characteristic of the disease. These pustules were painful, and a number of them had also erupted inside Fanny's throat, making it difficult for her to swallow food and water. Her temperature climbed alarmingly, while her pulse began to weaken. Dr Cooper warned William that nothing further could be done and that his 'wife' had but a few days left to live.

Fanny was also aware that she was dying and, between fever-inspired deliriums, made arrangements for the end. She requested to see her attorney, Mr Morse, to confirm with him that her will was still valid and that William's inheritance could not be legally denied to him. Mr Morse came to the house and assured her that this was correct. Even so, Fanny requested that the will be made even more strongly in favour of William, but Mr Morse refused, saying that it was sufficient as it stood.

William overheard these proceedings and felt compelled to intercede. 'Do you not wish to give anything to your relations?' he said to Fanny.

'No,' she replied.

'Should I perhaps divide your clothes among your sisters?' he asked.

'I have nothing to give to anyone but you,' said Fanny with some emotion in her voice. She was exhausted and so there the matter rested.[7]

Later the same day Fanny received a visit from the Revd Stephen Aldrich, a priest at the nearby church of St John the Baptist, Clerkenwell, and an acquaintance of William's half-brother Thomas. Aldrich, while not delighted at William and Fanny's unmarried state, nonetheless offered Fanny comfort and assured her that she was still within the protection of the church.[8]

It was only after these matters had been cleared up that Fanny asked for her family to be informed of her illness. She requested that her sister Anne, who lived on London's Pall Mall, be sent for. William was wary of contacting any of the Lynes family, but also knew that he could not deny his dying partner this most basic of requests. On the 31 January a messenger was despatched to Pall Mall to alert Anne Lynes of the perilous health of her younger sister.

Anne was delighted to hear of her sister's whereabouts but distressed at the thought of her being so ill. Without delay Anne took a cab from Pall Mall to Bartlett Court. Here she was admitted by William, who must have known that, by alerting the Lynes to their sister's location, he was stirring up a hornet's nest. Luckily, Anne Lynes's primary concern was not the scandal of Fanny's elopement. She was simply happy to see her sister, so much so that that the seriousness of her situation did not at first sink in.

Seeing that Fanny was heavily pregnant must have been a shock to Anne, but this was immaterial in comparison to the effects of the smallpox. Fanny was bedridden with her body covered in blistering sores, many of which were weeping pus. She had taken no food for several days, was drinking very little water and could only just speak. William had warned Anne of her sister's imminent death, but she did not believe him and instead said that Fanny was 'in a fair way of doing well'. Fanny requested that Anne come the next day; she replied she was busy but that she would send a servant to ask after her.

The next day saw Fanny's health decline further. She barely drank anything at all and then only when forced to do so by Dr Cooper.

As promised, Anne Lynes's servant came and went, reporting back to her mistress that Fanny was 'doing well' and was even sitting up in bed. If this was true, then it must have been a temporary let-up, for that night Fanny began to slide in and out of consciousness, a condition that heralded the beginning of the end of her life. Fanny's last hours of life were a traumatic experience both for her and for those who sat at her bedside. Dr Cooper was present throughout and later gave a harrowing description of her decline.

For near fifty hours before she died [wrote Cooper], she hardly swallowed a pint of any fluid whatever, and that only, when myself, or the apothecary were present to administer it to her. The last morning of her life we found her extremely low, her eyes sunk, her speech failing, and her intellects very imperfect; we told Mr Kent, she could not then live twelve hours. Accordingly, a short time after we left her, her speech was wholly taken from her, she became senseless, a little convulsed, and expired in the evening, viz., on the 2nd of February.[9]

The death of Fanny initiated a mental collapse in William Kent, who had lost not just his beloved Fanny but also his child, who had been only a matter of weeks away from being born when smallpox struck. His grief was overwhelming and was for a while a cause of concern to those around him. Both Dr Cooper and Aldrich stressed to him that Fanny had died of a highly infectious disease and that little time should be wasted in getting her body removed and buried. A sturdy coffin with an inner liner was ordered, and at the same time a message was sent to Anne Lynes, to inform her of her sister's death. The funeral was scheduled for the morning of 5 February at the Revd Aldrich's church of St John the Baptist, Clerkenwell.

For the next three nights Fanny's body lay in state at Bartlett Court, watched over by Carrots and William. Shortly after dawn on 5 February the few mourners who were to attend the funeral arrived at William's house. The sole representative for the Lynes family was Anne, who arrived in an agitated state, having been convinced that her sister would recover. The lid on the coffin had already been screwed down as a precaution against infection, but Anne insisted that the lid of the coffin be removed. This done, she fell upon her sister's body and wept uncontrollably for several minutes before the lid was replaced and screwed down and the coffin carried to St John the Baptist's church.

The funeral service itself was 'as decent as circumstances could permit', but, when it came to the paperwork, William was left with a dilemma. Fanny's burial would have to be entered into the church's burial register, but which name should he use? He and Fanny may have been living together as man and wife, but he had no legal right to claim that they were married. If he registered Fanny's burial under his own surname of Kent, he might later fall foul of the law, but, if put down her real name, then it would be obvious to all that the couple had been living in sin. In the end William put her reputation before his and registered the burial as 'Frances Kent'. William was faced with the same dilemma over the coffin's nameplate; should he use his surname again? In the end he resolved the issue by refusing to fix a nameplate at all, a fact that caught Anne Lynes's eye and troubled her greatly. The anonymous coffin was solemnly carried down into the crypt at St John the Baptist's and laid to rest among dozens of other randomly stacked coffins.

After laying Fanny to rest, the mourners returned to Bartlett Court for the wake. Here a tearful William offered Anne all her sister's clothes, but she refused. According to William, Anne told him: 'Your behaviour toward my sister was the same as if you had been married to her and so you are welcome to all that she possessed.'

As the mourners left the house William believed that he and Anne Lynes were parting on good terms and that she might even put in a good word for him when John Lynes found out about his sister's death. If this was so, then Anne's goodwill towards him did last for long.[10]

Despite William's insistence that he and Anne parted on good terms, she was still unsettled by the lack of nameplate on the coffin and so decided to call in on a family relation by the name of Robert Browne who lived nearby at Amen Corner.[11] Anne told Browne the whole sorry saga of William Kent and his turbulent relationship with the Lynes family. She ended with a description of the funeral and told him that it was troubling her. Browne too was uneasy and agreed to help Anne in any way he could.

The day after Fanny's funeral William took her will before the local church court in order to get it proved (that is, declared legally valid). Anne was invited to attend the will's reading and naturally assumed that she would be one of the main legatees, along with her brothers and sisters. She was in for a shock. Anne and the rest of her family had not anticipated quite how strong the bond between Fanny and William had been. They assumed that most of Fanny's money and possessions would be split between her brother and three sisters, as her brother Thomas had done. William, if he was mentioned at all, would surely get only a token amount of her estate. It proved to be the other way around. Apart from half a crown for each of her siblings, William got the whole of Fanny's estate.

'I give unto William Kent,' wrote Fanny, 'all my real estate [. . .] money, plate, wearing apparel and all other my personal estate whatsoever, wheresoever and of what nature, kind or quality soever to be at his sole and absolute disposal'. Fanny had written in such emphatic terms that her intention could be interpreted in only one way; William was to get the lot.[12]

To the Lynes this was not just a blow to their self-esteem; it also meant that they owed William money. Thomas Lynes, who had died the previous August, had left Fanny a share of some land in Norfolk that, when sold by John Lynes, had raised almost exactly £1,000, of which Fanny's portion was £94 12s 4d, a tidy sum. The money had never been paid to Fanny, as she had been hiding in London since June. However, as

William was now Fanny's legal heir, Thomas's legacy would have to be paid to him, along with any other monies or possessions that Fanny had left behind in Norfolk. Furthermore, William was Fanny's named executor, which meant that it was his responsibility to ensure that her instructions were carried out to the letter. If the Lynes refused to hand over Fanny's possessions and money, then the law would step in and force them to do so.

On learning this, Anne Lynes became enraged and tried to enter a caveat, requesting that the will be annulled. Messers Leavy and Morse had done exactly as they had been requested to do: the will was legally watertight and Fanny was free to leave her estate to whomsoever she chose. Whether she was married to William was immaterial in the eyes of the law. Anne's objection was overruled, and on 6 February 1760 the will was granted probate.

William Kent believed that the reading of Fanny's will would be the end of this terrible phase in his life. His links to Norfolk had been entirely severed, and, once John Lynes had handed over Fanny's money and possessions, he could think of no earthly reason why they would need to be in contact again. On their part, the Lynes were beside themselves with anger, especially John, whose loathing of William was now vehement. In his eyes, William had corrupted and killed two of the sisters that his late parents had asked him to watch over. John was determined not to let matters rest where they were. He determined that he would get even with William Kent, no matter how long it took him to do so.

5

A GHOST IN COCK LANE?

While she had lain dying, news of Fanny's illness became a daily topic of conversation through St Sepulchre's parish. Richard Parsons was certainly making the most of the situation. He openly promoted the idea that the smallpox was God's revenge on his former tenants for what he perceived to be their inexcusable behaviour towards him. Such unsavoury opinions were to be expected from a person such as Richard Parsons, but before long he could be heard making a more unusual claim. Mr Parsons insisted that his Cock Lane house was home to a noisy ghost.

In the days after William and Fanny's departure from Cock Lane the strange knocking noise that had so disturbed the household a couple of months earlier returned, and this time it was more violent than ever. Occasionally the thumps and bangs were so loud that they drew complaints from neighbours, but Richard Parsons could tell them only that the noises were not of his making and that they were beyond his control. Then, in late January 1760, while Fanny lay dying at Bartlett Court, matters took a further turn towards the bizarre.

For some days Richard Parsons had been complaining about the knocking noise to James Franzen, the landlord of the Wheat Sheaf public house, located a few doors up from Parsons's own house. Parsons spent a great deal of time and money at the Wheat Sheaf and one evening invited Franzen over to his house to witness the noises for himself. James Franzen was a highly strung man who had a great fear of the supernatural, but he accepted Richard's invitation and, after the pub had shut for the night, made his way to the supposed haunted house.

Richard was allegedly out on an errand when Franzen called, but Elizabeth Parsons insisted he come in for a drink. As he waited in the parlour, where Betty Parsons was also seated, a series of loud knocks rang from the parlour wall. Franzen jumped at the sound, which he later described as being 'like knuckles knocking against the wainscot'. Next came a prolonged bout of scratching that, to Franzen's ears, sounded like a wild animal clawing at the wall. During this commotion Elizabeth and Betty remained quite calm and merely commented these noises could now be heard day and night. Another bout of knocking resumed, prompting the increasingly nervous Franzen to ask if the name of the ghost was known to the family. Mrs Parsons told him that the noises had started during William and Fanny's time at the house and had remained there ever since. The spirit, said Mrs Parsons, must therefore be the first Mrs Kent (that is, Elizabeth Lynes), who was angry and upset at her husband William's behaviour during his time in Cock Lane. Franzen became very frightened indeed and, on hearing more scratching noises, stood up and told Mrs Parsons that he believed that their house was haunted. He then requested that he be allowed to leave. Given the look of terror on his face, his hosts could hardly refuse, and so he stood up and made his way downstairs towards the front door.

Franzen had reached the bottom of the stairs and had just started to open the kitchen door when there was a sudden movement behind him. He turned round to see a ghostly white figure brush past him in the corridor and run up the stairs. The figure, which was 'seemingly covered in a sheet', paused on the stairs for a moment before stretching out an arm and, with a long finger, slowly beckoning him. Franzen, though greatly frightened, moved as though to follow the ghost, but before he had taken a step Betty Parsons appeared and slammed the door to the stairs. She warned him that it was best not to follow the apparition.

Franzen heeded the advice and took to his heels, running straight from the Parsons' house back to his pub, where he sat by the fire in the kitchen, his head in his hands. Being too afraid to go to bed, he remained there for several minutes and was still trying to make sense of all that had happened when there was a knock at the door, which he at first ignored. The knocking became more urgent, forcing Franzen to stir himself. He opened the door to find Richard Parsons on his doorstep, who also appeared to be in a state of nervousness. Parsons barged his way into Franzen's kitchen and demanded that he be given the largest brandy that the house could provide.

'Why, whatever is the matter?' said Franzen, observing Parsons's trembling hands.

'Oh Franzen,' replied Parsons, 'I was going into my house just now when I saw a ghost!'

'So did I!' said Franzen 'And I have been frightened ever since.'

'Bless me!' retorted Richard, 'Whatever can be the meaning of it? It is very unaccountable.'

Franzen fetched two glasses of brandy which they drank in haste. After draining his glass Richard made good his exit, leaving the petrified publican to face a sleepless night alone.

The unfortunate Franzen never did reconcile his encounter with the Parsons' ghost. Even two and half years later, when he was forced to recount the tale in court, he visibly shook at the thought of his brush with the supernatural, causing one court reporter to note that 'poor Franzen hardly seemed recovered from his fright'. The same was not true of Richard Parsons, who, for all his protestation of being frightened, returned to his haunted house and continued to live there with his family. In fact, all the Parsons family seemed rather fond of their noisy ghost and would speak of it regularly, still insisting that it was the vengeful spirit of William's first wife. However, not everybody was so keen on the idea of living in a haunted house.

Catherine Friend, a lodger at the Parsons' house after William and Fanny, was tormented by the noises for several weeks. She complained about them to Richard, but he could comment only that he himself was disturbed by them and also wished that they would stop. Eventually

Catherine got fed up with the continual disturbance to her sleep and left Cock Lane for new (and quieter) lodgings. She later noted that the noises were said to have continued long after she had left.[1]

It was quickly apparent to all who witnessed them that the knocking and scratching noises would only occur in a room when young Betty Parsons was also present. Those who were of a suspicious nature may even have expressed the belief that Betty herself was making the noises and that the mysterious ghost seen by the publican was nothing more than Richard Parsons covered in a white sheet. But this was an age where the idea that a house might contain a ghost was no less believable than the idea that it might contain rats and mice. It was also difficult to see what the Parsons family could gain by promoting their house as being haunted (other than a certain amount of local notoriety). After all, the strange noises had already driven away one lodger, depriving the family of much-needed rental money.

Whatever their cause, the mysterious noises continued to reverberate periodically about the house and it was taken for granted locally that, among its other attractions, Cock Lane now had a *bona fide* haunted house.

6

John Moore, Philip Quaque and William Cudjoe

The Revd John Moore was a well-meaning and honest man but one whose naivety would occasionally land him in trouble. Moore was the Lecturer of St Sepulchre's parish church, an elective position that he had held for many years. As such he was one of Richard Parsons's superiors and must therefore have come into near daily contact with the heavy-drinking officiating clerk.[1]

At the time of Fanny Lynes's death John Moore was just 27 years old and strongly wedded to his faith. He was well known in the parish, not least because he could often be seen in the company of two young African boys. Black people were a comparative rarity in Hanoverian London and were often still enslaved to their Caribbean plantation owners. Indeed, it was then not unusual to see slaves advertised in the papers. In 1761 the *Daily Ledger* announced the sale of a 'healthy Negro girl aged about fifteen years, speaks English and has had the smallpox'.[2]

The two Africans in Moore's care, whose names were Philip Quaque and William Cudjoe, were bound to nobody, although they often took to following Moore as he went about his parish duties. It would be through their curiosity that Moore was to become aware of the mischievous ghost in the Parsons' house. They would also become two of the few people to witness the phenomenon at very close quarters.

Quaque and Cudjoe's arrival in St Sepulchre's parish was largely involuntary. They were born around 1741 on a remote stretch of the West African coast at Cape Coast Castle in the country that we now call Ghana. Of the two, it is Philip's history that is the better known.

His father was Cabosheer Cudjoe, the tribal leader of Cape Coast Castle and a paid employee of the African Company of Merchants.[3] Cudjoe was a born administrator and diplomat who used the slave trade to great effect, permitting the Europeans to operate out of Cape Coast Castle in return for money, goods and the development of the local infrastructure.

The slave ships would come and go, but few Europeans dared to live permanently at Cape Coast Castle. The heat, humidity and a host of tropical diseases (most notably malaria) claimed the lives of many European settlers. The region was justifiably known as 'the white man's grave'.

However, hardship and the prospect of an untimely death were prospects that appealed to some, and to none more so than Christian missionaries. The Revd Thomas Thompson was one such zealot. He was an Anglican priest who resigned a Fellowship at Christ's College, Cambridge, to follow his long-held desire to preach abroad. The Society for the Propagation of the Gospel in Foreign Parts granted his wish, and in 1752 he landed at Cape Coast Castle ready to preach the word of God to the supposedly unenlightened Africans.[4]

Cabosheer Cudjoe had other ideas. He met the Revd Thompson and told him that his people needed education, not God. After a battle of wills, Thompson agreed that he would educate the villagers if they would listen to his preaching. Thompson's attempt at converting Cudjoe's people proved to be largely ineffective with the Cabosheer himself remaining 'firm and unshaken in his superstition'. His people would generally attend church only if given liquor. It was a hopeless task, and, as predicted by many, the climate soon took a toll on Thompson's health. In 1756 he was evacuated back to England. 'All things considered,' wrote one commentator, 'the prejudice of the people against him and his frequent interruptions by sickness, he could not well have had better success.'[5] Thompson's successor chose not to take up his post.

Although his time in West Africa was fraught with problems, Thompson did initiate one programme that was to make his mark on the region. Somehow Thompson managed to persuade Cape Coast Castle's ruling elite to allow him to send some of their sons to England. Here they would be educated and, in time, returned to the colony so that they could then teach their peers.

Three boys, all under 12 years of age and all the sons of local rulers, were selected. There was Philip Quaque, the aforementioned son of Cabosheer Cudjoe, William Cudjoe and Thomas Coboro; they arrived in London in October 1754 and were placed, by the Society for the Propagation of the Gospel, into the care of Mr Hickman's Islington Parish Charity School. Naturally, Thompson made sure that their education was to have a strong religious dimension. Seven weeks after their arrival the Society for the Propagation of the Gospel was pleased to hear from Hickman that 'one of them could say the Lord's prayer and the Apostles' Creed, and the other two answered well'.[6]

The African boys continued to progress well, and in time all three children agreed to be baptised into the Christian faith. However, London's filthy streets held as many potential dangers for the African immigrants as the rainforests of Ghana did for the Europeans. Thomas Coboro soon succumbed to smallpox but recovered only to be struck down with tuberculosis. He died in 1758, after which Mr Hickman surrendered care of Philip and William into the hands of a close friend of his, the Revd John Moore.[7]

Philip Quaque, William Cudjoe and Moore got on well with one another and the boys' education continued to progress well. Part of Moore's evangelical ambitions included a plan not only to educate his two African students but also to get them ordained, so that they might one day return to Cape Coast Castle as missionaries. The theory that Moore worked on was that a returning African minister would be more likely to convert his own people than a European one. To this end Moore had made sure that the two young men were receiving more than just average charity school learning. He had begun to teach them Latin and the classics and was doubtless introducing them to wider theological issues as well.

Moore was pleased with Philip and William's progress, informing the Society for the Propagation of the Gospel that the young men had a 'teachable disposition and good behaviour'. Moore would probably have arranged for Philip and William to be educated at the Charity School in Cock Lane, the only one that was local to St Sepulchre's. This school, as fate would have it, was located directly opposite Richard Parsons's house.[8]

It had long been known in the neighbourhood that the Parsons' house was reputed to be haunted, but few had witnessed the ghost for themselves, it having been silent for some time. However, towards the end of December 1761 strange knocking noises began to be heard outside the house once again, and the rumours about ghosts were revived. The noises were even loud enough to be heard by the masters and students in the Charity School.[9] Playground gossip must have centred on what kinds of spectres, devils and phantoms were inhabiting the house opposite. Philip and William were several years older than most of their classmates and more sober-minded, but surely even they could not ignore the resounding knocks that would occasionally drift across the schoolyard.

Of the two boys, Philip is portrayed as being the more intelligent, and one suspects that he would have been confused by the gossip about ghosts and so sought the advice of his patron, John Moore; perhaps he would know what to make of this strange phenomenon. Moore was exceedingly interested in news of the noisy ghost and asked Philip if he knew to whom the haunted house belonged. The father of Betty Parsons, replied Philip. Moore knew of Betty Parsons, and he therefore also knew that the house concerned belonged to the officiating clerk at his church of St Sepulchre's.

Thus it was that on a cold December day Richard Parsons found himself being approached by the distinctive figure of the Revd John Moore, who was anxious to talk to him about the strange happenings at his Cock Lane house.

7

METHODISM AND THE
SUPERNATURAL

A s a clergyman, John Moore might have been expected to
have an interest in the apparently supernatural happenings
in Cock Lane, but in fact his interest in the ghost went far
deeper than this. Although an Anglican priest, Moore was
also known to be sympathetic to the Wesleyan Methodist movement.

When one looks at Moore's personality, his interest in Methodism is
not all that surprising. He had an evangelical bent and was keen on the
promotion of Christianity to the masses. He was active within the
Society for the Propagation of the Gospel, an organisation that promoted
Christianity to native Asians, Africans and Americans and that
contained many Methodist sympathisers. In an age when many middle-
and upper-class people were apathetic about religion, the Methodists'
ability to stir the masses was appealing to people like Moore. By 1760
he was active within the movement and had made several key contacts
within George Whitefield's great Methodist Tabernacle located on the
Tottenham Court Road.[1]

It was largely Moore's Methodist faith that would lift the Cock Lane
ghost from the level of a local curiosity to a national and then inter-
national sensation. In the process the ghost was to become a battleground
between those who supported the Methodist movement and those who
despised everything it stood for. To understand why Methodism is so
important to the Cock Lane ghost story, one has first to appreciate
something of the origins of the movement in the beliefs and experiences
of John Wesley, one of its founders.

In 1750s London Methodism was still a comparatively young movement, but its ability to gather converts, especially among the poor, was alarming the church hierarchy and many establishment figures. In origin Methodism dated back to 1738, when the brothers John and Charles Wesley began to utilise the many local societies that existed within the Church of England. The Wesleys, both of whom were ordained Anglicans, used these societies to promote an evangelical doctrine that emphasised the role of personal experience in the process of salvation. During the 1740s they and George Whitefield, an associate, took the message further by travelling the country preaching to large and enthusiastic crowds of working people. The Methodist movement quickly gathered a large following, which sometimes led to confrontations with the authorities.[2]

In the late eighteenth century Methodism was one of the few church movements to be actively recruiting new members; it still appealed primarily to working people, with Wesley himself once describing his congregation as being 'poor to a man'. John Wesley's passionate preaching about the evils of materialism and the achievement of salvation through self-discipline and prayer were purposefully aimed at the dispossessed.

Asked by James Boswell, his young friend and faithful biographer, why Methodists were so much more successful at preaching than the Anglican clergy, Dr Samuel Johnson thundered: 'It is owing to their expressing themselves in a plain and familiar manner, it is the only way to do good to the common people. To insist against drunkenness as a crime, because it debases reason, would be of no service to the common people: but to tell them that they may die in a fit of drunkenness, and show them how dreadful that would be, cannot fail to make a deep impression.'[3]

Johnson was not wrong, and by 1767 there were an estimated 24,000 Methodists in England, making it a force to be reckoned with. Methodism may have been popular at a grass-roots level, but it was deeply distrusted by many middle- and upper-class Anglicans. Some, such as the Duchess of Buckingham, hated it because of its egalitarian preaching. She complained that 'it is monstrous to be told [by Methodists] that you have a heart as sinful as the common wretches that crawl on the Earth. This is highly offensive and insulting and at variance with high rank and good breeding.'[4] Others, including many leading Anglicans, were scared by the Methodists' popularity, fearing that that their mass of 'unwashed' supporters might threaten the Church of England's status quo. For this reason the Establishment turned on the Methodists, who became a target that could be criticised and mocked without fear of reproach. Indeed, the middle classes delighted in the satirical plays, newspaper sketches and cartoons that portrayed the Wesleys' supporters in a poor light.

One particularly strong vein mined by satirists was the Methodists' strong belief in the supernatural. It was common to see Methodists portrayed as credulous and willing to believe in all manner of strange and unusual things without question. The caricature was founded in truth, for the Methodists did indeed have a predilection for the supernatural; the *Arminian Magazine*, the Methodist journal, was filled with stories relating to ghosts, witches, demons, curses and second sight, many of them supplied by John Wesley himself.

The lecturer M.J. Naylor once wrote of Wesley that his followers 'ascribed to him an almost Papal infallibility and dared not to reject what he advanced. Their conviction has insensibly spread amongst the multitudes connected with them by the common intercourse of society and once more re-illuminated the fading flame of vulgar superstition.'[5]

As Naylor indicates, the Methodists' fascination with the supernatural came mostly from John Wesley, whose personal journals and writings are filled with references to the paranormal. He was a firm believer in the supernatural world and was frustrated that others could not see the spiritual dangers that it presented. That frustration would sometimes boil over; it was an annoyed Wesley who complained that 'the English in general, and most of the men of learning in Europe, have given up all accounts of witches and apparitions as mere old wives' tales. I am sorry for it for the giving up of witchcraft is, in effect, giving up the Bible. Did I ever see an apparition myself? No. Nor did I ever see a murder, yet I believe there is such a thing.'[6]

Wesley believed that he could help convert people to his cause by seeking out supernatural events, especially those involving premonitions and ghosts, and publishing their details. Most cases were second-hand and had obviously suffered from some exaggeration, so it was hard for many to take them seriously. He was particularly famous for his 'investigation' into Elizabeth Hobson, a girl from Sunderland who claimed to have had a string of strange and perplexing experiences involving premonitions, visions and apparitions. Wesley did not witness any of these himself but nonetheless took great pains to record her stories. He then promoted them as *bone fide* examples of the ways in which the 'invisible world' can affect our lives.[7]

This caused much amusement among the chattering classes, but the accounts were taken seriously by James Boswell, who, in 1778, approached Dr Johnson on the subject, asking him what he thought of Elizabeth Hobson.

'Wesley believes it,' Johnson told Boswell, 'but not on sufficient authority. He did not take time enough to examine the girl. I am sorry that he did not take more pains to inquire into the evidence for it.'[8]

The origin of Wesley's faith in the supernatural is not hard to uncover, for the first case that he ever investigated actually concerned his own family. It is clear that the strange nature of this case and its many eyewitnesses, all of whom were well known to Wesley, had a profound effect on his attitude towards the paranormal. It also has a direct bearing on the Cock Lane scandal.

The case of which I speak started in 1715 when the 12-year-old John Wesley was away at boarding school. The rest of his family were at this time residing at Epworth, a remote hamlet in the Lincolnshire fens, where his father Samuel had been rector since 1695. In 1715 the Wesley family consisted of Samuel, his wife, Susannah, their daughters Susannah,

Ann, Emily, Molly, Nancy and Hetty, and a young son, Charles (John's elder brother Samuel was also away at school). All lived in a large but basically furnished rectory house.

Life in Epworth had been far from comfortable for the Wesleys; they found the fenland climate harsh and the scenery bleak and unremitting, but worst of all were the local parishioners, who were 'boorish and uncultivated, as wild a set of men as could be found in England'.[9] The locals disliked the church in general and Samuel Wesley in particular: they burned his crops, maimed his animals and even tried to burn the rectory to the ground.

'Most of my friends', wrote Samuel Wesley in 1705, 'advise me to leave Epworth if I e'er I [sic] should get from hence. I confess that I am not of that mind, because I may yet do good there, and 'tis like a coward, to desert my post because the enemy fire thick upon me. They have only wounded me yet, and I believe CAN'T kill me.'[10]

Samuel Wesley may have relished the challenge, but the rest of his family did not. In particular, his daughters disliked not only where they lived, but also the perpetual poverty and hardships brought by their father's financial mismanagement. They would write to their absent brothers complaining about their lack of decent clothing and their father's debts. Life was tough for the Wesley girls.

In the winter of 1715 the inhabitants of Epworth rectory were to find themselves at the centre of a series of bizarre and inexplicable events that were later to be documented in detail by John Wesley. Even so, few biographies of Wesley mention them, partly because around 1800 there was a conscious effort by the Methodist movement to distance itself from the supernaturalism that had pervaded the thinking of its founder.

The trouble began without warning on the night of 1 December, when one of the Wesleys' maids reported having heard the sound of groaning from the dining room 'like a person in extremes, at the point of death'. The family did not take her seriously, until, a few days later, the house began to resound with strange knocking noises that appeared to emanate from the walls, floors and furniture. The knockings generally came in threes and fours and would stop and start suddenly.

At first Mrs Wesley attempted to keep knowledge of the phenomenon from her husband, but within days the activity escalated to include a range of other noises that included scratching, rustling and even the sound of breaking glass. By Christmas the entire family was aware that something unusual was happening in the house, but, strangely, none of them seems to have been particularly scared (the same was not true of the servants, all of whom were terrified). It was quickly apparent that the phenomenon was closely associated with the Wesley daughters, especially Hetty, who was often close by when the sounds started.

Samuel Wesley was a pragmatic man and at first thought that the villagers were playing pranks on his family. However, the regularity of the knockings and their ability to appear deep within the house at any hour convinced him otherwise. He noticed that the knockings would become violent during prayers, especially those that asked for the health of King George to be preserved. On this he commented that 'the ghost must be a Jacobite'. It was suggested to Wesley that the noises were made by a supernatural intelligence and the children even gave it a name: Old Jeffrey.

On Boxing Day 1715 Samuel Wesley set out to communicate with Old Jeffrey. He recorded the attempt in his journal:

After or a little before ten, my daughter Emilia heard the signal of its beginning to play, with which she was perfectly acquainted; it was like the strong winding up of a jack.

She called us, and I went into the nursery, where it used to be most violent. The rest of the children were asleep. It began with knocking in the kitchen underneath, then seemed to be at the bed's feet, then under the bed, and at last at the head of it. I went downstairs, and knocked with my stick against the joists of the kitchen. It answered me as often and as loud as I knocked; but

I knocked, as I usually do, at my door, 1–23456–7, but this puzzled it, and it did not answer, or not in the same method, though the children heard it do the same twice or thrice after.

I went upstairs and still found it knocking hard, though with some respite, sometimes under the bed, sometimes at the bed's head . . . I asked what it was, and why it disturbed innocent children, and did not come to me in my study if it had anything to me to say. Soon after it gave one knock on the outside of the house. All the rest were within, and knocked off for that night.[11]

Old Jeffrey continued to disturb the family through Christmas and into the New Year, by which time several clergymen were urging Wesley to leave the house. 'I will never flee from the Devil: let the Devil flee from me!' was his reply. His stance was vindicated when, at the end of January, the noises began to fade. By February they had stopped altogether.

The family disagreed about the true nature of Old Jeffrey. Samuel Wesley and his wife suspected that a disembodied spirit was at work, but his daughters were convinced that witchcraft was to blame, citing an example of devilry from a nearby village. The elder son, Samuel, who was away at college, was clearly sceptical about the whole thing. In his letters to his mother he asked a whole string of questions about the whereabouts of various servants and family members (especially his sisters) when the noises took place. His mother assured him that fraud was most unlikely.[12]

Throughout this period of turbulence the young John Wesley was away from the house and so does not feature in the tale at all. This is not to say that he was not interested in what had been happening; on his next visit home John wrote an account of the haunting, using his father's journal and the family's personal recollections. Later, in 1726, he gathered first-hand accounts of the strange knockings from his mother and sisters, as well as from servants and visitors to the house. He also made use of the letters between his family and his brother Samuel.[13]

It has often been suggested that Wesley's interest in the paranormal was sparked off by the Epworth knockings.[14] It is certainly clear that by 1726 John Wesley had a strong interest in the supernatural and was intent on getting hold of evidence that could help prove its reality. The antics of Old Jeffrey certainly helped to reinforce strongly his belief in this area. All these first-hand accounts were condensed by Wesley into an article for the *Arminian Magazine*, drawing them to the attention of the wider world.

By the 1760s the strange experiences at Epworth were known to John Wesley's followers and were cited as examples of the supernatural in action. One of the places where its influence was to be felt most keenly was Cock Lane, where another noisy ghost had taken up residence and one whose behaviour was not dissimilar to that of Old Jeffrey.

8

THOMAS LYNES'S LEGACY

In the months following Fanny's death William Kent started to pick up the threads of his life once more. The building work at his Bartlett Court house was completed, and he began to earn himself a living, although what exactly his line of business was is not clear. Shortly after the funeral Fanny's servant Carrots left William's employ, but the two parted on good terms and William was sorry to see her go.

Even William's troubles with the Lynes appeared to ease. In November 1760 John Lynes reluctantly fulfilled his dead sister's bequest and handed to William all her money and goods. It was not done with good grace, but afterwards William did not hear anything further from his Norfolk enemies, which was something of a relief to him. With time the wound created by Fanny's death healed and the year afterwards William fell in love again, this time with a woman named Bathsheba Bowers, who, by all accounts, was quite wealthy. On 31 August 1761 the couple were married in the London church of St John Zachary.[1]

Contrary to William's hopes, the Lynes family most certainly had not forgotten him. While William settled into married life in London, John Lynes found himself in a spot of financial bother that concerned Thomas Lynes's will.

Thomas died in August 1758 leaving a will that contained some very generous provisions for his friends and family. It was his desire that his sisters Catherine, Anne, Susan and Fanny each be given £150 and that a further £20 be given to his brother-in-law Stephen Hordlett. The money for this was to be partially raised by the sale of some land that Thomas owned in a neighbouring parish. It was sold to a James Shittle for £400, and in November 1760 John Lynes distributed the money.

The amount raised by the sale was not quite enough to give Thomas's surviving sisters and William Kent (who was due to get Fanny's share) the £150 he had wanted; instead each received just under £100 in cash. John believed that his duties as an executor had been fully discharged.[2]

In the spring of the following year John Lynes was made aware that some of Thomas's land had in fact been rented and not owned outright, as he had believed. The person to whom he had sold the land was furious when he found out that he had been sold the land illegally and demanded that John refund him £245.[3]

At the beginning of May, John Lynes wrote to the beneficiaries of his late brother's will requesting their presence at the Unicorn Inn, Mileham, on the 20th of the month. The meeting was duly held (minus William Kent, who refused to attend), and it was agreed that Thomas's legatees should pay John Lynes back for the money he been forced to refund. The only person who would not agree was William Kent. When asked to repay his share of the costs, he refused point blank, explaining that the legacy had 'been used to pay for Fanny's debts and funeral expenses, the sum of which amounted to upwards of one hundred pounds'. William claimed that he was not liable for John Lynes's mistake. After years of mutual distrust and loathing, the two arch enemies were about to confront one another.

Throughout the summer of 1761 John Lynes brooded on the issue and became increasingly angry at his ex-brother-in-law. William, on the other hand, barely gave the matter any thought at all. By the autumn John's patience snapped, and, left with no alternative, he decided to take William to court. A Bill of Complaint was submitted to the Lord Chancellor on 31 October 1761. This lengthy document outlined John Lynes's perceived case against William and was the first step in persuading the Chancellor that William Kent had a case to answer. If the Chancellor agreed, then William would be invited to reply to the charges, beginning a lengthy process that would end in the case being tried in court.

A Bill of Complaint is supposed to be a reasoned and unbiased document that sticks to the facts of the case, but during its drafting John Lynes was at times unable to control his anger. He displays a certain amount of paranoia surrounding William's refusal to repay any money, and connects this with some grander plot against the Lynes family. John hints at a conspiracy, accusing William of 'combining and confederating with diverse other persons at present unknown whose names, when discovered, may be added party hereto with apt words to charge them and contriving how to defraud your orator {i.e. John Lynes] of his just demand'.

He also disbelieved William's explanation about having spent the money on Fanny's debts and funeral expenses and openly accuses him of

> pretending to have applied the sum of money that he so received in payment of the debts of the said Frances Lynes without notice of the said mistake whereas your orator charges that he the said William Kent was sole executor and chief legacee of the said Frances Lynes and his personal estate after payment of her debts legacy and funeral expenses amounted to the sum of one hundred pounds upward which he has consorted to his own use and that of the said confederates . . . all which is contrary to equity and good conscience.

John finishes by asking the judge to subpoena William so that he can be interrogated about the true cost of Fanny's debts and expenses and then be made to pay his share of the refunded money to John Lynes.[4]

The Bill of Complaint was submitted while William was abroad on a business trip. On his return he was surprised to find himself the subject of John Lynes's wrath. Even so, William was not especially concerned, as he was convinced that the so-called debt was generated by a mistake that was not of his making and the case would surely fall apart as soon as it reached the courts. William was wrong to be so flippant. Not only was John Lynes taking the matter extremely seriously; he had also initiated a campaign of harassment against his former brother-in-law.

Many months later William would complain that from the moment of the lawsuit's commencement the Lynes family had 'pursued him with implacable resentment' and that their 'animosity was carried to the highest pitch'. It would appear that part of this animosity included their conducting an investigation into the time that he and Fanny had spent in London, probably in the hopes of uncovering information that could later be included as part of the court case.[5]

The person persuaded by the Lynes to probe into William's affairs was Robert Browne, a distant relation and the man who had comforted Anne after Fanny's funeral. Browne had already made some enquiries into William's life in the weeks after Fanny's death and had even arranged to meet William's friend John Leavy on 25 February 1760. The meeting resulted in Leavy giving Browne a written account of William and Fanny's elopement from Norfolk to London. This testimonial had been given by Leavy in good faith and was meant to reassure the Lynes that Fanny had travelled to London of her own free will. In fact, Leavy's account of Fanny's flight from Norfolk did little to reassure them and in time his words would be used by Browne to accuse William of murder.[6]

By trade Robert Browne was a master builder and a successful one at that, and it is possible that Browne's wealth gave him the necessary spare time to look into William's affairs.[7] His investigation commenced in early December 1761 and, naturally enough, saw Mr Browne paying a visit to the parish of St Sepulchre, where William and Fanny had lodged for some months. Browne may have been surprised to learn that William and Fanny had long been the subject of neighbourhood gossip. According to the rumours, William Kent had been a gold-digger who had defrauded his landlord and who had later poisoned his 'wife' in order to get at her fortune. The trail would quickly have led Browne to the house of Richard Parsons, where he would doubtless have discovered that the name of William Kent was most unwelcome.

Even two years after William's departure, Richard Parsons's gin-soaked mind still held a great deal of bitterness against his ex-lodger and with good reason. In the weeks after Fanny's death William had successfully sued him for the twelve-guinea debt that had been the cause of their falling-out. Browne listened to the Parsons' version of events, in which they were the innocent victims of a swindler and an adulterer who had upped and left their house at only a few hours' notice. A story like this would have served to reinforce Browne's low opinion of William, but the flow of information was not all one way.

During this exchange Richard Parsons would have learned from Browne of John Lynes's lawsuit against William. This must have tickled the Parsons family and may have led them to think about causing some mischief of their own. Can it really be a coincidence that shortly after Mr Browne's visit the mysterious knocking noises were again to be heard in Cock Lane? William certainly did not think so; he openly stated that the 'infernal agent arrived to strengthen [the Lynes'] plea'. Robert Browne's snooping was beginning to bring together several hitherto separate strands from William's past life. The results were to be disastrous.[8]

9

THE RETURN OF THE NOISES

In Cock Lane it had been two years since the publican James Franzen had encountered the white-sheeted ghost in Richard Parsons's house, but he still trembled at the thought of it. He avoided the house whenever possible, but would occasionally shuttle a pot of beer between the Wheat Sheaf and the Parsons' kitchen.

In December 1761 Franzen paid just such a visit and found the Parsons family, including the children, seated together in an upstairs room. As they sat talking, a strange scratching sound like an animal could be heard emanating from a wall. Franzen tried to think nothing of it; after all, mice were as much a part of London domestic life as were dust and mud. The scratching finished, followed a few seconds later by a resounding thud. Franzen, who had been witness to the first set of ghostly noises, looked nervous but said nothing. A few seconds later and a series of knocks reverberated about the room in such quick succession that it was impossible for him to say where they were coming from. Franzen looked up at his hosts, the terror evident on his face. It was Mrs Parsons who gave voice to his worst fears. 'The ghost has returned,' she said dispassionately.

'The spirit of Elizabeth Lynes has returned?' he asked.

'Not Elizabeth,' replied Mrs Parsons. 'This time we think that it is Fanny Lynes, come to revenge her murder at the hands of her husband.' Franzen did not hang around to exchange pleasantries. At the first opportunity he left and returned to the Wheat Sheaf for a stiff brandy.[1]

The return of the knocking noises to the Parsons' house took the neighbourhood by surprise. That the house had once been haunted by the ghost of Elizabeth Lynes was common knowledge, but the spirit had not made its presence felt for over a year. Yet now it was evident to all but the deafest members of the community that it was back. The thumps and knocks could be heard clearly in the street outside, but they were quite random in nature, although they were more likely to be heard in the late evening, after Betty Parsons had gone to bed. News of the noises spread quickly, and by Christmas the Parsons found themselves receiving visitors, curious to hear the ghost for themselves. One such visitor was the Revd John Moore, whose chat with his African student Philip Quaque had left him anxious to find out more about the Parsons' alleged ghost.

Richard Parsons must have been alarmed that he had attracted the attention of Moore, who was, after all, one of his superiors at the church. On the other hand, Parsons must also have known of Moore's strong Methodist leanings and would therefore have realised he would not be sceptical about the ghost. On this last point he would have been absolutely right, as Moore vehemently believed that the 'invisible world' was capable of interacting with the corporeal one.[2] This fascination with the 'invisible world' meant that, at the first sign of a ghost or a witch in a neighbourhood, Methodist sympathisers such as Moore would arrive on the scene.

In the mid-eighteenth century ghosts occupied an odd position in society. Only a century earlier supernatural occurrences were near universally accepted and widely feared, even among the most learned members of society. Indeed, some protagonists, most notably the self-styled witch-finder general Matthew Hopkins, were able to mobilise the masses with talk of witchcraft and ghosts. However, the dawning of the eighteenth century brought with it the 'Age of Enlightenment', in which the approach of rationalism was applied to religious and other matters. Many intellectuals used rationalism and primitive scientific deduction to dismiss the supernatural (though not the Bible) as the folly of an earlier less-enlightened age.

However, belief in the supernatural remained strong among the poor and working classes, some of whom preferred to blame their lot on forces beyond their control rather than on themselves or the authorities. This division between the sceptical intellectuals and the credulous masses is illustrated by the author Joseph Addison, who, in 1711, describes an experience he had while staying at a house in London:

> I remember last winter there were several young girls of the neighbourhood sitting about the fire with my landlady's daughters, and telling stories of spirits and apparitions. I seated myself by the candle that stood on a table at one end of the room; and pretending to read a book that I took out of my pocket, heard several dreadful stories of ghosts as pale as ashes that had stood at the feet of a bed, or walked across a churchyard by moonlight, with many other old women's fables of the like nature. As one spirit raised another, I observed that at the end of every story the whole company closed their ranks and crowded about the fire: I took notice of a little boy, who was so attentive to every story, that I am mistaken if he ventures to go to bed by himself this [year]. Indeed, they talked so long that the imaginations of the whole assembly were manifestly crazed, and I am sure will be the worse for it as long as they live. I took the candle into my hand, and went up into my chamber, not without wondering at the unaccountable weakness in reasonable creatures, that they should love to astonish and terrify one another.[3]

As the eighteenth century progressed, so this division between well-heeled sceptics and poor believers grew noticeably wider. It was a facet of English society that Methodist leaders observed with interest and believed they could use to their advantage. John Wesley himself had noted that, while the English were generally laissez-faire about religion, they could still be moved by talk of disembodied spirits, devils and other supernatural phenomena. Many Methodists hoped that, by taking their concerns about the supernatural seriously (as opposed to denying its existence like the 'enlightened' Anglicans), they might attract people to their movement.[4] This was true of Moore, who, like many Methodists, believed that a dead person's soul could return to Earth as a ghost only if it had cause to do so (for example, to right a wrong done to it in life).[5] It was with all this in mind that Moore began interrogating Richard Parsons about the nature of his haunted house. His questions came quickly. What was the nature of the phenomenon? How long had it been happening? How did it start? What was the cause?

Parsons explained that the ghost was suspected of being Fanny Lynes, an ex-lodger of his who was alleged to have been murdered by her husband. The spirit would give regular demonstrations of its powers, knocking and scratching at the walls of the house, disturbing the family and neighbours. Naturally, Moore asked if he could witness the phenomenon for himself. Having sold the ghost in such positive tones, Parsons found it difficult to say no, but even he must have sensed that he was drawing undue attention to himself. Nonetheless, it was agreed that Moore should pay a visit to Cock Lane on a forthcoming evening.

At the time that Moore was taking an interest in the Cock Lane ghost, news of the alleged spirit was beginning to spread beyond the parish boundaries. By the New Year of 1762 Cock Lane was being visited by people who were curious to hear the ghost for themselves, and they would rarely leave disappointed, for the spirit was highly active, especially at night, and loved nothing more than an audience to perform to. The thumps and knocks, while originating from inside the house, could be clearly heard outside. Only a privileged few would actually be invited into the inner sanctum of the Parsons' house. John Moore was to be one of these, and, in early January 1762, he buttoned up his coat against the cold of the evening and set off on the short walk between his house and Cock Lane.

Moore was admitted into the Parsons' cramped and musty house and led up a steep, narrow staircase to the room of young Betty Parsons and her sister Anne, both of whom lay under the covers in the same bed. Here Moore found Richard and Elizabeth Parsons sitting in the semi-darkness, the only light coming from a small candle at one end of the room. Also present was a friend of theirs, Mary Fraser, a woman from neighbouring Hosier Lane whose reputation as a local troublemaker was on a par with that of Richard Parsons himself.

Greetings were made and pleasantries exchanged; then the party settled down to the matter in hand. A few minutes passed and nothing was heard, but, just as Moore was getting restless, a faint scratching noise came from a corner of the room. It was followed by a hollow knock.

'She is here,' announced Mary Fraser, adding, 'Fanny, do speak to us. Pray tell us something.'

More knocks came, interspersed with further scratching noises. They appeared at one moment to come from the walls and skirting board, and at another from the girls' bed. A string of especially loud knocks emerged from the bedstead, then silence followed.

'Pray which rooms of the house are afflicted with the noises?' asked Moore of Mrs Parsons.

'Whichever room the girls are in,' she replied; 'the spirit follows them about, especially Betty. Fanny and she were close friends you see.'

Moore was amazed at this and requested that the girls be taken to another room to see if the noises followed. Parsons obliged and took the two girls and their blankets into a small room on the second floor. There was a few minutes' silence and then the knocking erupted again. The banging occurred randomly for a short while, after which only the occasional scratching sound could be heard.

If the accounts are to believed, Moore was immediately convinced by what he had seen and heard. It was the most clear-cut example of a supernatural phenomenon that he had encountered and would have to be properly investigated. By the time he left the house it was gone midnight, but even so he found that there were a dozen or so people standing in the street who had been listening to the sound of the Cock Lane ghost.[6]

In the coming few days, Richard and Elizabeth Parsons received several more visits from John Moore. On one occasion he brought with him Bateman Griffith, a carpenter who lived a few doors up from Parsons, to see if he could find a natural cause. Mr Griffith could find no obvious cause for the noises and so resorted to removing the wainscoting in several of the rooms where the knocking was most prevalent. It was to no avail and the origin of the knocking remained a mystery.[7]

Moore was right to look for a physical cause. Apart from the possibility that his officiating clerk and his family were trying to pull a fast one on him, the dense and ramshackle nature of London housing and the lack of soundproofing between buildings meant that unusual noises were a fact of life. In a busy city like London unexplained knocking noises were (and still are) a continual source of worry and trouble to householders. For example, the seventeenth-century diarist Samuel Pepys, who was certainly one of life's worriers, was on one occasion vexed by a knocking noise that bears a marked resemblance to those experienced in the Parsons' house. They turned out to have a natural cause, but the following entry from Pepys's diary (November 1667) shows how superstitious people can react to such things:

Waked about seven o'clock this morning with a noise I supposed I heard, near our chamber, of knocking, which, by and by, increased: and I, more awake, could, distinguish it better. I then waked my wife, and both of us wondered at it, and lay so a great while, while that increased, and at last heard it plainer, knocking, as if it were breaking down a window for people to get out; and then removing of stools and chairs; and plainly, by and by, going up and down our stairs. We lay, both of us, afeard; yet I would have rose, but my wife would not let me. Besides, I could not do it without making noise; and we did both conclude that thieves were in the house, but wondered what our people did, whom we thought either killed, or afeard, as we were. Thus we lay till the clock struck eight, and high day. At last, I removed my gown and slippers safely to the other side of the bed over my wife: and there safely rose, and put on my gown and breeches, and then, with a firebrand in my hand, safely opened the door, and saw nor heard any thing. Then (with fear, I confess) went to the maid's chamber-door, and all quiet and safe. Called Jane up, and went down safely, and opened my chamber door, where all well. Then more freely about, and to the kitchen, where the cook-maid up, and all safe. So up again, and when Jane come, and we demanded whether she heard no noise, she said, 'yes, and was afeard,' but rose with the other maid, and found nothing; but heard a noise in the great stack of chimnies that goes from Sir J. Minnes through our house; and so we sent, and their chimnies have been swept this morning, and the noise was that, and nothing else . . . we do sometimes think this morning that the house might be haunted.[8]

The timid Samuel Pepys was lucky. The sweeping of his neighbour's chimneys turned out to be the cause of the trouble, but one can see how quickly a supernatural explanation was sought, not just by the servants but also by Pepys, a future president of the Royal Society.

Unlike Pepys, Moore could find no natural explanation for the noises in the Parsons' house, and so he continued to believe that a supernatural agent must be the cause. It does not seem to have crossed his mind that a human agent might have had a hand in the proceedings. In addition to his physical investigation, Moore also began to dig deeper into Fanny Lynes's history. Richard Parsons was only too happy to tell Moore his version of events, where William and Fanny had left his property in a hurry after the discovery of their elopement. He also told Moore that, shortly after leaving Cock Lane, Fanny had fallen ill and died, probably because she had been poisoned by Kent. With this in mind, Parsons suggested to Moore that his resident ghost was not the troubled spirit of Elizabeth Lynes, as had originally been supposed a couple of years previously, but instead that of her sister Fanny, who had returned to seek revenge on William Kent, her murdering husband.

The fact that the knocking noises (and indeed the white ghost seen by James Franzen) had already been in existence before Fanny's death did not seem to matter. As far as Richard Parsons was concerned, having a ghost that cast doubt on William Kent's reputation suited him just fine.[9]

10

THE PERFORMANCES BEGIN

In 1761 the Methodist community in England was small but well connected, and in the months before the Cock Lane ghost's resurgence it had become associated with two other prominent ghost cases. One of these was in Warwickshire, but surviving details are obscure. Horace Walpole notes of it that 'the Methodists endeavoured to establish, not only the belief, but the actual existence of ghosts'.[1] Then, only a matter of weeks before the knocking noises recommenced at the Parsons' house, strange happenings at the Lamb Inn in Bristol drew the attention of several local Methodist supporters.

The Lamb Inn case, which was to continue for nearly a year, shows some remarkable similarities to the Cock Lane ghost. The family that lived at the Lamb Inn, the public house at the centre of the case, consisted of Richard Giles, his wife and two daughters aged 13 and 8. Like the home of the Parsons family, in November 1761 the inn was invaded by scratching and knocking noises that seemed to follow the children from room to room. By Christmas 1761 the Lamb Inn ghost had attracted the interest of several clergymen, all of whom were sympathetic to the Methodist movement. They immediately suspected that a local witch had been paid to bewitch Mr Giles and his family.[2]

The clergy attending the Lamb Inn ghost in Bristol must have been aware of the Wesleys' Epworth Rectory experience and of Samuel Wesley's attempts to get Old Jeffrey to communicate with him. In the Lamb Inn they were able to get the ghost to mimic their own knocking noises, as Samuel Wesley had done. Based on this, someone had the idea of trying to get the noises to answer questions by the use of a simple code. A question would be asked and then the 'spirit' asked to respond by knocking once for 'yes' or twice for 'no'. The technique worked and allowed the clergymen and the ghost to hold stilted conversations for hours at a time.[3]

Back in Cock Lane, John Moore was also confronted with a ghost that would make only random knocking noises and yet he too was keen to communicate with it. Moore was still relatively young and was inexperienced in matters of the supernatural, and so he turned to his friend and mentor, the Revd Thomas Broughton.

Broughton was an early convert to Methodism and had been instrumental in the movement's promotion during the early 1740s. Like most of the early Methodist clergy, Broughton had not alienated himself from the Church of England and was the Lecturer at Bishopsgate Within and All Hallows churches. Both were within spitting distance of Moore's own churches of St Sepulchre and St Bartholomew-the-Great. It was Broughton who had initiated Moore's interest in Methodism and afterwards continued to counsel him. Thus, when Moore found himself confronted with the Parsons' ghost in Cock Lane, it was to Broughton that he turned.[4]

At the time the Lamb Inn case was a major talking point among the Methodist clergy, and it is probable that the Revd Broughton was familiar with the case. If so, then it was probably Broughton who advised his friend Moore to try establishing a channel of communication with the Cock Lane spirit. If such a channel could be established, as it had been in Bristol, then it might be possible to find out what the spirit wanted and how it could be helped to depart this world in peace. Moore arranged to visit the Cock Lane house with Thomas Broughton on the evening of 5 January with the idea that they would be able to establish contact with the spirit.[5]

In the meantime, the knocking noises continued to emanate from the house, drawing ever larger crowds. Needless to say, Richard Parsons was already turning the matter to his advantage and had started to charge people for the privilege of being in his house with the ghost. When Moore found out about this, he was deeply unhappy. He wanted the phenomenon to be taken seriously, and that meant not making the ghost look like a fairground sideshow. In reply to Moore's reproaches, Parsons complained that having the ghost in his house was costing him dearly. It had scared away any potential lodgers, while the stress and sleeplessness were affecting his family and work life. The ghost, said Parsons, was driving him steadily towards bankruptcy. If he could not charge people, then his family might soon be destitute.

Even at this early stage Moore was already obsessed with the Parsons' supernatural manifestation and was anxious not to lose the cooperation of the family. He had access to his church's funds and also, it seems, to a financial source associated with the Methodist movement. Moore approached Richard with a proposal: if he desisted from charging the public, then the church would make good any perceived loss of income, but only so long as the ghost remained active.[6]

Richard Parsons could not believe his luck. The ghost of Fanny Lynes looked as though it was actually going to recoup some of the money that he had been forced to pay back to William Kent. The nature of the deal also meant that it was in the family's interest to have the ghost resident with them for a while longer yet.

On the evening of 5 January the Revd Moore arrived to find Cock Lane thronged with people, with a dense crowd outside the Parsons' ramshackle property. Moore entered the house and was taken to the children's dimly lit first-floor bedroom. As before, Betty Parsons and her younger sister were tucked into a large bed, apparently asleep, while around them stood half a dozen people. Richard and Elizabeth Parsons were there, as were Mary Fraser and the trembling figure of James Franzen. The other bystanders were all neighbours or relations of the Parsons, positioned at various points about the room. A few minutes later the Revd Thomas Broughton arrived and the proceedings began.

Since the previous visit by Moore, the meetings had become better organised. Rather than letting the noises appear spontaneously, Richard

Parsons had appointed their troublesome neighbour Mary Fraser as mistress of ceremonies. She would summon the ghost and act as its chairman, interpreting the spirit's mood and ensuring that the crowd did not get too rowdy.

Fraser requested silence from the crowd and, when everyone had settled down, started to walk slowly round the room asking: 'Fanny, Fanny, are you there? Please come to us. Dear Fanny, please come.'

After a few seconds' silence there was a low scratching noise, which seemed to emanate from under or close to the children's bed.

'Fanny, Fanny, is that you? Are you here?' asked Fraser. A more distinct scratching followed, again coming from the vicinity of the children.

'Fanny dear, there are some people here who want to ask you some questions; will you answer them?' A series of loud and heavy thumps followed.

Fraser turned to Moore and bade him to ask her what he would. Under more normal circumstances Moore was an assertive person, but on this occasion he was hesitant. 'Spirit, I am a clergyman and I am anxious that we might talk. Will you talk to me?' The scratching noise came again.

'The spirit cannot talk,' interjected Fraser; 'it can only make noises.'

'In that case will you answer my questions by knocking?' A series of knocks followed.

'If it pleases you, then you could answer my question in the following manner. If your response to my question is yes, then will you knock one time. If the answer is no, then knock twice. Is this agreeable?' A short silence followed, then one loud knock rang out.

'Good,' said Moore and began his questioning. 'Spirit, are you the soul of a departed person?'

One knock followed.

'Are you the soul of a person once living in this house?'

One knock.

'Are you the departed soul of Miss Frances Lynes?'

A brief pause occurred before another single knock occurred. Moore looked flustered.

'Are you returned for a purpose?'

One knock.

'In life were you harmed by someone?'

Again, one knock.

'Were you murdered?'

This time there was silence. Moore paused and then tried a different tack.

'Were you poisoned?'

There was another brief pause and then a furious knocking erupted about the room. Moore had trouble keeping pace but reckoned that he had counted thirty-one knocks. Assuming this to be a positive response, he continued to ask questions.

'Was the person who administered the poison known to you?'

One knock.

'Was this person William Kent?'

One knock.

This revelation caused a low murmur to erupt about the room. Moore, whose face was probably a mixture of delight and concern, took leave of the questioning.

In his place came Thomas Broughton, who began to ask the ghost of Miss Fanny questions of a much more theological nature. At first the ghost was keen to cooperate with Broughton, but as his questions became more arcane and difficult to answer, the knocking noise quickly degenerated into a series of irritated scratching noises. At this point Mary Fraser intervened.

'Miss Fanny is tired,' she said. 'We should leave her be.'

Both Broughton and Moore were keen to carry on the questioning, but Richard Parsons was insistent that the spirit be left to rest for the evening. He did, however, assure the clergymen that they would have plenty of other opportunities to question the ghost on subsequent occasions.[7] One by one the people in the room filed past the sleeping children and began to troop down the narrow staircase and into the road outside, pushing past the crowd of curious onlookers assembled on the Parsons' doorstep.

Moore and Broughton set off along Cock Lane; both were enthused and excited with what they had witnessed. They agreed with one another that there was no discernible explanation for the phenomenon and that it must therefore be a genuine example of a ghost returned to Earth in order to avenge its murder. They also agreed that the ghost of Miss Fanny could be used to the Methodists' great advantage and might even be a useful vehicle for attracting new converts to the Wesleyan cause.

Thomas Broughton was a cautious man and, although enthusiastic about the ghost's potential, he was unhappy about the accusation of murder against William Kent. He decided (wisely as it turned out) that, as the ghost had chosen to manifest itself in Moore's parish and not his, that it should be up to Moore to handle the affair in his own manner.

Moore wanted to take a less cautious approach and was enthusiastic to promote his new discovery and he thought that the best way to do this was to prove that the ghost's allegations were true. If he could find evidence that suggested Fanny Lynes had been poisoned, then there could be no doubting the ghost's veracity. Moore had a new mission in life – to prove that William Kent had murdered his former lover.

The days following the 5 January séance were busy ones for Moore as he turned detective in his hunt for proof of Fanny Lynes's murder. Finding out information about William and Fanny's time in Cock Lane was not difficult. For a good while the couple had been the talk of the parish, and Moore was soon being given gossip and speculation pertaining to their elopement from Norfolk and the fact that Fanny was the unmarried sister of William's first wife. Moore was also told of the accusation of murder and the details of William's inheritance from Fanny. After hearing all this he felt that there were enough suspicious circumstances to back up the spirit's accusation of poisoning.

Moore arranged several further meetings with Richard Parsons and his performing ghost. Sometimes these would be held in the Cock Lane house, sometimes in nearby properties, but the question-and-answer format was always the same. From this it became apparent to Moore that, unless young Betty Parsons was present, the ghost would not make an appearance. Indeed, the relationship between Betty and the ghost was such that she told Moore that she had on one occasion seen it, describing it as a glowing white figure with no hands. The bond between Betty and the ghost would eventually be exploited by those seeking to uncover the truth of the affair.

One of Moore's chief sources of information about William and Fanny was Richard Parsons and his wife. In the Parsons' hands William Kent changed from the bumbling country gentleman whom they had known to a short-tempered and dangerous womaniser who was permanently short of money. The trusting Moore does not seem to have considered the possibility that the Parsons had a vested interest in denigrating William Kent, the person who had successfully sued them for twelve guineas.

It may also have been Richard Parsons who put Moore in touch with Robert Browne, the Lynes' relation who had been making his own investigation into William's affairs. Browne had no hesitation in offering an opinion on William Kent: he told Moore how Anne Lynes had been prevented from seeing Fanny's body and how the coffin had been placed in the crypt without a nameplate on it. Again, to a person with a suspicious mind, all these little bits of evidence could easily be built into a case for murder against William Kent.

Moore was convinced that the ghost of Fanny Lynes was real and that William was the person responsible for her murder. In fact Moore was so convinced that he made a rash move and placed an advertisement in the *Public Ledger*, a London newspaper with a reputation for carrying gossip. As a result it would be only a few days before everybody in London knew what had been happening in the narrow thoroughfare behind St Sepulchre's church known as Cock Lane.

11

WILLIAM ENTERS THE AFFRAY

It was in the second week of January 1762 that William's good friend John Leavy, the man who had helped Fanny come to London, purchased a copy of the *Public Ledger* and settled down to read the latest news from London, Britain and abroad. It was a quiet time, and much of the *Ledger*'s news was pretty mundane stuff. War had been declared on Spain, a terrible fire in St Saviour's dock had destroyed a warehouse plus eight adjoining houses and a man had been robbed of five guineas in St George's Fields.[1] However, there was one small item that stood out from the rest.

'We hear', ran the item, 'of the bringing of a young lady out of Norfolk to a person in Greenwich and from there she was taken to a lodging house in St S——'s, London. Shortly after it was supposed she was murdered by poison which was given her in a drink.'[2]

The details were scanty, but to Leavy it seemed that this paragraph could only have been referring to William and Fanny's flight from Norfolk and their arrival in London, an act in which he had played an integral part. However, the referral to Fanny having been poisoned was more perplexing and not a little unnerving. Unsure what to do, Leavy set off from his Greenwich house to find William, whom he felt sure would want to know about this strange news item.

Leavy made the short boat journey from Greenwich to Clerkenwell, where he found William in good spirits. He had recently discovered that his new bride was pregnant and that his brother-in-law was keen to enter into a business arrangement with him. But when he read the *Ledger*'s report, William's mood changed. The newspaper was evidently referring to him and Fanny, yet there, in plain print, was a charge of murder against him. How did such a thing find its way into a newspaper, and, more importantly, who was making this serious accusation?

The newspaper gave no clues as to the article's author nor to the purpose of its publication. William, highly strung at the best of times, confessed to Leavy that he could not understand the meaning of it all and then became upset. Eventually he took to his bedroom, where he gave 'vent to the passions and commotions in his breast arising from such an accusation'. He remained there for some time, caught in the throes of depression and anger.[3]

It took all Leavy's powers of persuasion to convince him that the newspaper report was nothing more than idle gossip, but it was a downcast William who left his room to rejoin his friends and family. He complained to them that he had 'behaved in the most kind and affectionate manner to Fanny, right until her death'. Leavy could vouch for this and told him not to dwell on the report any further. It was a piece of mischief-making by one of his enemies and thus not to be taken seriously.

For the next couple of days William bought copies of all the London papers, scouring them anxiously for any further mention of Fanny's death. Initially he believed himself to be safe, but on the third day, when the next edition of the *Public Ledger* was published, his hopes were dashed. In it was another article, which set out the allegations against William in more detail. It also gave William his first clue as to who might be behind this slanderous accusation. The article read:

The following surprising relation gains, at this time, the particular attention of most of the neighbourhood: that, for these two years a great knocking and scratching had been heard in the night in the first floor of the house of the Officiating Parish Clerk of Saint Sepulchre's, in Cock Lane, near West Smithfield, to the great terror of him and his family. To find out the cause he ordered the wainscot to be taken down, but to no effect; for the knocking and scratching was more violently renewed upon a bedstead whereon the two children lay; the eldest is about twelve years of age. These children were afterwards removed into the two pair of stairs room, where the same noise followed and was frequently heard all night.

Some time since as a publican in the neighbourhood was in the house below stairs, in the evening, he saw a shadow much like a woman, who passed by him and beckoned him, upon which he was so terrified that he ran home and was very sick; the clerk soon after having occasion to go into another room saw the same appearance; this happened within an hour.

Upon these things being told in the neighbourhood a report was spread that the house was haunted, which induced many persons to sit up all night, several gentlemen, and a worthy clergyman attended; the noise of scratching and knocking was continued in a violent manner.

The clergyman addressed himself in this manner. If any injury has been done to any person that had lived in that house, he might be answered in the affirmative by one single knock, if on the contrary, by two knocks; which was immediately answered by one knock.

He then asked several questions, all of which were most reasonably answered, and the following account is taken from the responses, viz., That she was a woman, her name F——; that she lived with Mr. K——, in a familiar manner; that two years since she was taken ill with the small pox, and seeing her illness he poisoned her; that she was buried at Saint John the Baptist's Clerkenwell, etc.

The above affair being now grown so serious and engulfing the general conversation of Saint Sepulchre's parish, we are credibly informed one of the clergymen, who has entered decently into this mysterious affair, has made regular minutes of all the interrogatories which have passed between the spirit and him; and we doubt not but he will shortly oblige the Public with the whole detail, to the conviction of the incredulous.[4]

This time, rather than being upset, William became angry. The article made it clear that the source of his trouble lay in Cock Lane and therefore suggested that Richard Parsons was his chief accuser.

Knowing this gave William strength, for he had already successfully sued Parsons once and could do so again, but even so there were many items within the article that were both strange and worrying. Most perplexing of all was the report that William's accuser was a spiritual presence that knocked out its charges of murder on a skirting board. What was the meaning of this? The fact that there seemed to be a local clergyman involved was also worrying, as was the article's assertion that the affair was engulfing the entire neighbourhood. Could any of this be true?

William needed to place a stop to this nonsense and so set out on the short journey from his own house in Clerkenwell to Cock Lane. Here he learned from bystanders that the investigation was being coordinated by the Revd Moore of the local parish church. Luck was on William's side, for when he arrived at the church he found Moore there, busy dealing with parish matters. William approached him and, without revealing who he was, showed him the two articles from the *Public Ledger*.[5]

'Do you know anything about these?' he demanded.

'I do,' replied Moore, 'but they are not entirely accurate. There is an error in one of them.'

At this point William revealed his identity to Moore. The clergyman was taken aback and, realising that he was within earshot of other people, asked that they go somewhere private to discuss the matter. Once away from the limelight, Moore gave William an honest and accurate account of his involvement with the Parsons' ghost. William asked Moore if the *Ledger* had been right when it said that he was keeping a written record of the ghost's performances. Moore replied that this was true and offered to show William some of his notes.

Moore's notes consisted largely of a list of the questions that had been asked of the ghost with its answers pencilled in beside. William read them out loud to Moore, who showed very little emotion until they reached the point where the spirit had been asked whether Fanny and William had been married, to which the reply had been two knocks – for no. Moore stopped William and asked him whether in fact he and Fanny had been married.

William said that they had not been able to wed because of a quirk of Canon Law. Moore expressed his disapproval of this, but explained that he was not surprised to hear it, as the spirit had told him as much a couple of evenings earlier. It was, he explained, information like this that helped prove the ghost's reality, otherwise how could it have known about his living in sin with Fanny.

'Richard Parsons and his wife knew of Fanny and me,' replied William, 'and is not the ghost in their house? I am surprised that a man such as you could be taken in by a common prank such as this.'

At this Moore became defensive. 'You need not take my word for it,' he retorted; 'the spirit appears nightly. If you go to the Parsons' house then you too can witness it and become convinced of its reality. Mark my words, there is something dark lurking behind all this.'

William could see that he was making little headway against Moore, who was convinced both of the ghost's reality and that he was guilty of murder. Nonetheless, William needed to clear his name and that meant unmasking the ghost, a job that he was going to have to do for himself. Before he took his leave of Moore, it was agreed that William should go to Richard Parsons's house on the following evening, 12 January, so that he might witness the events for himself.

William's meeting with Moore served to convince him of the seriousness of the situation. It was becoming apparent that he was the victim of a conspiracy concocted by Richard Parsons's drunken brain in revenge for being forced to repay the twelve-guinea loan. Moore, on the other hand, was probably just a misguided clergyman whose head was filled with thoughts of ghosts and witches. Unfortunately, his faith was adding intellectual weight to the ghost's claims, and it occurred to

William that, if Parsons's aim was to get him hanged for Fanny's murder, then Moore's support might just see the job done. Thus his main hope for breaking this conspiracy was to turn Moore against Parsons, which meant convincing the clergyman that the ghost was not telling the truth. William needed evidence that his dear Fanny had not been poisoned but had instead died a natural death, but where was such evidence to be obtained?

The next morning William set out to find those people who had witnessed the torment of Fanny's last few days, and the two people best placed to do this were the physicians who had attended her deathbed. William went first to Dr Thomas Cooper, the medical practitioner who had treated Fanny from the discovery of her pregnancy through to her death. When he heard about the accusation of poisoning, Dr Cooper agreed to help William clear his name.

'Will you come with me this evening to Cock Lane?' asked William, 'I would welcome a witness so that this deception might be unmasked.'

'I will be there,' was Cooper's reply.

With Cooper's cooperation assured, William next made his way across town to Soho, a mazelike district of the West End filled with dozens of narrow lanes, blind alleys and pedestrian thoroughfares. Here, in Grafton Street, was the business of James Jones, the apothecary who had been called in to treat Fanny by Dr Cooper as soon as smallpox had been diagnosed.

Jones and Dr Cooper were friends, and, as soon as the apothecary heard of William's plight, he also agreed to be a witness to the events in Cock Lane that night. William returned home, hopeful that he had outmanoeuvred Richard Parsons. With two such credible witnesses, would the Parsons family and Moore still claim that Fanny had died from poisoning?[6]

For much of January 1762 the weather in London had been unsettled, with strong winds driving scattered showers of rain across the capital's already waterlogged streets. On Tuesday 12 January the already blustery conditions began to deteriorate into one of the worst winter storms of recent years. During the afternoon the strength of the wind increased, sending ships in the Thames estuary scurrying for the safety of the port. By lunchtime the rain had arrived, coming down in torrential sheets, soaking anyone foolish enough to step outside. Accompanying this were spectacular displays of lightning and thunder that shook house timbers and sent children running to their mothers. This was not a night for people to be abroad in the town.

The weather was of no consequence to William Kent. Regardless of the flooded streets and high winds, he was determined to face his accusers in the hope that he could silence them once and for all. He had arranged to meet Dr Cooper and Mr Jones in a local tavern from where they would travel on to Richard Parsons's house together. By the time the trio had met and taken a carriage to Cock Lane the weather had worsened to such a degree that fragments of roof slate and chimney pot littered the cobbled streets. In places the rain had flooded septic tanks, sending raw sewage into the road, but fortunately the houses in Cock Lane had been built with London's often flooded streets in mind. Each house had its ground floor a foot or so above the street level, which prevented any water and sewage from flowing under the front door, as it could in other parts of town. The storm was not going to disrupt that night's events, although the lightning and crashing thunder would certainly add a theatrical atmosphere to the proceedings.[7]

Kent and the two physicians pulled up outside the Parsons' house, which, because of the weather, was probably free from the curious tourists who had recently tended to besiege it. The sober-looking trio were greeted on the doorstep by the less than sober Richard Parsons. We can imagine that William must have struggled to utter any pleasantries to his former landlord and that he and his colleagues would have trooped upstairs to the children's bedchamber in silence.

The room was, as ever, in near complete darkness, the sole flickering candle providing just enough light to see the bed and the silhouettes of the few people gathered there. On the instructions of the Revd Moore, the number of witnesses in the room had been kept to a minimum. Other than Richard Parsons, his wife Elizabeth and John Moore, the only other people present were the Revd Thomas Broughton, the Parsons' friend Mary Fraser, who had adopted the role of the ghost's medium, and a man named Richard James, a local businessman and colleague of Moore's.

Moore was pleased to see William arrive but was not so happy to learn who his two guests were and why they had been brought as witnesses. With introductions made and false pleasantries exchanged, Moore asked Mary Fraser to make contact with the ghost of Miss Fanny. Without delay Mrs Fraser moved into the centre of the room and shouted: 'Fanny, Fanny, are you there dear Fanny?'

Apart from that the increasingly fierce storm outside, no noise was heard. Mrs Fraser began to move about the room, her head looking in all directions as though searching for a missing pet.

'Fanny, Fanny; why don't you come? Do come!'

Nothing was heard. Mrs Fraser, looking agitated, began to run about the room, her voice trying to coax the ghost into action.

'Pray Fanny come; dear Fanny come!'

The scene was rapidly becoming farcical, and Moore, observing the incredulous look upon the faces of William, Cooper and Jones, cut Mrs Fraser short.

'Enough!' he said to her. 'You make too much noise!'

He turned to address William and his friends.

'This ghost is a sulky, touchy thing,' said the clergyman, 'and we must take her as she runs. If you will leave the room and wait downstairs I will try and bring her myself. I will stamp my foot on the floor when she is here.'[8]

William and his learned colleagues did as they were bade and descended into the kitchen below. Here they waited for a few minutes, talking in low whispers that would occasionally be drowned out by claps of thunder and the sound of rain beating on the window panes. Eventually they heard the thump of a booted foot on the ceiling above and once again traipsed, single file, up the narrow staircase to the small bedroom.

'The ghost is here,' said Moore. As if to confirm this, a hollow knock emanated from somewhere near the centre of the room, where Betty Parsons and her sister lay in bed, apparently sleeping.

'I should like to hear you put the same questions to her as you have done before now,' said William to Moore.

'Agreed,' said Moore. 'Parsons and I have settled on a scheme whereby one knock is an affirmative and two a negative.' At this Moore produced a piece of paper on which were written the list of questions that had been shown to William the previous day. He began to speak in an earnest tone.

'Has any injury been done to any person that has lived in this house?'

There followed a short silence then, above the din of the rain and the wind, came a single but distinct knock. Its loudness took William by surprise, but even so he found it difficult to say from whence in the room it had come.

Moore noted the ghost's reply on his piece of paper in a matter-of-fact manner and then read the next question.

'Are you a woman?'

One knock.

'Are you Frances Lynes?'

One knock. On hearing this William looked uncomfortable.

'How many years is it since your death?'

Two knocks rang out, symbolising the two years since Fanny's decease.

'Was your death by natural means?'

Two knocks.

'Were you poisoned?'

One knock.

'Is your murderer known to you?'

One knock. At this Moore departed from his written script.

'Is your murderer in this room?'

A short pause and then one further single knock rang out. At this William became agitated and started to object, but before he could do so a voice rang out from the opposite side of the room. It was Richard Parsons.

'Kent!' he shouted. 'Ask the ghost if you shall be hanged!'

William was wrong-footed by this outburst and, for reasons best known to himself, did as he had been bade.

'Well then,' William demanded of the ghost. 'Am I to be hanged?'

The reply was almost immediate and came in the form of the loudest knock of the evening; a single hollow thump that came from one of the walls. One can imagine that in the half-light Richard Parsons was smiling broadly.

'Thou art a lying spirit,' shouted William into the gloom. 'Thou art not the ghost of my Fanny! She would never say such a thing!'[9]

Realising that he walked wide-eyed into a trap of Richard Parsons's making, William refused to hear another word. He stormed from the house, dragging Dr Cooper and Mr Jones with him. With his parting words William warned Moore that he would be hearing from him shortly.

It was approaching midnight, and outside the tempest was approaching its peak. Along the River Thames boats were being ripped free of their moorings and dashed to matchwood on the river bank. As the wind and tide combined, a surge of water travelled back along the river from the North Sea and into the London basin, spilling over the river defences into the low-lying land in Westminster and Millbank. It was the worst storm to hit the city for nearly twenty years, and by the morning several houses had blown down and a number of people lay dead. As such it was a very apposite omen of the storm that the Cock Lane ghost was about to cause in London society.[10]

The tempestuous events of 12 January made William Kent aware of several things, chief of which was that the charge of murder against him was going to be harder to shift than he had hitherto expected. It was quite clear in his mind that Richard Parsons, plus several of his friends and family, had devised means of faking ghostly knocks and that Moore had somehow been taken in by the scam. In fact, the clergyman seemed hell-bent on establishing that the ghost was real by proving that its central allegation of murder was true.

In the days that followed William was contacted by Dr Cooper, who said that he and Jones the apothecary would be happy to provide signed testimonies setting out the circumstances of Fanny's death. William declined, saying he hoped that it would not come to this and that the matter could be settled amicably and without resorting to the law.

Indeed, William had good cause to want to avoid any undue fuss. He had been economical with the truth about the tragedy of Fanny's death, and, although he had mentioned it to his new wife, he had neglected to tell her that they were not married at the time. He had also neglected to mention that his first wife Elizabeth and Fanny had been sisters. Were the truth of William's complex relationship with the Lynes family to get out, then he would have some explaining to do, especially to his brother-in-law, with whom he was about to enter into business.

William's hopes of a peaceful settlement were to be quickly dashed. In St Sepulchre's, people were already finding new and inventive ways of exploiting the presence of the ghost in Cock Lane.

As a close friend of Moore and also a probable Methodist sympathiser, Richard James had been invited to the meeting on 12 January as a witness to the proceedings. James was a well-known local businessman who ran a profitable gold-beating service in nearby Giltspur Street.[11] Like his clergyman friend, James was anxious to prove that the ghost of Fanny Lynes was real and felt that the case would benefit from a bit of free publicity in the newspapers. Moore concurred and gave permission for James to use his transcriptions of the ghost's question-and-answer sessions as the basis a newspaper article. James wasted no time in putting pen to paper, and later that week the following article appeared in the *Public Ledger*:

Between eleven and twelve o'clock at night, a respectable
clergyman was sent for, who, addressing himself to the supposed
spirit, desired, that if any injury had been done to the person who
had lived in that house, he might be answered in the affirmative by
one single knock; if the contrary, by two knocks. This was
immediately answered by one knock.

He then asked several questions, which were all very rationally
answered, and from which the following particulars were learned;
'That the spirit was a woman, her name Frances L——s; that she
had lived in fornication with Mr K——, whose first wife was her
sister, and that he had poisoned her by arsenic, and administering it
to her when ill of the small-pox'.[12]

It was through this article that the world outside St Sepulchre's parish
learned of the strange happenings taking place in Cock Lane. Londoners
loved nothing more than a good ghost story, especially one that hinted at
sexual misconduct and murder most foul. The same was true of the
newspaper editors. January was traditionally a time of no news and low
circulation figures, making the arrival of such a newsworthy item an
editor's dream come true. If Londoners wanted to know more about this
intriguing story, the newspapers would be only too happy to furnish
them with further details. The fact that much of what would be printed
was based on gossip and hearsay was not of great concern. Thanks to
Richard James the cat was out of the bag and there was to be no easy
means of getting it back inside again.

Faced with the unmovable certainty of John Moore's religious faith,
William decided to fight him head on, and so, after his first visit to the
ghost, he arranged a meeting with his local parish priest, the Revd
Stephen Aldrich. William may initially have approached Aldrich to ask
him to testify that Fanny's death was natural, as it was he who had given
Fanny absolution in her dying days. Her body also lay in the crypt of his

church of St John the Baptist, Clerkenwell. Fortunately, the Revd Aldrich decided that he wanted to be a good deal more involved with the Cock Lane ghost than this.

Aldrich was an ageing priest but also an experienced one. His academic credentials were impeccable: he had graduated from Emmanuel College, Cambridge, in 1730 and worked at a number of schools and churches. Aldrich was a no-nonsense character who disliked Methodism and who had no patience with superstition or the supernatural. He was also pragmatic and well connected, and, when he heard of William's troubles, he volunteered to help him look into the affair and, if possible, to unmask the fraud.[13]

William had by then organised with the Revd Moore to be present at another of the ghost's séances on 18 January. Aldrich agreed with William that he would attend and do his utmost to get the matter stopped dead in its tracks. William did not yet know it, but Aldrich would prove to be his greatest ally in his battle with Richard Parsons and John Moore.

12

ALDRICH AND THE MAYOR

A little after ten o'clock in the evening of 18 January 1762 a carriage drew up in Cock Lane. Inside was a determined-looking William Kent, James Jones the apothecary, the Revd Stephen Aldrich and a lawyer named Mr Selman. William was convinced that the ghost's tomfoolery was not going to stop of its own accord and so thought that the sight of an eminent priest and a lawyer might scare Moore and Parsons into submission.[1]

William and his colleagues were surprised to find that Cock Lane was so full of people that it took several minutes to force their carriage through the crowd to the Parsons' house. It was evident that the newspaper reports were dragging in the curious from all parts of the city.

The arrival of William's party must have caused a stir among the crowd. He would have been jeered at as he left his carriage, the accusations of murder and adultery echoing down the street after him. The commotion drew Mrs Parsons to the door; she ushered the gentlemen inside and asked them to be quiet. The ghost had arrived early and was already scratching and knocking in the children's room.

The company shuffled upstairs, where they found John Moore, Richard Parsons, his two daughters, Richard James and Mary Fraser already in attendance. Also present was Charles Watson, a friend of Moore's who lived just round the corner from St Sepulchre's church in Red Lion Court.[2] Whispered introductions were made, during which William was pleased to note Moore's displeasure at seeing Stephen Aldrich enter the room. When the assembled crowd had settled Mary Fraser stood up and began to call out into the darkened room:

'Fanny, are you come my dear? Pray tell me, what is it o'clock?'

An angry scratching noise was heard, signifying the spirit's displeasure.

'Do, my dear, don't be ill-natured,' said Fraser, 'Tell me what is it o'clock?'

On this a full ten knocks rang out, signifying that it was ten o'clock.

'How much after ten o'clock?'

One knock rang out, which Fraser interpreted as meaning a quarter past ten.

'The spirit is mistaken,' countered Aldrich; 'it is 35 minutes after ten.'

Aldrich arose and went to stand by the children's bed. Here he stamped his foot down hard on the floorboards, for which he received another angry scratching noise. He stamped again and in reply received a further bout of scratching. It was evident that Aldrich was trying to discover the exact location of the noise, but after several minutes of alternate stamping and scratching he could get no closer to a solution, as it was too dark to determine the noise's provenance with certainty.

Moore was anxious not to upset the elderly priest, but eventually he interceded. 'If we might carry on,' he said to Aldrich. 'I have many questions to put to the ghost and I don't want her upset.' The elderly clergyman agreed and withdrew to the side of the room.

'Fanny,' called out Fraser again, 'will you answer our questions? Answer do.'

One knock rang out, which, as Moore pointed out, meant 'yes'. Moore stepped forward with his sheet of prepared questions and began to read them out aloud, pausing after each one so that the ghost might reply.

'Is Mr Kent in the room?' asked Moore.

One knock.

'Have you been seen by any living person?'

One knock.

'Have you been seen by Mister Parsons and his daughter and Mr Franzen?'

One knock. At this point Aldrich again interjected.

'If then', he ventured, 'you have been seen by these people, then will you show yourself to those here present?'

Two very loud knocks rang out.

'What then', continued Aldrich, 'if Mr Kent were to be left in the room alone. Would you then appear to him?'

Again two knocks. Aldrich tried one more time.

'If Mr Kent was to leave the room, then would you appear to those of us that remain.'

Two knocks. Aldrich signalled to Moore that he had finished and that he could continue with his prepared questions.

'Are you the wife of William Kent?' asked Moore.

One knock.

'Did you die of natural causes?'

Two knocks. William shifted uneasily, knowing full well what was to follow.

'Did you die by poison?'

One knock.

'Did any person other than Mr Kent administer it to you?'

Two knocks.

'Was it given in water-gruel, beer or any other liquid?'

As Moore said the word beer the knocks rang out; this caused William to interject.

'But my Fanny had never drank beer in her life; she preferred to drink purl [a drink that is a mix of ale and spirits, usually gin, often with sugar and ginger added].'

On hearing this Moore rephrased the question.

'Was the poison given in beer or purl?'

The ghost knocked for purl. William's outburst had only served to correct the error.

'How long did you live after receiving the poison?'

Three knocks followed, which, according to Moore, signified three hours.

'Did the girl named Carrots know that you had been poisoned?'

One knock. Moore noted this reply with some satisfaction, believing that he might at last have found evidence of a witness to William's murderous deed.

'Should Mr Kent be taken up for your murder?'

One knock.

At this point Aldrich took one of the room's few lighted candles and walked over to the children's bed. He stooped down and used the candle to look beneath the bed; he could see nothing untoward and again returned to his position.

'Should Mr Kent speak to you?' asked Moore of the ghost, but he received no reply. He asked again but to no avail.

'It is the candle,' said Mary Fraser. 'Fanny does not like the light and shies away from it. If we are patient then she may return.'

A few minutes later and the scratching noise returned again, signalling the ghost's renewed presence. Moore took up the questioning once more.

'How many clergyman are here present?' he asked.

One knock.

'Are there not two of us?' asked the Revd Aldrich of the Revd Moore.

'Ah yes,' countered Moore, 'but you were not known to the ghost before now.'

In fact, Aldrich had been known to Fanny, as he was at her bedside during the last hours of her life, but, unlike William, he decided not to argue the toss, preferring to leave the ghost in error. Instead, Aldrich took the opportunity to ask some questions of his own.

'Are you Fanny Lynes?'

One knock.

'Was Mr Jones or Mr Selman your apothecary?'

On this the angry scratching noise was heard. Mary Fraser quickly stepped in and asked 'Was Mr Jones your apothecary?' To this the ghost answered with one knock. Aldrich was annoyed at this, being convinced that Fraser had given the ghost the answer to a question that had hitherto stumped it.

Other people in the room began to ask their own questions. Some were frivolous, such as Elizabeth Parsons asking whether or not she was sat on a chair (one knock was given); others were more serious, especially those asked by Stephen Aldrich.

'Will you appear at my house?' asked Aldrich. He was pleased to receive an affirmative one knock in return, but before he could capitalise on this Richard Parsons, who had been remarkably quiet thus far, could contain himself no more.

'Will you be pleased if William Kent is hanged?' he shouted out. The ghost knocked once, signalling that, yes, she would indeed be pleased. Parsons observed the look of displeasure on William's face and lapsed back into silence, his mischief having been made.

Mr Selman, the lawyer, took his turn, asking the ghost how long it had been dead (two knocks signifying two years), whether it would knock on the bedpost (two knocks) and, most bizarrely, whether or not she could hear if he spoke in a whisper. Selman said this in such a low voice that the ghost evidently didn't hear him and did not reply.

The final question of the evening came from Aldrich.

'If you really want Mr Kent to be taken up then appear before us now. Do this and we will gladly give you the satisfaction that you desire.' After this there followed a series of angry scratching noises, after which the ghost went silent and could not be persuaded to reappear.[3]

As the meeting broke up Aldrich had seen enough to know that he had just been witness to a clever sideshow orchestrated by the Parsons, Mary Fraser and others. He said as much to Moore, who was affronted by his fellow clergyman's scepticism. Moore told Aldrich that he believed that the next night would provide proof of the ghost's reality, for he had arranged for Carrots, Miss Fanny's servant, to come before the ghost. According to Moore, only Carrots could provide the evidence necessary to bring William to justice.

Aldrich said that for the time being he had seen enough and would not be attending the next evening. William, on the other hand, was anxious to keep some measure of control over the proceedings and agreed to come. If Carrots was to give evidence against him, then he wanted to be around to hear it.

Outside the Parsons' house the crowd remained as thick as ever; they had been listening to the knocking from outside, although they had not been able to hear the questions that went with it. For these they would have to wait for the report in the newspapers. William and his friends emerged into the street to cat calls and further jeering. Ignoring the rabble, they boarded their carriage and left Cock Lane.

Although he was still unsure how he had managed to find himself in this position, William felt certain that, with people such as Aldrich on his side, the issue would somehow be resolved in his favour. Furthermore, Mr Selman advised that, on the basis of what he had seen that evening, there were strong grounds for bringing an action of libel against the Parsons family and Moore, but to do so successfully they would first need to unmask the human agents behind the ghost.

On the morning of Tuesday 19 January John Moore set about making his plans for that evening's séance. He was convinced that, when Carrots was placed before the ghost, she would corroborate its accusation of murder. Her confession could then be used to obtain a warrant for the arrest of William Kent.

Moore was anxious to have as many eminent witnesses to that evening's events as was possible and so he spent much of the day trying to persuade his friends and peers that they should attend the Parsons' house that night. Most of them were well aware of what had been happening in Cock Lane and wanted nothing to do with it. Doubtless some believed that Moore's enthusiasm for the ghost was blinding him to the potential danger of the situation. Others probably did not want to become involved in an affair that would surely end up in the courts with either William on trial for his life or Moore on trial for libel. Even so, a few people agreed to accompany Moore to the Parsons' house that night.

The first to do so were Philip Quaque and William Cudjoe, Moore's young African students. It was they who had first alerted Moore to the knocking noises in Cock Lane and they had evidently remained curious about the ghost. As both boys had ambitions of a career in the church, Moore probably felt that they would make reliable witnesses.[4]

Moore also managed to recruit a further two Methodist clergymen. One of these was his old friend and confidant Thomas Broughton, the other was the Revd William Dodd, a controversial character who was well known in London society. Dodd was a couple of years older than Moore but was noted for being 'young, thoughtless, volatile and inexperienced' and also something of an egotist.[5] He had at one time been a writer and then a private tutor before finally entering the Church, a job into which he had only fitfully settled. Dodd, who came from a humble background, liked luxurious living, and the lack of money associated with his church career worried him. At the time that Moore approached him he was in the process of ingratiating himself with the senior clergy in London, and as a consequence was starting to become quite well known. (Indeed, a few months later he would be made chaplain to the King.) Never one to turn down an opportunity for self-promotion, Dodd was happy to let himself be associated with the increasingly famous Cock Lane ghost.

In addition, Moore also arranged for James Franzen to be present (probably because Carrots seemed to trust him), as well as Mary Fraser, Charles Watson, a Mr Gibson and others.[6]

Charles Watson was a Methodist sympathiser and a friend of Moore's and had been invited to witness the ghost on at least one other occasion. Unlike the trusting Moore, Watson was not fully convinced of the ghost's veracity and, as a local resident, would have been fully aware of Richard Parsons's poor reputation. The appearance of Mary Fraser (another local bad apple) in the role of ghost raiser *extraordinaire* only served to increase his doubt. The sight of William arriving with the Revd Aldrich and Mr Selman the lawyer made Watson even more uneasy. He sensed trouble brewing for the ghost's supporters and felt that it was his duty to try and head it off.

On 19 January, while Moore was trying to find 'reliable witnesses' for that evening's performance, Charles Watson took the liberty of alerting his local Alderman to the developing situation in Cock Lane. London's Aldermen were there to act as a barrier against corruption and oppression within the city. By 1762 there were twenty-six of them, each representing a particular ward. The position was an elected one, although only Freemen of London (that is, important people such as politicians and businessmen) were entitled to vote. Since 1741 the Aldermen had been empowered to act as Justices of the Peace within the city, a position that permitted them to sit in judgment in cases of petty crime or disturbance. The Aldermen quickly became a first port of call when it came to settling matters that were likely to lead to a breach of the peace.[7]

The Alderman for Ludgate, the ward in which Cock Lane is situated, was Francis Gosling, a successful City banker and noted philanthropist.[8] Watson arrived at Alderman Gosling's Fleet Street house in the morning. He was granted an immediate appointment and outlined to Gosling what was happening at Cock Lane. 'This affair is likely to gain much ground yet,' warned Watson, 'I think that you should interpose before events begin to run out of control, as they surely will.'

Alderman Gosling was no fool and realised that what Watson was saying was true. It sounded as though Cock Lane was providing Londoners with an explosive mixture of supernatural happenings, sexual misconduct and, for good measure, an accusation of murder. Rioting was a popular pastime among the common sort, and the foundations for a good riot were being laid in west Smithfield. Gosling was not a timid man by nature, but his authority went only so far, and he was not keen to take on the sole responsibility for sorting out this mess.

'I do not care to interfere in this matter alone,' he informed Watson. 'I should be happier if we had the authority of the Lord Mayor on our side. We should acquaint him with this matter. Go presently and fetch the Revd Moore and we will shall see the Lord Mayor together.'

This was not exactly what Watson wanted to hear, but he did as he was asked and returned a short while later with Moore, who must have been less than delighted to find out that his ghost was now drawing the attention of the London authorities. Gosling, Moore and Watson travelled together to the Lord Mayor's office, where they were swiftly granted an appointment.[9]

In 1762 the Lord Mayor of London was Sir Samuel Fludyer, the 58-year-old descendant of a wealthy clothier. His tenure as Mayor had begun the year before, with his first duty being to host a banquet for King George III and Queen Charlotte. Here Fludyer was surprised to learn that, under an ancient tradition, the only members of the feast permitted to have a knife, fork and napkin were himself and the King and Queen: everybody else had either to bring their own or use their hands.[10]

As the ghost's greatest supporter, Moore had the responsibility of explaining to the Mayor what had been happening in Cock Lane. He was at pains to stress the reality of the situation: that he had personally investigated the affair and had been unable to determine the origin of the noises. Moore's testimony ended with a plea that the Lord Mayor order the arrest of William Kent on the charge of murdering Fanny Lynes. He promised that proof would be forthcoming from the testimony of Carrots, who was due to face the ghost that very evening. Watson grudgingly supported his friend, but Gosling kept quiet, not wishing to become any further embroiled in this affair than was absolutely necessary. The Mayor felt much the same way as his Alderman.

'I cannot say that I would choose to stir much in this affair,' he said to the assembled trio, 'and I am not yet satisfied that there is enough evidence to order Kent's arrest. However, I will give you four days in which to procure this evidence – I hereby grant you a full hearing on 23 January.'

Mayor Fludyer was not at all grateful to Gosling for having deposited this particular problem on his doorstep and hoped that the matter could be resolved before the 23rd came round. Moore's description of mysterious noises, an unproven accusation of murder and, worst of all, seething crowds of people in Cock Lane took the Mayor's mind back to another extraordinary affair that had occurred several years earlier.

'I am sorely reminded of the Elizabeth Canning affair,' he told Moore, 'and that worries me.' Fludyer had good cause to worry, for the recollection of the Elizabeth Canning affair was enough to make the blood of any Lord Mayor of London run cold.[11]

Prior to the appearance of the Cock Lane ghost, London had been remarkably free from scandal for several years. Much of this was to do with the so-called Elizabeth Canning affair, a baffling mystery that, like the Cock Lane ghost, had the whole of London up in arms. In this instance both the 'mob' (that is, London's working masses) and the authorities had had their fingers badly burnt, so much so that afterwards great pains were taken to avoid a similar situation arising again. Unfortunately the Cock Lane ghost was not only to slip through the net; it was to become a far bigger scandal than the one that had surrounded Elizabeth Canning.

The 'Canning affair' began on 1 January 1753 when Elizabeth Canning, then a girl in her early twenties, took a short walk from her mother's London house to see her aunt and uncle. On the way home she was (by her account) assaulted and kidnapped by two men who robbed and bound her and then dragged her semi-conscious to the house of one Susannah Wells. Here she was kept prisoner for a month by Mary Squires, a gipsy, and two other girls. Squires allegedly asked Elizabeth to become a prostitute and when she refused all but her underclothes were removed and she was locked in a hayloft. For one month Elizabeth alleged that she managed to live on a few crusts of bread, a mince pie and a single pitcher of water. She also claimed that she had not gone to the toilet during this whole time. After twenty-eight days Elizabeth managed to break out of her jail and made her way home to her mother.

After Elizabeth had told her tale to the authorities, Susannah Wells and Mary Squires were arrested, though both of them denied having ever seen Elizabeth before in their lives. However, a servant of Wells and Squires (named Virtue Hall) confirmed Elizabeth's story but only after herself being threatened with prison. Based on Virtue's evidence Squires and Wells were convicted at the Old Bailey and sentenced to lengthy jail terms. Also jailed were three gentlemen (John Gibson, William Clerk and Thomas Grevil) who had offered evidence against Canning. They had sworn that they had seen Squires living in Dorset at the time of her supposed imprisonment. The case was widely publicised in the newspapers, and the convictions were welcomed by Londoners. However, not everybody was convinced by what they had heard.

Several eminent gentlemen smelt something fishy about Elizabeth's testimony. Could she really have lived for a month on such a small amount of bread and water and still have had the strength to escape? Could she really have gone for a month without urinating and defecating? They seriously doubted it and between them gathered enough evidence to prove that, at the time of Canning's supposed kidnap and imprisonment in London, Mary Squires had been living near Abbotsbury, Dorset. As a consequence, in June 1753 Squires and the others were pardoned, much to the anger of the London mob, the majority of whom believed them to be guilty. The thought of Squires being released created an uneasy atmosphere in London, something that was further stoked by the newspapers' sensationalist reporting of the affair.

The Lord Mayor of the day, Sir Crisp Gascoyne, decided to investigate the affair himself in an attempt to find on which side the guilt lay. His enquiries were exhaustive and followed avidly by the media. As it became clear that Gascoyne was coming out against Elizabeth Canning, so the anger of the mob increased, leading to demonstrations and, eventually, rioting.

Ignoring the mob's displeasure, the Lord Mayor decided that there was enough evidence to prosecute Elizabeth Canning, and so, in May 1754, she was brought before the Old Bailey. Mary Squires was able to produce over thirty reliable witnesses to her having been in Dorset the previous January, while Canning could provide only character witnesses. Elizabeth was duly convicted and sentenced to transportation to America for seven years. News of this prompted yet more rioting, but the sentence was carried out.

The real reason as to why Elizabeth Canning should have gone missing for a month and then blamed her disappearance on complete strangers was never discovered, although many suspected that an illicit love affair might have been the cause. The 'Canning affair', as it was commonly referred to, shook and alarmed all Londoners. One contemporary source said of it:

> No affair did so much to excite the curiosity or divide the opinion of the public; the newspapers and magazines were for a long time filled with little else than accounts of Canning and Squires. Ten thousand quarrels arose from, and fifty thousand wagers were laid on, this business. All of Great Britain and Ireland seemed to be interested in the event: the first question in the morning was, 'What news of Canning?' and the last squabble at night was whether she was honest or perjured.[12]

Once acquainted with the events surrounding the Cock Lane ghost, both Alderman Gosling and Mayor Fludyer could recognise that the mob was becoming excited in the same way as it had over the Canning affair. If the Mayor had acted immediately, he might have had the chance to sort out the mess before any trouble could start, but, for fear of denting his reputation, he chose to leave the Cock Lane matter to its own devices for several days. This was a bad error of judgement, for it was in those few days that the brewing scandal in Cock Lane took on a life of its own and in the process became uncontrollable.[13]

13

THE RETURN OF CARROTS

Shortly after dark on 19 January 1762, James Franzen went to fetch Esther Carlisle (the red-headed servant otherwise known as Carrots) and took her back to Richard Parsons's house. Moore had requested that Carrots be brought to the house ahead of the ghost's performance so that he could interview her in front of witnesses. Franzen showed Carrots into a downstairs room, where she found Moore, Mrs Parsons and Mary Fraser already assembled.

On seeing the young girl, Moore asked her to sit down. The two had not met before, and it appears that Moore did not even know Esther's real name, referring to her only as Carrots. He was also unaware of her strong personality and stubborn nature and the fact that, despite the potentially unnerving circumstance in which she found herself, she was not one to be intimidated. Moore began by explaining the background to the ghost's arrival in Cock Lane.

'This house has been troubled by knocking and scratching noises for nearly three years,' he explained. 'We have deduced that the agent behind these noises is the ghost of your former mistress, Miss Fanny Lynes. The ghost tells us that she was given poison two to three hours before she died and you were witness to this. Miss Fanny says that she told you who gave her poison just before her decease. We believe that the murderer was your old master, Mr William Kent.'

Carrots listened patiently and then said in reply: 'I'm sure that Miss Fanny did no such thing for my master and mistress were very loving and lived very happily together.'

Moore ignored this and continued to pursue Fanny's presumed murderer. 'Ah,' said he, 'but the ghost tells me that if you were taken up and carried before a magistrate you would give an account of the murder for she told nobody but you about her fate.'

'Sir,' said Carrots, 'I assure you that I know nothing at all about this affair. My mistress could not speak for nigh on four days before her death.'

'But you must know something,' said Moore earnestly, 'and I now insist that you tell me the truth!'

'I do not know what you mean by the truth,' said Carrots, 'for I know nothing of this matter.'

Moore's line of questioning troubled Carrots, as did the insistent tone in his voice. The talk of magistrates and murder was unsettling and it was clear that he was not going to take 'no' for an answer. Carrots decided that it was time for her to make her excuses and leave. She stood up.

'I am wanted at another place,' she said sharply, 'and I must be there this evening.' Moore moved to block her way.

'Nay,' he said, 'you must stay and hear the knocking for yourself. You have nothing to fear from us and we shall ensure that you are provided for. You need not fear this place.'

Moore's offer of money persuaded Carrots to stay, but she had no intention of playing along with his story. She decided to take part in whatever charade Richard Parsons had concocted for that evening and then never return to Cock Lane again.[1]

At around ten o'clock the other witnesses started to arrive, including William Kent. In total around twenty people managed to squeeze themselves into the children's small room, many of whom were there for the first time. Kent must have wondered what revelations awaited him that night, especially considering that his former servant had also been summoned to appear before the ghost.

With so many important people in the audience, Moore wanted to give them a show trial that could leave no one in the slightest doubt of the ghost's veracity. The first thing he did was to order Philip Quaque and William Cudjoe to strip the children's bed and to search for any concealed devices therein. The two young men obliged.

With the bed returned to its made-up state, and the children tucked under the bedclothes, the ghost-raising routine began. As before, Mary Fraser opened the proceedings by moving about the room, banging on the skirting boards and requesting that Fanny answer back.

'Fanny, Fanny, are you coming? Fanny, are you coming dear lady?'

The ghost arrived promptly and Moore began to put questions to it, most of which concerned Fanny's supposed murder.

'Did you come to an untimely end by poison?'

One knock.

'In what was the poison given, purl or beer?'

Knock for purl.

'How long before your end was it given?'

Three hours.

'Is the person called Carrots able to give information about the poison?'

One knock.

'Was any person other than Mr Kent concerned with the poisoning?'

Two knocks.

'Can you leave this house?'

One knock.

'Will you follow Betty Parsons everywhere she goes?'

One knock.

'Are you pleased to be asked these questions?'

One knock, followed by a sound described as being like 'the fluttering of wings'. The questions became serious once more.

'How long before your death did you tell Carrots, your servant, that you had been poisoned?'

One knock, taken to mean one hour. At this Carrots spoke up.

'I protest. My mistress was not capable of speaking for days before her death.'

'Ah,' replied Moore, 'but she may have done so though you might not have understood it.' And, returning to his questioning, he asked: 'How many days did Carrots live as a servant with you?'

Four knocks, taken to signify the four days that Carrots lived with Fanny before her death. Carrots confirmed that this was true.

'Is Carrots in this room?'

One knock.

'Does she know anything of the murder?'

One knock.

'Is your murderer here?'

One knock.

'If Carrots and her master are taken up before a magistrate, will they confess?'

One knock. At this Carrots interceded again.

'Are you really my mistress?' she asked. (One knock.) 'Then I am sure, madam, you may be ashamed of yourself, for I never hurt you in my life!'

After this brave outburst Carrots stood up and fled from the room, rushing down the stairs and into the mass of onlookers that filled Cock Lane.

With his star witness gone, Moore was unsettled. After all, he had wanted to extract a confession to William's guilt from her. Moore's questioning began to take a different tack as he resorted to asking the ghost questions that he hoped would prove that it was not of this Earth.

'How many clergyman are there in the room?' he asked.

Three knocks. This was correct.

'And how many negroes?'

Two knocks; one each for Philip and William.

'And what colour is my watch?'

It knocked for black, which was apparently true.

The séance continued in this fashion for some hours before, at around four in the morning, the ghost finally took its leave of the house. The tired witnesses filed out into the street to make their weary way home. The remaining bystanders outside, aware that there would be no more noises that night, also began to drift homeward.

William was much encouraged by what he had seen and was now certain that the ghost had been created by Richard Parsons and his cronies. William must have known that Parsons was a fool who could be scared easily with threats of legal action, but dealing with him while he was under the protection of Moore was problematic. Before leaving, William pulled Moore to one side and gave him a warning.

'If you carry on with this affair,' he said to the clergyman, 'then you will suffer for it in the end. The ghost is an impostor.'

Moore was not downhearted and denied this. 'No, the ghost is real enough and I shall prove it.'[2]

Kent left the house and strode off into the night. Moore had had his chance. The next day Kent would put the legal wheels in motion.

Back in the Parsons' house everybody had left apart from James Franzen and Mary Fraser, who alone remained in the children's room. Franzen had been so frightened at what he had seen that he literally could not move through fear.

'When do you think the ghost will come again, Mrs Fraser?' asked the petrified Franzen.

'Oh,' she replied, 'she will come again soon. Let us go to prayer.'

Mrs Fraser picked up a copy of *The Book of Common Prayer* and started to read the Lord's Prayer. This somewhat surprised Franzen, as he had hitherto supposed her to be 'a bad woman'.

'Why do you not pray?' she asked of Franzen, who had remained silent.

'I wish I could pray,' replied he, 'but I am too frightened to say the words.'

Fraser seemed to be annoyed by this and threw down the book, shouting: 'Damn that ghost! I'll fetch her presently!'

With that the knocking noises started again. Franzen was so scared that he could think of only one question to ask the ghost.

'Will I be frightened to death?' he stammered.

One knock was returned, signifying that he would. The terrified publican fled from the Parsons' house back to the Wheat Sheaf. Here he and his wife spent a nerve-racking night listening to strange knocking noises that seemed to have followed them into their bedroom.

This was the last time that Franzen would witness the ghost. His fear of the supernatural had got the better of him, and memories of the experience followed him for years afterward, causing him to tremble whenever he recounted the occurrence.[3]

14

A CIRCULATION WAR

When the events of the evenings of 18 and 19 January 1762 hit the newspapers, they lifted the Cock Lane ghost from being a local curiosity to a national phenomenon. In the eyes of Moore and his supporters they now had ample evidence to order the arrest of William Kent on a charge of murder, but it was Richard James (Moore's businessmen friend) who was to be the instigator of the Cock Lane ghost's rise to superstar status.

James, who had witnessed the ghost on more than one occasion, had already placed an article in the *Public Ledger* in the hope that it might attract further information about William and Fanny's time in London. However, instead of providing more information on William and Fanny, the articles had served only to excite the curiosity of the *Ledger*'s readers, many of whom had later travelled to Cock Lane to witness the ghost for themselves. Others had contacted the paper personally, in the hope of getting further information. From this reaction it was obvious to the *Public Ledger*'s publishers that the Cock Lane ghost was going to be big news. The London newspaper world was a small and competitive one, and soon other publishers turned their attention to the ghost's story.

The *Public Ledger* had been founded in January 1760, so at the time of the Cock Lane ghost it was barely 2 years old. Despite its youth, this daily newspaper had already proved itself to be innovative and forward thinking. It was, for example, the first newspaper to use a four-column page, something that would become an industry standard within a decade. It had also developed a means of discreet advertising whereby a person could place an advertisement in the paper that only hinted at

22 Denmark Road
Exeter
EX1 1SL
23.5.16

Dear Adam

Does this fill in some gaps for
you?

I could write reams on these
are various ~ bones in this
precis of my family's lives but

when
think.
If you have any queries let
me know.
Lots of love
Joan

what was being offered. Those attracted could then travel to the *Public
Ledger*'s head office and, on the payment of three pence, see the full text
along with the details of the person who had placed it. In addition, each
edition of the *Public Ledger* included an index to the advertisements
carried by all other English newspapers, something that made it very
popular to both advertisers and readers.

The *Public Ledger*'s subtitle, the *Daily Register of Commerce and
Intelligence*, reveals the nature of its intended readership – namely,
London's commercial sector, a rich source of literate middle-class men
who had the time and money to take a daily paper. By choosing to target
this lucrative market, the *Public Ledger* immediately put itself in direct
competition with the *Daily Gazetteer*, a best-selling London daily that
had been in existence since 1735.

The appearance of the *Public Ledger* wrong-footed the *Daily Gazetteer*,
and for several months it found itself trying to catch up with the new
periodical. In the year following the appearance of the *Public Ledger*, the
Daily Gazetteer had been forced to mimic its four-column style and to
introduce a 'commercial register' in competition to its rival's popular
'commercial index'. This 'commercial register' included for the first time
a list of current commodity prices, something that was difficult and
time-consuming to compile. Within two months the *Public Ledger* had
launched its own 'price current', conveying the same information.[1]

The battle for readers, which included a price war, continued
throughout 1761 and into 1762. Both papers were anxious to please
their target audience, and the popularity of the Cock Lane ghost was an
opportunity they could not miss.

The printer (and therefore the managing editor) of the *Daily Gazetteer*
was Charles Green Say, whose offices were in Newgate Street, barely a
stone's throw from Cock Lane.[2] Say kept a close eye on the *Public Ledger*'s
content and would often pick up on stories that it had covered (the
Ledger would do the same to the *Daily Gazetteer*). The newspaper
industry may have been relatively young, but plagiarism was already a

way of life. Say had read the *Public Ledger*'s account of the Cock Lane
séance held on 12 January but may not have dwelt much upon it until a
few days later when news started to trickle in of large crowds gathering
in Cock Lane eager to witness the phantom for themselves. Considering
how close he was to Cock Lane, Say may even have been tempted to pay
a visit himself. Whether he did or not, he did become interested in the
affair, and he somehow managed to poach the *Ledger*'s author. Richard
James, the local businessman who was in the inner circle of the Cock
Lane ghost's confidantes (and who may even have been bank-rolling
some of the expenses associated with the affair), was now working for
the *Daily Gazetteer*.[3]

Not to be outdone, the *Public Ledger* recruited a new special
correspondent of its own. The *Ledger*'s offices were based in the
churchyard of St Paul's Cathedral, and it did not need to go very far to
find someone willing to report for it. Near its own offices in the
churchyard was the shop of one William Bristow, a printer of
pamphlets. Bristow had already visited the scene of the ghost once and
had even interviewed Mrs Parsons. Bristow was the ideal candidate and
was easily recruited to the cause.[4] In the coming weeks the *Daily
Gazetteer* and the *Ledger* would do battle with one another over the
Cock Lane ghost. The ghost was selling newspapers and was also
drawing other printers into the affray. The story was about to become
headline news.

The opening salvo of the war came on 20 January, the day after poor
Carrots had been interrogated by Moore and his supposed ghost. The
editions of both the *Daily Gazetteer* and the *Public Ledger* carried Cock
Lane on their front pages, spreading news of what was happening in
Cock Lane across London and into the surrounding countryside. The
Public Ledger's report was the shorter of the two and slightly confused,
containing a mixture of information from the start of the affair through
to the questions of the 12 January séance. Evidently Mr Bristow had
been forced to cobble together the article at short notice.

Not so the *Daily Gazetteer*. Richard James was not only a witness to all that had happened in Cock Lane; he also had access to the detailed minutes that Moore had been making at each séance. His report was lengthy and included a complete list of the questions asked on 18 January as well as the answers given by the ghost and the reaction of key participants such as Kent and Moore.[5]

The tone of both articles implied at all times that the ghost was a real spirit and its answers truthful. The *Ledger*'s article ended with a plea to John Moore and a warning to William Kent. It asked Moore to 'oblige the public with the whole detail' so that it might lead 'to the conviction of the incredulous'. Like the modern press, eighteenth-century editors knew that readers preferred their news to be sensational and that they would rather be told that there was a ghost in Cock Lane than not.

Circulation figures regrettably are not available for newspapers at this time, but the coverage of the Cock Lane ghost must have had a noticeable effect on sales, for within a few days every single paper in London was reporting on the phenomenon. The majority of these other papers were not dailies but instead came out every two or three days. In the absence of any other source, most simply reprinted the lengthy *Daily Gazetteer* article by James that contained, word for word, all the questions and answers, but in at least one case the *Ledger*'s version was also reprinted.

By 21 January news of the Cock Lane ghost could be found in almost every London paper, including the *St James's Chronicle*, the *London Chronicle* and *Lloyd's Evening Post*, where it was front-page news. Only the *Public Advertiser*, which carried little public news, abstained from printing anything about the ghost, but eventually it too would join in the commotion.

Over the next few weeks Londoners would get used to reading about the latest news on the Cock Lane ghost in their periodicals, and in time people on the streets would talk of little else. However, the hitherto light-hearted manner in which the ghost had been treated would not last for long. A battle was developing between the ghost's supporters and its detractors, leading to a split in London society and the media that fed it.

By the evening of 20 January the whole of London was aflame with talk of the ghost of Miss Fanny. The newspapers and word of mouth had done their job well, and from midday onwards people started to arrive at Cock Lane, causing it to become clogged solid with human bodies and carriages. All were hoping that the ghost would put on a public display and once more openly accuse William Kent of murder.

The crowd was to be disappointed, for Richard Parsons, on seeing the increasing numbers of people arriving outside his house, had become greatly alarmed. With the aid of Moore, the Parsons family was removed to a house on the corner of Hosier Lane belonging to James Bruin, a pawnbroker, and his wife, Mary.[6] Although this refuge was only one street away from Cock Lane, the Parsons had somehow managed to escape detection by the mob and were safe there for the time being. However, although the Parsons had escaped the public's gaze, they would from then onwards find it increasingly difficult to escape the scrutiny of interested parties with a point to prove.

Earlier in the day Moore had been approached by three eminent gentlemen who, having read of the affair, wished to witness the ghost for themselves and, if possible, to test it to see if they could detect a fraud. Given that two of these gentlemen were the Earl of Northumberland and a prominent MP, Moore did not feel in a position to refuse. Besides which, if these gentlemen could be convinced of the ghost's veracity, then surely the Lord Mayor could not refuse to start a prosecution against William Kent and his accomplice, Carrots.[7]

In addition, Moore had also granted access to the Revd Stephen Aldrich, the sceptical clergyman who had previously visited the ghost with William Kent. As public interest in the ghost had increased, so Aldrich had become more involved with the affair and had begun gathering evidence against Richard Parsons and the other ghost-raisers. William, on the other hand, wanted nothing further to do with the ghost and, faced with the real danger of being lynched by the mob, had retired to Greenwich, where the crowds could not trouble him. Before leaving, William handed over the task of unmasking the deception to Aldrich.

When Richard Parsons found out that Moore's guest list now included peers, MPs and assorted learned gentlemen, he must have been less than happy. Thus far the Parsons family had fared well from the ghost's activities. Richard was in receipt of a stipend from Moore, and he had been promised a lump sum should the ghost be able to secure a prosecution against William Kent. The Parsons benefited from large quantities of food and drink brought to the house by curious visitors and by local businessmen, many of whom were grateful for the extra tourist trade being drummed up by the ghost. However, perhaps the greatest incentive of all was an offer by Moore to secure Richard Parsons the job of clerk in the Methodist Tabernacle on the Tottenham Court Road. This was the Methodists' main meeting hall, located in the fashionable west end of London, and so this would be a plum job that would see the Parsons move into a much better neighbourhood.[8]

However, such benefits now looked to be coming at a price, as Richard Parsons found himself caught between Moore's enthusiasm to see William prosecuted and the London authorities' desire to see the ghost proved to be a fraud. There were also rumours, printed with glee by the newspapers, that William was preparing a lawsuit against the ghost's supporters. In his more sober moments Parsons could perhaps see himself being dragged into a dangerous court case by this affair, but the ball was rolling and there was little he could do to stop it. To call a halt would be to risk losing his job and house as well as increasing the possibility of his being arrested for fraud or sued by William. Although Parsons wished the ghost would now fade away, he had no choice but to continue playing along with Moore's plans in the hope that the public would lose interest in the affair. It was a vain hope.

From the late evening onwards the visitors started to arrive at Mr Bruin's house in Hosier Lane. The coach containing the Earl of Northumberland and his colleagues got there shortly before ten o'clock, and the gentlemen were directed upstairs to where Betty Parsons lay in bed on her own. The young Anne Parsons, who had previously shared a bed with her sister, had been removed to another room; she would play no further part in the Cock Lane affair. From then onwards the spotlight would be focused on Betty, but the publicity and disturbed nights were already taking their toll on her health. She was also scared of the situation in which she found herself and had recently become melancholic and prone to sudden shaking fits.

That evening was the first occasion on which the ghost was forced to perform without many of its usual followers being present. Mary Fraser, the 'bad woman' who normally acted as the ghost's interlocutrix, was absent, as was Mrs Parsons, Richard James, Charles Watson and several others. At the request of the Earl of Northumberland, they had not been permitted to remain with Betty, although her father, Moore and two of his clergymen friends were allowed to be in the room.

Stephen Aldrich had also been invited and when he arrived at the house, at a little after ten, the performance had already started. He was shown upstairs but was not permitted to enter the room, as the Earl had requested that he be alone with Betty, so that he might interview the ghost alone. The rest of the crowd, including the Earl's two friends, was forced to wait outside, listening to the proceedings from behind a closed door.

The scratching noises duly arrived and the questioning began. The Earl was a sceptic and was not questioning the ghost with regard to finding out information with which to prosecute William. He suspected Betty of making the noises herself and wanted to see if he could catch her out. Northumberland managed to ask some mundane questions ('Were you poisoned?', etc.) before his friends, overcome with excitement, burst into the room. The noises immediately stopped. One of the men placed himself at Betty's side, leaning on the bed. At the sight of this Moore interjected, asking him not to sit in that way. The gentleman replied angrily: 'Sir, I came here with a design to know the truth of this affair, and I think that I have the right to place myself in any part of the room which I look on as most suspicious!'

An altercation between Moore and the eminent visitors followed, which ended with the three gentlemen storming out of the house. Before leaving, one of the men requested that the child be moved to his house, where she could be observed under strict conditions. Richard Parsons refused the offer. As they left a threat was hurled at Mr Parsons: 'I am authorised to say', shouted the man, 'that a person of distinction has interested himself in the discovery of this affair!'

Who this person of distinction is we cannot be sure for in the coming days and weeks a great many distinguished people would become embroiled with the ghost. The aggressive nature of the men's departure left Betty 'extraordinarily agitated', which caused one of the guests to express his surprise.

'That is because Miss Fanny has not yet been entertained,' explained Richard Parsons. Despite this, the ghost did not reappear that night, even though several people sat up through to the early hours. She did, however, return shortly after seven o'clock in the morning, and this time it was Stephen Aldrich who was permitted to ask the questions.

Aldrich had spent the previous day colluding with William, and between them they had devised a list of questions that they hoped would serve to prove the ghost a fraud and also give them grounds to take out a lawsuit for libel. In particular, William had provided Aldrich with a list of questions to which only he and Fanny were likely to know the answer.

Aldrich warmed up by asking several questions that were designed to get the ghost to confirm to him that its intention was to see William hanged. The establishment of this as a motive would be useful in any future court case. The ghost happily knocked out answers to Aldrich's questions, confirming to the assembled crowd that Fanny had been poisoned with arsenic concealed in purl by William. Then several questions were asked about William's private life. Was he now married? (Yes.) Was his new wife pregnant? (Yes.) Is he uneasy? (Yes.) All were answered correctly. It was when Aldrich started to ask the ghost about details of Fanny Lynes's life that things began to go awry. Suddenly the accuracy rate of the answers dropped markedly.

'Was your father's name John?' asked Aldrich.

Yes, replied the ghost, incorrectly (her father was Thomas Lynes).

'Was your father buried at Litcham?'

Again a yes was knocked; again it was wrong (he was buried at Little Dunham).

When the questioning moved round to details about William and Fanny's life in London, the success rate climbed again, the ghost being able to say correctly where they had stayed plus several other minor details. Then the line of questioning switched to the Lynes family.

'How many sisters have you alive?'

Three knocks. Correct.

'How many of your relatives were present at your sister's wedding?'

Six knocks. Wrong. (Only one, her sister Susan, was present.)

'When your sister was married, did you dine at Mr Kent's?'

Yes. Wrong.

As a finale Aldrich threw in a trap question for the ghost.

'Will you consent to make your appearance at my house?' asked Aldrich.

The ghost, which had answered many similar questions, rapped once for yes.

'That's well,' said Aldrich to Moore, 'she consents. We will have her under my roof tomorrow.'

Too late Moore spotted that Aldrich was attempting to move the proceedings to a place where he could better control them. He interceded.

'You mistake the meaning,' Moore said to Aldrich. 'She answers in the negative.'

A confrontation followed in which Moore gave a most extraordinary speech, which confirmed that his general interest in the ghost had become an obsession.

'Sir,' he said to Aldrich, 'the want of satisfactory answers is imputable only to a want of acquaintance with the temper and disposition of Miss Fanny. For my own part, I have now long made her the object of my attention and study and have such an influence and command over her as to be obeyed in almost everything I propose. Sir, I have at one time caused her to flutter and clap her wings like a dove. At another I have made her trip round the bed like a kitten.'9

Taken aback at this outburst, Aldrich agreed to ask the question again. Would the ghost consent to appear at his house? This time two knocks were given.

The list of questions being exhausted, the meeting broke up. It had been a long night and all concerned were exhausted, many now being grateful to be able to return to their own beds once more. Before leaving the room Mr Aldrich waylaid Richard Parsons.

'Mr Parsons,' he said, 'for the sake of the public and to put an end to the distress of your own family, and also that of Mr Kent, will you give your consent to the removal of your child Betty to my house?' Parsons, who was now a tired and distressed man, reluctantly gave his consent.

'And you?' asked Aldrich of the young girl in bed, 'Will you come?' Betty likewise consented.

'Then my plan is as follows,' continued Aldrich. 'Betty is to be brought to my house without her family. Mr Parsons, you shall be permitted to stay in the house but not in the same room as her. The girl shall be searched by a woman of honesty and good reputation and then placed in a room with just a bed and no other furniture. Those present will include clergymen, physicians and a Justice of the Peace.'

Richard Parsons did not like the sound of the plan but he was tired and wanted rid of Aldrich and the rest of his guests, so he agreed reluctantly. Aldrich was grateful to him.

'We shall call for the girl tomorrow morning,' he said. With no further ado Aldrich left the house and returned home. He had plans to make.[10]

From the outset the Revd Aldrich had always been sceptical about the Cock Lane ghost, but that evening's proceedings had convinced him that it was a clever fraud perpetrated by Richard Parsons and his friends. The ghost had been able to answer questions only about William and Fanny's time in London, which suggested that the knocking noises were being produced by a person or persons who had known the couple while they were in the city but not before. This was surely proof that the whole affair was a humbug.

Aldrich knew that the Parsons family was now under considerable pressure and that there might be a temptation for them to stop conjuring the ghost in the hope that the matter would then fade from the public's mind. However, if William's name was to be cleared, then this could not be allowed to happen. The only way that justice could be seen to be done was for the trickery behind the ghost to be unmasked and in a very public manner. It had thus been Aldrich's idea to take the girl to his house in order to get her to perform under controlled conditions and in front of a panel of learned men who could detect the fraud. To him, getting Richard and Betty Parsons to agree to this was a major breakthrough.

As he made his way home, Aldrich gave thought to how best to keep the pressure on the Cock Lane conspirators. He and William already had some evidence against the Parsons, and Aldrich evidently felt that, if he placed some of these facts into the public arena, it might cause the weight of opinion to swing their way. That morning he wrote down a lengthy and extended account of the previous night's events, highlighting the ghost's failure to answer some of the questions correctly. The account was despatched to the *London Chronicle*, which was only too happy to publish it. Aldrich had concluded his article by saying:

There is such a mixture of truth and contradiction that a person cannot help doubting of the veracity of the knocker. It is, we humbly presume, to be enquired into for the satisfaction of the Public, and to bring exemplary punishment to the impostor, or impostors, if we are to relieve a distressed family [i.e. the Kents], to profess the reputation of the innocent, or to vindicate the cause of the injured. The public are desired to believe that the fraud will be discovered; of this they may rest assured.[11]

Aldrich's article, which was published in the *London Chronicle*'s next edition on 23 January, was the first public display of scepticism against the ghost. It was a call by Aldrich to the learned people of London and acquainted them with the facts as he saw them. He was asking them to come out against the ghost – but would they do so?

15

ANNE LYNES PAYS A VISIT

By the last week of January the uproar being caused by the Cock Lane ghost could be felt across London. The streets were aflame with gossip about the ghost and it could hardly have failed to reach the ears of Anne Lynes and her relation Robert Browne. The whole of London was talking about the shame of Fanny's elopement with William and the thought that he may have poisoned her for an inheritance. To Anne and Robert it appeared that William had yet again managed to drag the Lynes' name through the mud. Furthermore, the accusations appeared to come from Fanny's ghost. What were they to make of it all?

We cannot say for certain whether the Lynes family actually believed that the ghost of Fanny had returned to the Parsons' house, but it seems somewhat unlikely. What is certain is that the family did view the situation as being an opportunity to seek revenge on William, whom they did genuinely believe capable of having murdered their sister.

To this effect Robert Browne, like so many others in this affair, decided to utilise the power of the newspapers. On 21 January, the morning after the traumatic séance with the Earl of Northumberland in Hosier Lane, Browne journeyed to the offices of the *St James's Chronicle* and gave the paper a lengthy article concerning William. The article, which had been written in collusion with Anne Lynes, sought to assassinate William's character by delivering two key pieces of information.

The first was the testimony that had been written by William's friend John Leavy in late February 1760. Leavy had written this as a favour to the Lynes and in the belief that it was for their eyes only. Browne and Anne now saw fit to let the *St James's Chronicle* publish it in full.

One Mr K., some time in the month of August 1759, employed a person to carry a letter to a young woman of a respectable family of Norfolk, and withal to bring her in a Post Chaise [coach] to the said Mr K.'s lodgings somewhere in or near The Strand. The Agent having performed his undertaking, arrived with the Lady at London late in the evening, and carried her to the said Mr K.'s lodgings, agreeable to his instructions; but when they came there, Mr K. had left directions to bring her directly to Greenwich (which was performed with the help of a pair of oars), where the said Mr K. was ready to receive the faithful girl, after the fatigue of a journey of about a hundred miles, performed in one day.

They continued some short time at Greenwich, where the said Mr K.'s Agent frequently visited; there being a great friendship between them . . . Mr K., during his stay at Greenwich, thought it necessary that the young Lady should make a will in his favour, which was no sooner thought of than put in execution . . . All things having had the desired effect, the Lady was removed to a lodgings somewhere near the Mansion House. There they did not continue long, the people of the house not altogether approving of their conduct; and from thence they removed to lodgings behind Saint Sepulchre's church, Snow Hill . . . where he continued to cohabit with the young Lady.

[signed] J.A.L., 25 February 1760.[1]

The testimony was a reasonably honest relation of how Leavy had helped reunite the two lovers and how, after a brief stay in Greenwich with himself, they had decamped to central London. Apart from the bit about William insisting that Fanny make a will in his favour (an allegation that Leavy later claimed to have been 'misinterpreted' by Browne), there was nothing overly suspicious in the account. However, Browne continued the story in his own words, painting William and Fanny's relationship in a much darker light:

Sometime around the latter end of January, 1760, the young Lady was taken ill of the smallpox, and on or about the 31 of the same month, her sister, who lived in good reputation in Pall Mall, was made acquainted with her illness, and being overjoyed to hear where she was, went immediately to her, and found her ill, but in a fair way of doing well. She lamented her unhappy situation, and on parting requested, if possible, that her sister would come and see her the next day; but the sister not being able to comply with her request, sent a person to enquire how she did; who brought her word that her sister was purely [better], and had sat up in her bed that day. On the morning following, however, word was brought to the sister in Pall Mall, that her sister at Clerkenwell was dead, which greatly surprised her, as she had received so favourable an account of the state of her sister's health the day before.

The deceased died the second day of February, 1760, and was buried two or three days afterwards at the church of Saint John, Clerkenwell: the sister in Pall Mall, at the request of [Mr Kent], attended the corpse to the grave, but was deprived of the pleasure of seeing her dear sister's body, as the coffin had been screwed down some time before she came to the house. She was buried by the name of [Kent], as appears by the Parish Register.

Soon after her decease [Mr Kent] proved the Will in Doctors Commons, namely the 6 February, 1760 (though a caveat was entered by the deceased's sister), and availed himself of all her fortune, in prejudice of her brother and sisters, who lived in great harmony and love together before this fatal accident.[2]

Browne and Anne Lynes had managed to paint a subtle but damning picture of William's involvement in Fanny's death. At no point did they directly accuse him of poisoning Fanny, but the implication is obvious, not least from the description of her death as an 'accident'. Anne's contention that she was not allowed to view the body implies that

William did not want her to see the corpse in case she noticed that her sister's body had none of the physical marks associated with smallpox. Finally, the article makes mention of the haste with which William had proved the will, thus 'availing himself of all her fortune'.

Naturally, this account was a greatly exaggerated one, blended from a mixture of half-truths, exaggerations and selective reporting, but it nonetheless did the trick. When the article appeared in the *St James's Chronicle*, it served to confirm the suspicions of many ordinary Londoners – namely, that the ghost was telling the truth about William, who had evidently murdered Fanny for her money.

It was 21 January, and, as the day progressed, so a crowd began to gather in Cock Lane. However, the Parsons were still residing in Hosier Lane, and, when the mob discovered that the house in Cock Lane was deserted they became restless. With the ghost the number one topic of conversation in London, it did not take long for someone to discover where Betty Parsons had been moved to. Thereafter the pawnbroker's in Hosier Lane was besieged by the ghost-seekers, but by good fortune the mob's tenacity had been foreseen by Moore, who, hours earlier, had moved Richard and Betty Parsons to the house of another sympathetic parishioner in nearby Crown and Cushion Court, a small cul-de-sac at the top end of Cow Lane.

Despite protests from the Parsons family, Moore wanted yet more of his clergy friends to witness the ghost and so decreed that there should be another séance held that evening. As the evening progressed so the familiar members of the Cock Lane cast, which this night included Mary Fraser and Elizabeth Parsons, started to gather. The Revd Stephen Aldrich was once again present, determined to keep up the pressure on Richard Parsons.

The knocking noises began at around eleven o'clock, much to the satisfaction of Moore and his colleagues. Aldrich, however, was not so happy. Early on in the proceedings he had been prevented from examining Betty closely and at this had lost his temper. For the first time he directly accused the girl of being an impostor. 'This is a trick of yours,' he shouted at her. As soon as he had done so Betty burst into tears and then cried uncontrollably for several minutes; from around the room came several loud knockings followed by silence.

Moore took advantage of this and turned Aldrich out of the house, asking him to control his temper. Following Aldrich's departure, Betty was seized with a terrible trembling fit that made her shake from head to toe. Afterwards the knocking returned briefly but only to tell the assembly that Fanny would not answer questions until the next morning. A noise like fluttering wings, which Moore interpreted as the spirit's departure from the house, was heard; then all was silent.

The ghost did as it had promised and returned the next morning, but by this time a new visitor had arrived – Anne Lynes had come to witness the supposed communication from her dead sister. Although there is no record of it, it is likely that she was accompanied by Robert Browne.

Anne was allowed to put several questions to the ghost. She began by asking how many days before Fanny's death had she been to visit her. Three knocks were given, which was correct. The ghost then confirmed to Anne that it was indeed her dead sister and that she had been poisoned by William; the latter being done by nine solemn knocks. Two other questions were then asked, both of which would have serious repercussions later on:

'Would it give you satisfaction to have your body taken up?' asked one of the clergymen present. 'Yes,' was the reply.

'Would the taking up and opening of your body lead to any material discovery?' Again the result was affirmative.[3]

As before, the details of these happenings were dutifully transcribed and passed, via Richard James, to the newspapers for publication. Fuelled by the media reports of Browne and James, the mood among the common folk of London was running against William Kent, who, for his own safety, remained living in Greenwich.

The morning of Friday 22 January saw the end of Aldrich's patience with the Cock Lane ghost. He was now ready to see a conclusion to the charade and believed that he had witnessed enough to allow him to catch and reel in the impostors. The time had come to test the Cock Lane ghost under his own terms rather than those of Moore and Richard Parsons.

Just before midday Aldrich, together with an unnamed 'man of veracity and fortune' and his sister, travelled to Cock Lane, where Richard Parsons was residing after the excitement of the previous two nights. Aldrich's intent was to take Betty into his own custody, as he believed had been agreed with her and her father the day before. Aldrich knocked on the door, which was thrust open by the rough-looking Richard Parsons.

'What do you want?' he asked angrily.

'We have come for your daughter. Is she here?' said Aldrich.

'No, she is not.'

'Where is she?'

'I will not tell you!'

'But did not you and she both consent to go to my house?'

'No matter for that: she will go nowhere!'

With that the door was shut in Aldrich's face, infuriating him all the more. His carefully laid plan to expose the ghost had been scuppered. It was clear that Richard Parsons had been warned by Moore against cooperating with Aldrich's plan.[4]

Aldrich and his two companions left Cock Lane annoyed but not yet beaten. Aldrich had hoped to avoid taking legal action, but this was now the only route open to him. Later that day he met William and began to assemble a legal case against the Cock Lane conspirators.

Richard Parsons was telling the truth when he said that Betty was not in Cock Lane. The public madness surrounding the family meant that she had been placed in yet another safe house, this time belonging to a matron from the neighbouring St Bartholomew's Hospital. Her address was kept a strict secret, but, as ever, Betty was required to perform that night. This she did in front of a crowd of almost twenty people, the names of whom are unknown but which included many supporters of the ghost (presumably Moore's clergymen friends again) and only a minority of dissenters.

The mysterious noises did not come until six in the morning, at which time Betty appeared to be in a deep sleep. A scratching sound 'like a cat on a cane chair' was heard, but, before any questions could be asked a heated conversation, conducted in whispered tones, erupted among the men present.

The row commenced after at least one person expressed disbelief at the supposed supernatural origin of the noise. Another disagreed, and before long everyone in the room was arguing. The theme of the argument shifted onto the fate of Richard Parsons should the ghost prove to be fraudulent. Some of the more sceptical members of the party had forthright views on what his fate should be, prison, the pillory and transportation to America doubtless being mentioned. In fact, the argument became so absorbing that the company failed to notice that the scratching noises had stopped altogether.

The argument caused Betty to suddenly burst into fits of tears. Moore tried to calm her down, saying that no harm would come to her and that she was perfectly safe. 'But what of my father?' she wailed. 'He shall be ruined if the ghost is proved to be false.'

'I thought you were sound asleep when we were discussing this,' said someone.

'Aye,' replied Betty, 'but not so sound; I could hear all you said!'

This revelation caused disquiet among the assembly. If the girl was prepared to fake sleep, then what else would she be capable of? Could she also be faking the noises?

As ever, an account of that night's events found its way into the papers, but for the first time some of the reporters began to express some scepticism. On hearing of Betty's pretending to be asleep, one of them commented that this should 'have been sufficient to open the eyes of all who were not wilfully blind'.[5]

Regardless of this banter, the matter was about to leave the hands of Moore and Parsons, as the London authorities finally became involved in the affair. Later that day the Lord Mayor was scheduled to hear pleas from both sides regarding the ghost. It was expected that the Lord Mayor would either rule in favour of Moore and order William's arrest, or would rule for the Revd Aldrich, which would open the path for a prosecution against the entire Parsons family. London held its breath.

16

THE COMMITTEE OF GENTLEMEN

Sir Samuel Fludyer, the Lord Mayor of London, had acted unwisely in deferring his judgment on the Cock Lane ghost for four days. He had done so because he had seen similarities between the ghost and the Elizabeth Canning case and believed that, by ignoring the problem, it would go away. In fact the reverse had occurred, and the Cock Lane ghost now obsessed all London, just as the Canning affair had done several years earlier. A casual glance at the newspapers would reveal as much.

'The plot thickens,' commented the *St James's Chronicle*, 'and we may expect further entertainments, as often, and as authentically as we can muster together the particulars of a story, that now may be said to engross the conversation in the town. The clergy and the laity, the nobility and the commonality continue their nightly attendance upon the invisible agent. Nor are the ladies less curious upon the present than upon most other occasions; insomuch that the narrow avenue of Cock Lane is become some sort of midnight rendezvous, occupied by a string of coaches from one end to the other.'[1]

The appointed time for both groups to see the Mayor was on the afternoon of Saturday 23 January, where, at around 3 p.m., the Revds Moore and Aldrich, plus select members of their entourage, arrived at the Mayor's Guildhall office. Unfortunately, the detail of what occurred inside the Mayor's office is not preserved, but its consequences are.

On 19 January Mayor Fludyer had been faced only with Moore's petition, which he could easily have turned down. Now, four days further on, he also had one from the vociferous Revd Aldrich. Both sides wanted the same thing – the arrest of their opponent. Moore wanted William

Kent arrested for murder; Aldrich wanted Richard Parsons arrested on a charge of conspiring against William.

Fludyer knew that, whichever way his decision fell, it would cause upset. If he favoured Aldrich, then the London mob, who backed the ghost, would perceive a miscarriage of justice and become restless, as they had during the Canning case. If he favoured Moore, then the intellectuals and politicians that were his powerbase, and who were generally against the ghost, would feel insulted.

In the end the Mayor managed to dodge the issue. He gathered Moore and Aldrich in front of him and told them that neither had the burden of proof required for him to issue a warrant of arrest. To get such a warrant, the Mayor declared that the ghost's existence would have to be proved or disproved beyond all doubt. However, rather than leaving the matter to hang in the air, as he had done before, the Mayor, who did not believe the ghost was real, decided to settle the matter by utilising Aldrich's previous plan to unmask the ghost.

Fludyer instructed Moore to release Betty Parsons into Aldrich's custody so that she could be examined by a select committee of learned people under controlled conditions. If this should lead to the matter being settled decisively one way or the other, then a warrant would be issued.[2]

Aldrich left the Mayor's office a happy man, confident that he could expose the fraud and save William from the gallows. He returned to his house to convey the good news to William. John Moore was not so pleased. He returned to Cock Lane to convey the bad news to Richard Parsons and his family.

Despite this blow, that night Moore insisted that the ghost perform again in Crown and Cushion Court, but even he was now harbouring doubts. He asked a lady to lie with Betty all night just in case there was a deception at work, but the spirit chose to remain silent throughout the night. Richard Parsons later claimed to Moore that the ghost had arrived after he and the other visitors had left the house and had continued loudly to make its presence felt for some hours. Conveniently, there was nobody else around to witness this.[3]

The plan outlined by the Lord Mayor to Moore was almost identical to the one Aldrich had put to Richard Parsons a few days earlier. Betty would be taken to his house and placed in a room with only a bed in it. There, in front of a committee of learned men, she would be asked to summon the ghost of Miss Fanny. It remained Aldrich's belief that under such close scrutiny the mechanism behind the fraud would be discovered. Naturally, he was anxious to resolve this matter as soon as possible and so, on the morning following his meeting with the Mayor, he set off from his Clerkenwell home to Cock Lane. He took with him James Penn, a good friend of his who was the lecturer from St Anne's Church in Aldersgate.

The Revds Aldrich and Penn arrived in Cock Lane, which was, as usual, filled with people. They managed to push their way to the front door of the Parsons' house and, after some effort, persuaded Richard to let them inside.

'What time will you be delivering Betty to my house?' asked Aldrich.

Richard Parsons had been forewarned of this by Moore and so knew that the weight of the law was massing against him. Even so, he was determined to go down fighting.

'I am ready to allow Betty to be examined by you,' he said, 'but you must permit a family friend to be present so that she might be diverted during the daytime.'

'That is not part of the plan,' said Aldrich, 'and I cannot permit it.'

'And I, Sir, cannot release the girl unless this condition is met.'

'Whom do you have in mind?' asked Aldrich.

'I believe that I have a suitable candidate. She is a local woman known to Betty but who is wholly unconnected with this affair and may be trusted to be impartial.'

'Send for her,' said Aldrich. 'I shall judge her character for myself.'

Richard Parsons sent for the woman, who arrived only a few minutes later. Aldrich recognised her immediately. It was Mary Fraser, the woman whom he had twice seen running around the room to raise the ghost of Miss Fanny.

'No!' said Aldrich firmly. 'This woman is not only familiar to me but is also intimately connected with the alleged ghost. She will not do!'

Mr Parsons must have expected this reaction but obviously felt that the gamble was worth a try. To have got Mary Fraser into the same room as Betty would have been a great coup indeed. Luckily he had a reserve plan.

'Very well,' said he, 'if Mary will not do then I can offer another woman, wholly unexceptional, who is a distant relation to me and the daughter of a gentleman of fortune.'

Aldrich, whose patience was once again wearing thin, questioned Parsons about this woman. After much prevarication Parsons confessed that, while the woman did indeed have a wealthy father, she had been disinherited after disobliging him. It is conceivable that Aldrich would have allowed an heiress into his house, but news of her having been abandoned by her family was a different matter. He had heard enough.

'Mr Parsons,' he said standing up, 'if you can procure any person or persons of strict character and reputation who are also housekeepers, such will be with pleasure admitted.'

'I need a little time to find someone suitable,' was the reply.

'Then take some time. Deliver your candidates to me at Clerkenwell by the end of the day.' Mr Parsons agreed to this, and with that both Aldrich and James Penn took their leave of his house.

Some hours passed before Aldrich was visited by William Lloyd, an emissary from Cock Lane, carrying a letter that read:

Mr Parsons chuses first to consult with his friends before he gives a positive answer concerning the removal of his daughter to the Reverend Mr Aldrich's.

(Signed) William Lloyd, Brook Street

Back in the parish of St Sepulchre's Richard Parsons had sought Moore's help, pleading with him to find a means of escaping Aldrich's plan. Moore, who was still suffering his own doubts about the ghost, said that, since his visit to the Lord Mayor, the matter was out of his hands. He could do nothing to prevent Aldrich from examining the girl.

Consequently, three hours later, Aldrich received another note from William Lloyd. It read:

> If the Lord Mayor will give his approbation, the child shall be removed to the Reverend Mr Aldrich's.
> (Signed) William Lloyd, Brook Street

This was an odd statement, given that Parsons was already aware that the Lord Mayor had ordered his daughter's removal. Aldrich was annoyed but decided to wait until the next day before confronting Richard Parsons again. In the meantime he set about putting together his committee of 'gentlemen of established character' who he hoped would be able to unmask the ghost.[4]

That evening was a solemn one in Cock Lane. Betty Parsons was back at her father's house, which was again at the centre of a demonstration. When it became apparent that Betty was at home, the crowd became ever more populous and excitable. Despite this mayhem, Moore had arranged for another séance to be performed for an eminent friend of his, the Revd Ross, another Methodist sympathiser. One can imagine that the last thing the Parsons wanted to do was to put on yet another performance. They were exhausted, having been forced to stay up almost every night for three weeks and shunted from house to house. They had also put up with the stress of confronting sceptical people and the constant public attention. Nonetheless, Moore insisted that performance had to go on, and to his relief Miss Fanny obliged him, knocking out her answers in her usual fashion. The Revd Ross was a man of deep theological thinking and much concerned with the nature of the afterlife. He was greatly entertained by the knockings and later said of his evening with the Cock Lane ghost:

'I heard the knockings and thought I would if possible find it out and therefore I took an opportunity to ask several questions. I began by asking it some philosophical questions; I first asked if it was clothed in a body? One knock. I asked whether in a body of flesh? Two knocks. I then asked if it was clothed in a body of light? One knock.' On hearing this description, a learned gentleman asked of Ross: 'Did you puzzle the ghost or did the ghost puzzle you?'[5]

Nothing else remarkable occurred during the rest of the evening, the same regular questions concerning William's guilt being asked and the same answers being received.

On the Monday, Aldrich continued to pursue Richard Parsons, who was again unwilling to release Betty into the clergyman's care. Aldrich warned him that such an action would draw a warrant from the Lord Mayor, followed swiftly by the arrest of the entire family. Parsons begged one more day so that he could consult his friends and family. As a consequence he contacted Moore and told him that there would be no public performance that night. Moore put out the equivalent of a press release, which announced: 'The fatigue undergone by Mr Parsons and his family has been such that he desires his house might be free from company for one night.'

Aldrich was annoyed at the Parsons' delaying tactics and so made up a press release of his own, detailing all that had gone on that weekend and especially highlighting Richard Parsons's slippery behaviour regarding the issue of releasing his daughter.

'We whose names are underwritten', began Aldrich, 'thought it proper, upon the Approbation of the Lord Mayor, to see Mr Parsons yesterday, and to ask him in respect of the time when his child should be brought to Clerkenwell . . .'. Aldrich then went on to describe Richard Parsons's evasive behaviour, quoting William Lloyd's missives in full.

The effect was to make it look as though the Parsons family had something to hide. Aldrich was past dressing up his feelings and, after restating his plan to examine the child, ended by saying: 'We have done, and are still ready to do everything in our power to detect an impostor, if any, of the most unhappy tendency, both to the public and individuals.'[6] The release went out in the *St James's Chronicle* and served to place further pressure on Richard Parsons.

Aldrich knew that Parsons had no choice but to comply with the Lord Mayor's decision. He would give him his extra day and then come down hard. As it was, Aldrich did not need to get heavy, for the next morning the Parsons capitulated.

Both the Parsons and Moore had seen Aldrich's press release in the *St James's Chronicle* and knew that they could hold out no longer. Word was sent to Aldrich that the girl would be released to him under the terms set out in his plan. It was agreed by all that she should be examined on the following Monday, six days hence. That would give Aldrich time enough to gather together his committee of learned gentlemen.

Richard Parsons was, however, gravely unhappy with Aldrich's press release, which had painted him in a very bad light. With the help of Richard James, he struck back by inserting his own notice in the *Public Ledger*:

Whereas several advertisements have appeared in the papers reflecting upon my character, who am father of the child which now engrosses the talk of the town; I do hereby declare publicly, that I have always been willing and am now ready to deliver up my child for trial into the hands of any number of candid and reasonable men, requiring only such security for a fair and gentle treatment of my child, as no father or man of candour would refuse.[7]

The words had been cleverly chosen to garner public sympathy, making it look as though Aldrich was the aggressor and that the Parsons had always been willing to release Betty. Aldrich was not going to stand for that. The next morning his reply to Mr Parsons appeared in *Lloyd's Evening Post*:

[The Revd Penn and I] are greatly puzzled to find Mr Parsons asserting that he hath been *always* willing *to deliver up* the child, when he refused a gentleman on Wednesday evening the 20th and even denied to us that he had given his consent. We assured him that his child should be treated with the utmost care and tenderness: to satisfy him of which we proposed, that a person or persons of character and reputation, housekeepers, of his own appointment, should be admitted to attend the child, provided that they had never been present, when any questions were proposed, and told him that some gentlemen, of whom he had a great opinion, would be there, but no such persons, as he recommended, who were highly exceptionable to all candid and reasonable men.[8]

Aldrich delivered the *coup de grâce* with his final written sentence. 'What is to be understood', he asked, 'by reasonable security?'

The implication was obvious. Was Richard Parsons really asking for money in return for the release of his daughter? Whether he was after money or not (and, based on his past form, this was not beyond him), Aldrich had skilfully placed that thought into the public domain. This was to be the start of a slow and painful public assassination of Richard Parsons's character. Sensibly, Richard Parsons chose not to reply to this; he had other plans to gain the public's sympathy.

With Richard Parsons now bound to hand over his daughter, Aldrich needed to put together a committee of people whose combined knowledge and experience would be enough to detect the fraud behind the Cock Lane ghost. First to be asked was William Legge, the second Earl of Dartmouth, a man in his early thirties with a passionate interest in theological matters. He was actually a Methodist sympathiser but had been horrified at the bad press that the Cock Lane ghost was giving Wesley's movement. He had no desire to see Moore humiliated but equally well he wanted a stop to the nonsense taking place in Cock Lane.

Between them, Lord Dartmouth and Aldrich selected the other members of the committee, contacting them one by one, asking for their participation. Some agreed, others turned them down. James Penn and William Kent were automatic choices, but the other members had to be vetted carefully.

Both Dartmouth and Aldrich were agreed that there should be a physician on the panel who might be able to detect if the noises were being made by any bodily means. Accordingly, Dr George Macaulay was asked, and subsequently agreed, to join them. Little is known of Dr Macaulay's life, partly because his achievements have been overshadowed by those of his wife Catherine, a talented historian. However, a friend of his, Richard Baron, describes him as being 'a most worthy and benevolent man'. It was presumably for these qualities, among others, that Aldrich wanted him to be one of the ghost's examiners.[9]

Next came the need for a woman who could be trusted to care for Betty and to search her for hidden devices. Dr Macaulay suggested Mrs Oakes, the matron from the lying-in hospital in Brownlow Street. She could act as lady-in-waiting to Betty Parsons.

Next to join was Captain Thomas Wilkinson, a neighbour of the Parsons who was evidently sceptical of the ghost and who perhaps had some local knowledge that could be of use to the committee. Wilkinson is a man about whom little is known other than that he was in the habit of carrying a loaded pistol. Neither Aldrich nor any of the other committee members appears to have been well acquainted with him, and it is possible that he was also the committee's military safeguard, just in case any trouble arose. Aldrich may have met Wilkinson at the séance held in Hosier Lane on 20 January. On that occasion Wilkinson had arrived with his pistol and was determined to 'fire at the place from whence the noises should proceed and then beat a retreat using a stick'. Luckily he did not carry out this threat, but it may just have earned him a place on Aldrich's committee.[10]

The next choice was a clever one. Aldrich desired that there should be a professional investigator on the panel – someone who was used to exposing impostors. There was only one real choice: Dr John Douglas, a Scottish priest who was famous for his work in detecting frauds. Douglas was intolerant of ghost stories and had frequently admonished the Methodists for their promotion of the supernatural.[11] He was also famous for having brought to book a number of rogues, with his most famous case being the unmasking of William Lauder in 1750.

Lauder, a Scottish schoolmaster, had for some years been making accusations of plagiarism against the writer John Milton, claiming that chunks of his most famous work *Paradise Lost* had been stolen from the works of various contemporary Latin poets. In 1750 Lauder laid out his accusations in a pamphlet entitled *An Essay on Milton's Use and Imitation of the Moderns in his Paradise Lost*. To add weight to his thoughts he managed to persuade a famous writer to add a preface and a postscript to the pamphlet in support of its thesis: that famous person was Dr Samuel Johnson.

On seeing Lauder's work, John Douglas set about demolishing it, proving that he had falsified his evidence against Milton as part of a long-running hate campaign against the writer's work. Douglas's conclusions were published in his own pamphlet (*The Vindication of Milton*), which destroyed Lauder's reputation while at the same time making Douglas's. Dr Johnson, who felt sheepish about his support for Lauder, was cleared of blame by Douglas, who made out that he had been an unwitting victim of Lauder's weasel words. Consequently Douglas and Johnson remained on good terms.[12]

Dr Douglas's knowledge and deductive powers made him an inspired choice for Aldrich's committee. On being contacted he agreed at once to participate, but he also had a suggestion of his own. The committee should have a literary man on it; someone who could record what was happening and who could then later write up the affair for the press. Why not, suggested Dr Douglas, invite Dr Samuel Johnson himself?

17

DR JOHNSON'S GHOSTS

Dr Samuel Johnson was a heavyweight, both physically and intellectually. His most enduringly famous work is his *Dictionary*, a mammoth task completed in 1755, but Dr Johnson was also the author of countless other valuable literary works. He was one of the best-known and most revered writers of his day and was at the centre of a new and exciting explosion in London intellectualism. He was, however, also noted for being opinionated, argumentative, boisterous and lazy. Many revered Dr Johnson for his genius but just as many others avoided his company whenever possible.

Throughout his life Dr Johnson had given the subject of ghosts much thought, trying to separate the lurid stories of chain-rattling phantoms, which would do the rounds in London's taverns and newspapers, from those apparitions that he felt might be genuine. He showed, for example, great faith in the experience of Edward Cave, a publisher friend of his who claimed to have once seen a 'shadowy being'.

'Cave did not like to talk of it,' said Johnson, 'and seemed to be in great horror whenever it was mentioned.' He mentioned Cave's experience on more than one occasion, adding that the witness was 'an honest man and a man of sense'.[1]

A few days after the death of his wife, Johnson implored God to allow her ghost to appear to him: 'O Lord!' he prayed, 'if thou has ordained the souls of the dead to minister to the Living, and appointed my departed wife to have care of me, grant that I may enjoy the good effects of her attention and ministration, whether exercised by appearance, impulses, dreams or in any other manner agreeable to thy Government. Amen.'[2]

Despite moments like this, Johnson was by nature a sceptic and by the 1760s had adopted an agnostic attitude towards ghosts and spectres. As a devoutly religious man, he could not rule them out entirely, but neither could he believe in the many spooky tales doing the rounds. He suspected most of the ghost stories told to him were nothing more than fanciful hallucinations.

'I make a distinction', said Johnson, 'between what a man may experience by the mere strength of his imagination and what imagination cannot possibly produce.' He illustrated his point with an example.

Suppose that I should think that I saw a form and heard a voice cry 'Johnson, you are a very wicked fellow, and unless you repent you will certainly be punished.' My own unworthiness is so deeply impressed upon my mind that I might imagine I thus saw and heard and therefore I should not believe that an external communication had been made to me. But if a form should appear, and a voice should tell me that a particular man had died at a particular place and at a particular hour: a fact which I had no apprehension of, nor any means of knowing. If this fact, with all its circumstances, should afterwards be unquestionably proved, I should in that case, be persuaded that I had supernatural intelligence imparted me.[3]

He reiterated this viewpoint many times, and it is a logical one. Any ghost brave enough to visit Dr Johnson would need to be able to provide him with independent proof of its existence, otherwise it should expect to be dismissed as a hallucination.

From James Boswell's careful documentation of Dr Johnson's life, it is clear that the great man suffered from not only a preoccupation with death but also a great fear of it. Once Johnson stumbled upon a half-buried skeleton in a churchyard; the sight caused him to recoil with horror and left him feeling faint. On a number of other occasions he expressed the view that all humans had a fear of death, whether they admitted to it or not. Boswell once remarked: 'David Hume said to me that he was no more uneasy to think he should not exist after this life, than that he had not been before he began to exist.'

'Sir, if he really thinks so, his perceptions are disturbed; he is mad,' replied Johnson; 'if he does not think so, he lies. He may tell you, he holds his finger in the flame of a candle without feeling pain; would you believe him? When he dies, he at least gives up all he has.'[4]

One function of Johnson's fear of death was an earnest desire to see proof of an afterlife so that he might be assured that there was something awaiting him beyond his mortal existence. However, with so much superstition abroad, Johnson laid down a rigid criterion: any incidence of communication with the dead could be considered genuine only if a piece of information was imparted to the living that could not be obtained in any natural way. Prior to the arrival of the Cock Lane ghost, Johnson had come across only one story that met his requirements.

In a 1749 article on the life of the Earl of Roscommon, Johnson relates that, as a boy, the Earl was playing happily when, for no apparent reason, he became distressed, blurting out, 'My father is dead!' Two weeks later news arrived from Ireland that his father had indeed died. Johnson makes much of this apparent example of supernatural foreknowledge:

The present age is very little inclined to favour any account of this kind, nor will the name of Aubrey much recommend it to credit: it ought not, however, to be omitted, because better evidence of a fact cannot easily be found than is here offered; and it must be by preserving such relations, that we may at last judge how much they are to be regarded. If we stay to examine this account, we shall see difficulties on both sides, here is a relation of a fact given by a man who has no interest to deceive, and who could not be deceived himself, and here is, on the other hand, a miracle which produces no effect; the order of nature is interrupted, to discover not a future but only a distant event, the knowledge of which is of no use to him to whom it is revealed. Between these difficulties, what way shall be found? Is reason or testimony to be rejected? I believe what Osborne says of an appearance of sanctity may be applied to such impulses or anticipations as this: 'Do not wholly slight them, because they may be true; but do not easily trust them, because they may be false.'⁵

Samuel Johnson was desperate for proof of an afterlife and there is little doubt that, from the moment he heard of it, the Cock Lane ghost absorbed him, but its potential value to him was more than just titillation.

Johnson's desire to see a ghost produce verifiable information unknown to any of its witnesses was apparently being met in Cock Lane. Here the ghost of Miss Fanny was telling people about her murder at the hands of her lover. If the charge could be proved, then the case was surely an example of supernatural intervention. Johnson quickly became obsessed by the Cock Lane ghost, searching around for titbits in the newspapers and asking his friends and visitors for further news of the spirit. His house, at 1 Temple Lane, was not far from Cock Lane, and it is not beyond the realm of imagination to think that he may even have paid a visit to the scene of the ghost itself, although there is no actual record of his having done so prior to his involvement with the Aldrich Committee.

So it was that John Douglas called on Dr Johnson to ask him to join Aldrich's committee. Johnson was never one to make a hasty decision and told Douglas that he would think about it. A short while later he gave word to a friend of Aldrich's that he would be delighted to take part in the proceedings.

The line-up was now complete. In only a short time Aldrich had managed to assemble a committee of eight eminent people containing three clergymen (Aldrich, Penn and Douglas), a physician (Macaulay), a soldier and a matron (Wilkinson and Oakes), William Kent and, to cap it all, the most famous literary person of the day (Dr Johnson). It was agreed that the committee would meet at Aldrich's Clerkenwell house between eight and nine on the evening of Monday 1 February; the examination of Betty would start thereafter.

In nearby Cock Lane Richard Parsons was feeling bruised from his slanging match with Aldrich conducted publicly through the newspapers. He recognised that he and Aldrich were now in a battle for the public's sympathy. There was less than a week to go before his daughter was taken from him and so, rather than try and scale down the ghost's activities, he decided that it was time to up the ante.

18

THE LETTER-WRITERS

Richard Parsons was aware that, by accepting Aldrich's terms and conditions, he and his family were in danger of falling foul of the law. He knew that both Aldrich and William had been gathering evidence against him and that, should the ghost fail to perform in front of Aldrich's committee, then that might be grounds enough for his arrest.

Such a high-risk outcome demanded a high-risk strategy to combat it, and so, rather than lie low for a few days to let the mania surrounding the ghost die down a bit, Richard Parsons instead opted to gather the weight of the London mob behind him. From Tuesday 26 January to the following Monday the Parsons family stayed in Cock Lane and nightly allowed the ghost to perform, much to the excitement of the crowd outside. Furthermore, these shows were not to be restricted to a handful of clerics of John Moore's choosing but were open to whoever could squeeze themselves through the front door of the Parsons' house.[1]

Predictably, a near riot ensued. With the ghost returned to its old haunt (so to speak), Cock Lane became jammed with pedestrians and coaches. The neighbouring public houses and pie shops overflowed with customers and the mass of people was such that it spread into surrounding streets. It was a scene of utter chaos – what could Richard Parsons possibly gain from generating such mayhem?

It was perhaps his hope that the performances would get the support of ordinary Londoners behind him and that the mood of the mob could then help dictate his family's fortune at the hands of the authorities. On the other hand, Parsons may just have been trying to milk the scandal of a few last bits and pieces of cash and other fringe benefits.

Richard James (Moore's businessman friend) had by this time stopped feeding details of each séance to the newspapers, and so, instead of lengthy lists of questions and other precise information, the papers began to be filled with gossip about the ghost from a variety of obscure sources.

The case now obsessed London more than ever and looked as though it might run seriously out of control. Some were alarmed by this. 'It is extremely to be wished', wrote the *St James's Chronicle*, 'that an affair which so much alarms the weak and superstitious, and is now exciting the attention of the first nobility and gentry in the kingdom, could be brought to a speedy conclusion.'[2]

To others it was an amusement. Horace Walpole was one such; he was a famous *bon viveur* and socialite as well as being a prestigious letter-writer noted for his humour and vivid caricatures of London life. On 29 January Walpole wrote to his friend Horace Mann saying;

I am much ashamed to tell you that we are again dipped into an egregious scene of folly. The reigning fashion is a ghost – a ghost, that would not pass muster in the paltriest convent in the Apennine. It only knocks and scratches; does not pretend to appear or to speak. The clergy give it their benediction; and all the world, whether believers or infidels, go to hear it. I, in which number you may guess, go tomorrow.[3]

Walpole did indeed visit the ghost the following night and wrote about it at length to his friend George Montagu, then living in Ireland. Walpole's description of his visit to Cock Lane is one of the few that gives a real impression of the chaos and madness that followed the ghost during the height of its fame:

Arlington Street
Tuesday 2 February 1762

To George Montagu,
You told me not a word of Mr McNaghton, and I have a great mind
to be as coolly indolent about our famous ghost in Cock Lane – why
should one steal half an hour from one's amusements to tell a story
to a friend in another island? I could send you volumes on the
ghost, and I believe if I was to say a little, I might send you its *Life*,
dedicated to my Lord Dartmouth, by the Ordinary of Newgate, its
two great patrons.

A drunken parish clerk set it on foot out of revenge, the
Methodists have adopted it, and the whole town of London think of
nothing else. Elizabeth Canning and the rabbit-woman were
modest impostors in comparison of this, which goes on without
saving the least appearances. The Archbishop, who would not suffer
The Minor to be acted in ridicule of the Methodists, permits this
farce to be played every night, and I shall not be surprised if they
perform in the great hall at Lambeth.

I went to hear it – for it is not an apparition, but an audition –
we set out from the opera, changed our clothes at Northumberland
House, the Duke of York, Lady Northumberland, Lady Mary Coke,
Lord Hertford and I, all in one hackney-coach and drove to the
spot; it rained torrents; yet the lane was full of mob, and the house
so full we could not get in – at last they discovered it was the Duke
of York, and the company squeezed themselves into one another's
pockets to make room for us.

The house, which is borrowed, and to which the ghost has
adjourned, is wretchedly small and miserable; when we opened the
chamber, in which were fifty people, with no light but one tallow
candle at the end, we tumbled over the bed of the child to whom
the ghost comes, and whom they are murdering there by inches in
such insufferable heat and stench. At the top of the room are ropes

to dry clothes – I asked, if we were to have rope-dancing between the acts – We had nothing; they told us, as they would at a puppet-show, that it would not come that night till seven in the morning – that is, when there are only prentices and old women. We stayed however till half an hour after one.

The Methodists have promised them contributions; provisions are sent in like forage, and all the taverns and alehouses in the neighbourhood make fortunes. The most diverting part, is to hear people wondering when it will be found out—as if there was anything to find out; as if the actors would make their noises where they can be discovered.

However, as this pantomime cannot last much longer, I hope Lady Fanny Shirley will set up a ghost of her own at Twickenham, and then you shall hear one. The Methodists, as Lord Aylsford assured Mr Chute two nights ago at Lord Dacre's, have attempted ghosts three times in Warwickshire. There! How good I am!

Yours ever,

H.W.[4]

Walpole's visit took place on the night of Saturday 30 January, and he was thus an attendee at the second-to-last public performance ever given by the ghost. However, Walpole was not the only person to be writing letters; the newspapers also found themselves deluged with the written opinions of their readers.

Most correspondents expressed their disgust at the idea of the ghost and were convinced that it was a fraud. Some were angry with the newspapers for giving space to the story. 'W' wrote to *Lloyd's Evening Post* congratulating the 'imaginary ghost of Cock Lane for its kind services in presenting you with food at a time of dearth of news'.[5] Others offered comic explanations for the phenomenon, including the idea that 'the girl has swallowed a mouse alive and that a cat may be easily sent down the same way, and put an end to the faint remains of scratchings and creeping of which no man was sensible'.[6]

The ghost, of course, also had its supporters, many of whom turned to the scriptures for evidence of the ghost's reality. Others recounted similar supernatural stories. Arthur Bedford wrote to tell the readers of the *St James's Chronicle* of a man he knew who had conjured 'little maids about a foot and a half high' that 'played in a circle'. With help from Arthur the man repented and his little maids disappeared.[7] The letter-writer named 'Fear', on the other hand, seemed to believe himself to be a ghost. 'Sometimes,' he wrote, 'when a cat has crept along behind the pewter, and thrown down every dish and plate on the shelf, I have instantly haunted the mind of every soul in the house.'[8]

However, the prize for the most original and amusing letter must go to the doctor who wrote to the *St James's Chronicle* with a highly inventive explanation as to how Betty Parsons could be producing the noises using only some peas and her rectum. It is difficult to know whether or not this letter is serious in its intent, but it must have raised a smile from many readers:

Sir,

Though I am far from denying the existence of a ghost, yet I very much doubt the possibility of its making itself visible or creating a sound or having and exerting the corporal sense; for, as I understand it, the ghost has no body, and how can it rap against the wainscot without knuckles or scratch without nails and fingers? We must therefore look for the cause of this amazing Cock Lane phenomenon in some material agency: and, instead of being made over to the clergy, I would have the child examined by the eminent naturalists of the Royal Society, or the College of Physicians.

Having been myself bred to physic, in the course of my reading I have found several wonderful relations of the like kind which at last have been discovered to have been produced by natural causes. The learned *Riverius* tells a story of a waggish girl at a boarding school who frightened all the rest of the scholars, by making a sound *per vaginam uteri*, into which she had artfully introduced a peascod [pea pod].

We have all heard of the woman who, having a tympanum, used to make a noise like a drum in knocking her belly: And I myself knew a man who could play a tune exactly like a bassoon, with his lower wind instrument [i.e. anus].

The *Choice Spirits* will furnish you with a hundred instances of persons who will crow like a cock, howl like a dog, mew like a cat or bray like an ass. May we not therefore reasonably suspect that the child in *Cock Lane* makes use of some artifice by which she can make strange noises of scratching and knocking? Considering the girl's age, I can hardly believe her to be capable of knocking from any such means as described by *Riverius*: I should rather conjecture that the sound proceeds from an artful contraction and dilation of the *sphincter ani*.

My advice therefore is that before her examination her intestines should be thoroughly cleaned by a purging clyster or a strong dose of Jalap: for upon enquiry I find that her diet has always been of the flatulent kind, particularly before her examinations; and who can tell the wonderful effects that may be produced from the eating of peas and pepper?

I am your humble servant,

A Physician[9]

19

A Visit to the Crypt

The events of Monday 1 February 1762 were to become part of London folklore for several generations afterwards. They were also to haunt the reputations of some of Aldrich's committee of gentlemen for years to come, most notably the eminent writer whom they had asked to join at the last minute.

Just before eight o'clock in the evening John Douglas collected Johnson and took him to Aldrich's house; they were the last people to arrive. While Aldrich sat downstairs briefing his committee of gentlemen, Mrs Oakes and three other ladies took Betty upstairs to a room that contained nothing save a bed. Betty was searched from head to toe, but no hidden devices could be found. Her father remained in a separate room downstairs, as Aldrich had requested, with only the Revd Moore for company.[1]

Aldrich had first to give his committee some news that had been relayed to him by Mr Parsons. He asserted that earlier in the day Miss Fanny had said that she would not consent to make an appearance at Aldrich's house that night. The news provoked outrage among the committee, many of whom took it as proof of the ghost's non-existence. Nonetheless the séance had to proceed, and so the disgruntled group of gentlemen filed upstairs into the bedroom, where Betty lay alone in bed in a room that was well lit by candles.[2]

Aldrich asked Betty whether what her father had said was true. Had the ghost really said that it would not appear that night? Betty confirmed that this was so. Aldrich remonstrated with Betty, warning her that this would not bode well for either her or her father.

At around ten o'clock the company settled down for the evening, standing at various points about the room or perching on wooden chairs.

There they remained, in total silence, for over an hour, waiting for Miss Fanny to begin her tricks, but Miss Fanny did not arrive and just after eleven o'clock the committee's patience snapped. The gentlemen stormed from the room leaving the four ladies to look after Betty.

The committee trooped downstairs to the parlour, where a nervous Richard Parsons had been waiting alone. Aldrich and his committee confronted him, openly accusing him of conducting a fraud. Parsons denied this in the strongest possible terms. The ghost is real, he protested. His refutations were met with disbelief and the interrogation continued.

It was during this questioning that Moore decided to mention that earlier in the week Miss Fanny had said that, if William Kent were ever to visit her coffin, then she would knock on the lid to signify her presence. Aldrich found this most interesting and believed that it could be used to their advantage, but, before he could dwell on it, a commotion began upstairs. Miss Fanny had decided to make an appearance after all.

Betty, having been left on her own with the four ladies, had mistakenly believed that Aldrich's committee had left the house altogether. Before long the ghostly scratching and knocking noises began to proceed forth from around the bed, sending one of the women fleeing from the room in tears of panic. On her way downstairs she alerted the gentlemen that the ghost had now arrived. They stopped questioning Parsons and went immediately to the bedroom. Betty told Aldrich that the ghost had indeed arrived. 'I felt it come like a mouse upon my back,' she said.

Mrs Oakes confirmed that she had heard the noises and, when asked to describe them, replied: 'It sounded like she was beating on her breastbone with a fist or perhaps thumping her two fists together.' On hearing this, Aldrich ordered the bed sheets be removed from Betty. The girl was seen to be lying in a position 'which best enabled her to use her hands under the bedclothes'. Mrs Oakes was asked to examine the girl's hands. She did so and observed that the girl's knuckles were covered in pads of skin and consequently remarkably hard.

'I suspect that they have long been used to the operation of answering Miss Fanny,' observed Aldrich. He ordered that Betty place her hands outside the blankets so that they could be visible to all in the room. The committee settled down to wait for the noises to begin again. Needless to say, they did not, although Betty still claimed that she could feel the spirit running up and down her spine.

Just prior to midnight it was obvious that Miss Fanny was not going to join them and so, perhaps at the suggestion of John Douglas, Aldrich changed tactics. He announced to the room that if Fanny would not appear to them at his house then they should make good her promise to appear in the crypt of St John the Baptist's church.

'William Kent, the person to whom you made this promise, will shortly descend into the vault of the church,' announced Aldrich to Betty. 'I expect Fanny to strike on the coffin as you advertised.'

This then was to be the spirit's big test. Fail this, said Aldrich, and it would never be believed in again. The entire committee of gentlemen, plus Moore, left the house for the church's vault. Richard Parsons and his daughter remained behind, waiting in dread for the company's return.

It took the group of men only a few minutes to cover the short distance between Aldrich's house and his church. English churches can be spooky places at the best of times, but at midnight and with the promise of a spiritual manifestation, St John the Baptist's must have seemed a very oppressive place indeed.

The door to the vault was opened, and, at Aldrich's insistence, William was asked to go down into the crypt alone. It was a task that he did not relish but he performed the duty nonetheless. Shaking with fear, William descended the steps and stood for several minutes in the cold, dank atmosphere of the large brick-arched vault, his only company being a large number of rough-stacked coffins and the rodents that scurried about them. When his candle started to burn low, William returned to the assembly in the church above. He had heard no unusual noises down there.

William Hogarth's *Credulity, Superstition and Fanaticism* was directly inspired by the Cock Lane affair. Several effigies of the ghost can be seen, including one on top of the thermometer. (From *Credulity, Superstition and Fanaticism*, Hogarth, 1762)

Richard Parsons's house on Cock Lane. William and Fanny lodged in the upper rooms. (From *Old and New London*, 1878)

COCK LANE.

For centuries the filthy, narrow thoroughfare known as Cock Lane was one of London's seedier streets. Richard Parsons's house is fourth on the right-hand side. (From *Old and New London*, 1878)

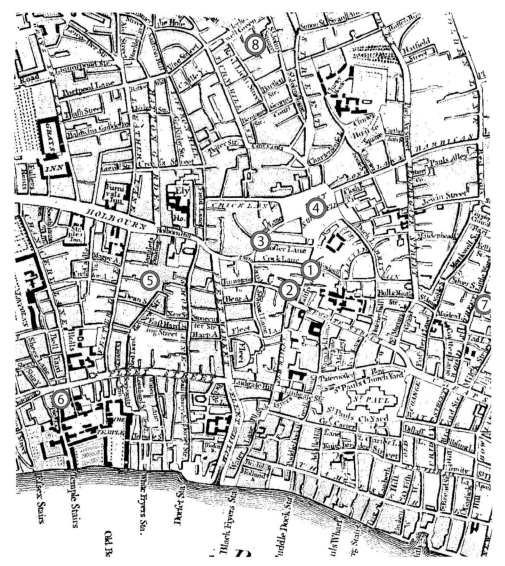

A 1761 map of London. 1 = Cock Lane; 2 = St Sepulchre's Church; 3 = Hosier Lane; 4 = Smithfield Market; 5 = Bartlett Court; 6 = Dr Johnson's House; 7 = The Guildhall; 8 = St John's Church. (From *London and its Environs Described*, 1761)

A detailed plan of the Cock Lane neighbourhood. (From Richard Horwood, *Plan of London*, 1975)

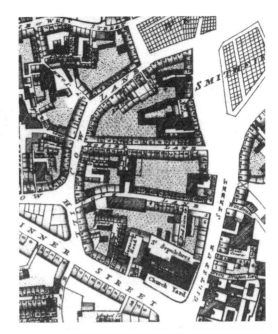

A historical map of the county of Norfolk.
1 = Litcham; 2 = Mileham; 3 = Swaffham;
4 = Stoke Ferry.

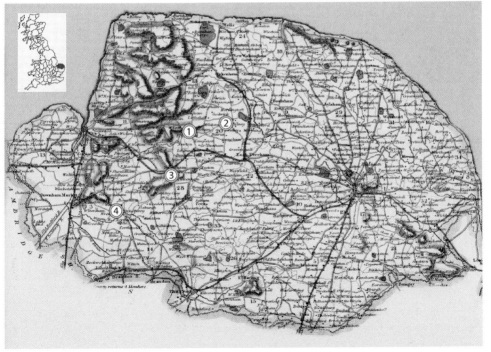

St Sepulchre's Church as it looked in 1762. (From *A History and Survey of London*, 1770)

This sketch parodies the work of Stephen Aldrich's Committee of Gentlemen, especially their visit to Fanny's coffin. The text beneath makes it plain that the artist thinks the whole affair is nothing more than a piece of street theatre. (From *The Cock Lane Uproar*)

For weeks the Cock Lane ghost was headline news, leading to heated arguments and discussions in coffee houses and on street corners. (From *Lloyd's Evening Post*, 25–27 January 1762)

EVENING POST, AND ITISH Chronicle. [Numb. 708.

d every MONDAY, WEDNESDAY, and FRIDAY.

JANUARY 25, to WEDNESDAY, JANUARY 27, 1762.

LONDON.

The fcratching and knocking in Cock-lane, Snow-hill, is by do means the firft thing of the kind that has been exhibited in London. The very fame farce of anfwering queftions by fcratching and number of knocks under a bed, whilft a boy was in it, was acted 25 years ago with great fuccefs, by a young Jew, who terrified the family not a little. The father, who was a man of fortune and character, knowing his fon to be more knave than fool, fufpected him of an impofture, and endeavoured to get the truth out of him by a fevere correction; but he was too hardened to be whipped into a confeffion; and went on many months; till a Gentleman, who pried clofer into the matter than other folks, difcovered that he had fifted wires under the bad, &c. in fuch a manner

On Thurfday evening faft Mr. King Cole, the elder, Brewer at Twickenham, fell into a tub of wort, and was fcalded to death.

We hear from Kingfton upon Thames, that in digging below the foundation of a malt houfe, which was upwards of an hundred years old, in order to build a new one on the fpot, three leaden coffins were found; in the firft of which was the body of a man, in the fecond a fkeleton of a horfe, and in the third that of a greyhound.

On Friday evening the Iflington ftage was ftopped on the New Road by a foot-pad; and, on his finding no perfon in the coach, he got up to the coachman, prefented a piftol to him, and took from him 18 s. and his watch. The coachman foon after cried out a foot-pad, ftop thief, &c. upon which he turned immediately back, and fhot the coachman thro' the flap of his great coat, and got

A comic depiction of one of the ghost's performances. Among the crowd are the playwright Samuel Foote and the blind magistrate Sir John Fielding, while on the wall hang portraits of the Bottle Conjurer and Elizabeth Canning. (From *English Credulity and the Invisible Ghost in Cock Lane*)

Scenes from Cock Lane. Top row: Fanny ill in bed; Franzen sees the ghost; middle row: crowds in Cock Lane; newspapers in the coffee shop; bottom row: Betty is discovered; Parsons in the pillory. (From *Harper's New Monthly Magazine*)

To be certain, Aldrich asked the entire committee, including Moore and Johnson, to go down to the vault. This they did and in the process created one of the most memorable scenes associated with the Cock Lane ghost. For a few minutes some of the most eminent and respected gentlemen in London society could be found standing in a dark, damp and smelly crypt at midnight waiting for a spectre to communicate with them by banging on a coffin lid.

Did people like Samuel Johnson, John Douglas and Lord Dartmouth really believe that the ghost would appear? It seems unlikely, but it was clearly important that all the ghost's promises be proved false. After a reasonable length of time, the committee agreed that the ghost was not going to make an appearance and took their leave of the church, returning to Aldrich's house once more.

Despite the late hour, Betty Parsons was roused and forced to undergo an interrogation by all the gentlemen present. Why had the ghost not appeared in the vault? Was the ghost even real? How do you make the noises? Is your father the person responsible for this fraud?

Betty continued to protest her and her family's innocence. Finally, at around two thirty in the morning, she became distressed and tearful and pleaded to be allowed to go home. Despite not having their confession, the committee relented and the distressed Betty was released into the custody of her father, who took her directly home.

In the house the committee met in conference. All were agreed that the ghost was a fraud, probably manufactured by the girl using her knuckles and hands to create the noises, either on parts of her body, or on the bed or some other hard object. It was also agreed that the girl could not be operating alone and that the likely mastermind behind the fraud was her father, who must have conceived the plan with the compliance of his family.

The committee no longer doubted that a fraud had been committed, but a problem remained: they had not witnessed the direct perpetration of that fraud and still could not say for certain how the knocking and scratching had been created. Without such proof it would be hard to obtain a prosecution against the Parsons. This would leave the matter in limbo, something that William did not want. He approached Moore and, in front of the others, confronted him.

'Do you still believe that my Fanny has returned?' he asked.

'No,' replied the downhearted clergyman. 'I think that you may be correct. The ghost is indeed an impostor.'

'Then you will assist me in the discovery of this fraud?'

Moore agreed that he would help in whatever way he could.

'Then I ask that you make an affidavit of what you know of this affair.' Moore was more hesitant and uncertain why William needed it.

'To clear my name and reputation!' came the curt reply. 'And also as a means of retrieving what I have lost in trade. Because of this I have lost a partnership with my brother-in-law. He is now refusing to enter into business with me.'

Now Moore was very hesitant. William had made him aware that he intended suing the ghost's main promoters, the majority of whom were also Moore's friends and/or parishioners. The clergyman began to backtrack.

'I am not yet fully convinced of the ghost's deceit,' he said. 'I believe that it may yet prove itself to be genuine.' The look on the faces of the gentlemen around him, particularly William's, must have left Moore feeling uncomfortable, for he added: 'William, I do not believe that you are a murderer, yet this ghost is surely a judgment upon you for living with your wife's sister unlawfully with respect to God and man.'

'This is your last chance,' warned William. 'I do not want to prosecute you, but without your cooperation I shall be forced to do so.'[3]

Moore would not be moved. He was flustered and aware that he had landed himself in hot water; he departed from Aldrich's house worried and confused. Privately he knew that he had been hoodwinked by Richard Parsons and his relatives, but Moore was a proud man, and to admit to his gullibility in public would see him turned into a laughing stock. He decided to try and ride the storm, but made a vow not to be seen in the company of Richard Parsons again.

POEMS AND SKETCHES

Despite a lack of sleep, on the morning after the visit to Aldrich's house, Samuel Johnson managed to settle down and write out an account of the committee's actions, the general content of which had been agreed upon by all the night before. As soon as his report was finished, it was taken to Stephen Aldrich, who rushed copies to all the newspaper editors, some of whom managed to include it in that day's edition.

However, and despite Johnson's haste, Richard Parsons had acted more quickly. After he had been released from Aldrich's house, he sought out Richard James and gave him an entirely different version of events. James had written this out and, first thing the next day, had taken it to the *Public Ledger*. Thus it was the ghost's supporters who got the first word about what had happened the previous night.

Regrettably, no copies exist of James's article, but from other sources it can be seen that one of its central allegations was that the ghost did not knock on the coffin because one or more members of Aldrich's committee had stolen Fanny Lynes's body from the crypt some hours earlier. With no body present, the ghost could not manifest the knocking noise. This rumour was widely circulated and was believed by many. In response to this, Aldrich wrote an additional introduction to Johnson's piece, which was be published in many later editions.

'I think it proper', wrote Aldrich, 'to acquaint the public that the following account of the proceedings of the Committee of Gentlemen who met at my house on Monday evening in order to enquire into the reality of the supposed visitation of a departed spirit at a house in Cock Lane is alone authentic, and was drawn up with the concurrence and approbation of the assembly, while they were present; and that the account in the *Ledger* contains many circumstances not found in truth.'

Johnson's article itself contained a straightforward account of the examination of Betty and the visit to the crypt. It ended by offering the Committee's view on the matter: 'It is the opinion of the whole assembly that the child has some art of making or counterfeiting particular noises and that there is no agency or any higher cause.'[1]

The view of the assembly coincided with that of London's middle and upper classes, the majority of whom had suspected as much all along. But the Cock Lane ghost was still widely believed in by London's working-class population. In fact, the Parsons' ghost had inspired a period of ghost mania in London, with stories of spooks and spectres popping up all over the place.

During the first week of February another knocking ghost started performing in Broad Street, near Covent Garden, but this time the authorities acted swiftly. Sir John Fielding, the Bow Street Magistrate, sent the householder 'his compliments with the intimation that it should not meet with that lenity the Cock Lane spirit did, but that it should knock hemp in Bridewell prison. On which the ghost, very discreetly, omitted the intended exhibition.'[2]

One ladies' charity school (ironically one that was supported by Dr Johnson) even placed a ban on the telling of ghost stories because of the fear that it inspired in the pupils there. The ghost had also attracted attention from much further afield than the confines of the city.

London's newspapers were a source of news to people living all over the country, and, to judge by the letters published, the ghost was causing quite a stir across the entire British Isles. People as far away as Bristol, Dublin and Aberdeen were discussing Miss Fanny's antics, and the matter had also reached the newspapers in Paris, Lisbon and Amsterdam. The dismissal of the ghost by the Aldrich Committee also sparked a certain amount of comic mimicry in the press, nearly all of it aimed at the Revd Moore.

One sketch had a fictional French correspondent from *Paris à la main*, who alleged that the ghost had moved to Paris, where it had taken root in 'Rue de Coq', where 'chief persons of the nation have assisted [in its discovery]; and what is extremely remarkable, a protestant clergyman has voluntarily administered MOORE than extreme unction'.

Even more savage was this parody from London, which gives a real clue as to Moore's standing in the community following the publication of Johnson's article:

We hear that the Revd Mr. Moore is preparing a new work for the use of families, especially children, to be published in weekly numbers, called *The Ghost's Catechism*; we have been favoured with a manuscript of the creed, which is as follows:

MR MOORE'S BELIEF

I believe in signs, omens, tokens, dreams, visions, spirits, ghosts, spectres and apparitions; and in Mary Tofts, who was brought to bed of a couple of rabbits; and in Elizabeth Canning, who lived a whole month without performing the usual offices of nature.

I believe in fairies, I believe in witches, I believe in hobgoblins, I believe in the shrieking-woman, I believe in the death-watch, I believe in the death-howl, I believe in raw-head and bloody-bones, I believe in all stories, tales, legends, etc., etc., etc., etc., etc., etc., etc., etc.

One paper even printed a mock séance in which Miss Fanny is found inside an empty beer bottle in a tavern and, in front of fifty members of the nobility, answers the following cheeky questions:

Q. What is the amount of the national debt?
　Above a hundred and thirty million knocks.
Q. How many years since the creation of the world?
　Above five thousand knocks.

Q. How many people are there in this room?
Fifty-eight knocks.
Q. And how many women?
Twelve knocks. Wrong. There was another lady in man's clothes.
Q. Can you say the Lord's Prayer backwards?
Much scratching, as if angry; after which the bottle suddenly cracked and no more answers were given.[3]

Nor were the newspaper sketch-writers the only ones to have fun at the expense of the Cock Lane participants. In early February the popular play *Apollo and Daphne* had an extra scene added that lampooned the events of the previous few weeks. In this new scene, which premiered before the King and Queen, Pantaloon and Mr Harlequin (the latter being an impersonation of Moore) pranced around a bed with a child in it listening to knocking and scratching noises.[4]

Several broadside ballads and poems also made their appearance (see Appendix Two), as well as a number of comic sketches, but none would be so subtle or as enduring as the work by Hogarth that was directly inspired by the ghost.

In 1739 Dr Samuel Johnson had a chance encounter with William Hogarth, the artist who was (and still is) famous for his prints satirising eighteenth-century urban society. Johnson was visiting the house of Samuel Richardson, the author of the novel *Clarissa*, when Hogarth burst in. He was anxious to talk to Richardson about a recent politically motivated execution. It was only halfway through this conversation that Hogarth noticed that Dr Johnson was in the room with them. In those days Johnson was not famous and so went unrecognised by Hogarth. The biographer James Boswell tells us what happened next:

While Hogarth was speaking, he perceived a person standing at a window in the room, shaking his head, and rolling himself about in a strange ridiculous manner. He concluded that he was an idiot, whom his relations had put under the care of Mr Richardson, as a very good man. To his great surprise, however, this figure stalked forwards to where he and Mr Richardson were sitting, and all at once took up the argument, and burst out into an invective against George the Second, as one, who, upon all occasions, was unrelenting and barbarous. He displayed such a power of eloquence that Hogarth looked at him with astonishment, and actually imagined that this idiot had been at the moment inspired. Neither Hogarth or Johnson were made known to each other at this interview.'[5]

Johnson and Hogarth do not seem to have had a particular fondness for one another. Whether this sprang from their above-described first encounter, where Hogarth seems to have taken him for a simpleton, or from Hogarth's famous artistic prints, which mercilessly poked fun at London society, we cannot be certain. As we shall see, Johnson had mixed feelings towards satirists, and it cannot have helped that a few years earlier Hogarth had portrayed Johnson's uncle as a drunken reveller in his print *Modern Midnight Conversation*.

By 1761 William Hogarth was entering his twilight years, having had a highly successful career as an artist. His political and sociological satires had made him popular with the people, but he was often disliked by establishment figures, especially politicians, who were a favoured target. Many of his prints held a mirror up to some of society's more unsavoury aspects. For example, his famous print *Gin Lane* displays the full horror of the 'gin craze', where emaciated alcoholics are splayed across London's pavements while around them the fabric of society is seen to be unravelling. Other prints are just as moralistic, depicting the effects of corruption, prostitution, hedonism and so on. The abiding interest in these prints is that the tragedy of the scene is usually offset by the artist's satirical portrayals of famous characters or other comic touches, designed to poke fun at authority.

In 1761, the year before the eruption of the Cock Lane scandal, Hogarth had turned his gaze towards the activities of the Church, an institution that seemed ripe for his waggish attention. The artist began working on his new piece in the spring of 1761 and spent hours transcribing his satirical thoughts about the Church into the fine engraved lines on a copperplate that would eventually form the final print. It was a slow and deliberate process that took some months to complete; he named the finished product *Enthusiasm Delineated*.[6]

Hogarth must have been uncertain about his new work, for he sought the advice of several colleagues before making the print commercially available. His friends, who were usually supportive of his work, were gravely concerned by what they saw. The print was indeed an attack on religion, but instead of making a subtle jibe, Hogarth had gone for an all-out assault on the Church.

The print depicts a meeting inside a darkened meeting house at which both the clergy and the congregation have become delirious. The preacher stands in his pulpit, high above his audience, spitting hellfire and damnation at them. Hogarth portrays the preacher both as a closet Catholic (as shown by the tonsured head hidden beneath his wig) and a fool (shown by his harlequin suit). In his hands the preacher holds a depiction of the Devil, while below him the audience are shown to be in a state of excitement (the 'enthusiasm' of the print's title), clinging to and even abusing effigies of Christ. This, together with the multitude of minor detail that is Hogarth's trademark, made the print look as though the artist was taking a swipe at religion in general; it was this that worried his colleagues.

John Ireland, a biographer of Hogarth's, later commented that the artist's friends warned him that the satire 'would be mistaken, and that there might be those who would suppose his arrows were aimed at religion in general'.[7] Another friend found an even greater problem with the print: for there, right in the middle of the picture, was the figure of Dr Samuel Johnson, whom Hogarth had depicted as delivering what looks to be a bombastic lecture from behind a lectern. On either side of Johnson is a cherub, whose presence serves to make him look more ridiculous still.[8] On observing the caricature of Johnson, Hogarth's friend John Hoadly advised him against publishing it. 'If Dr Johnson were to see this,' Hoadly warned, 'his opinion of you will be greatly diminished.'[9]

Johnson took his public image very seriously and, as will be seen later on, had in the past physically threatened those who had dared to parody him. Hogarth and Johnson were not the best of friends, and for the artist to make an enemy of so tenacious a character was ill advised in the extreme. With his friends so emphatically against it, Hogarth abandoned *Enthusiasm Delineated*. While he could withstand the acerbic comments of parliamentarians and those in authority whom he mocked, Hogarth could not risk alienating himself from the public at large. For the time being the copperplate containing *Enthusiasm Delineated* was shelved in Hogarth's workshop; his hard work had apparently been in vain.

A few months after having abandoned *Enthusiasm Delineated* Hogarth watched with increasing amusement as the events of the Cock Lane scandal unfolded through the city's newspapers and in coffee-house gossip. Hogarth was rarely one to satirise scandals of this nature (political farce was more his speciality), but there was a particular dimension to the events in Cock Lane that took his interest.

The prominent role of the Methodist clergy had been well publicised by the press, leaving few people in doubt as to who they should blame for the ghost's promotion. Hogarth looked at the accusations levelled against the Methodists and began to think again about *Enthusiasm Delineated* and his planned satire on religion. The actions of the Revd Moore and his colleagues had already drawn forth many comic sketches in the newspapers and the first satirical plays about the ghost were already being aired. From these it was apparent to Hogarth that one could write almost anything about the Methodists without being reproached: it was in effect open season on John Wesley and his followers.

Hogarth had found the answer to his problem. *Enthusiasm Delineated* had sprayed its venom at too great a target, risking widespread offence, so in its place he would create a new work that would utilise the events of the Cock Lane ghost to poke fun solely at the Methodists, a group of people that was already the subject of much mirth. Hogarth must have been titillated by what he was reading in the papers, for, although it can only have been begun in late January or early February 1762, the new work was ready in only a matter of weeks, it being on sale by 15 March. This time none of his friends disapproved, and the new work, entitled *Credulity, Superstition, and Fanaticism: A Medley*, received the general approval of the public.

To create *Credulity, Superstition, and Fanaticism* Hogarth had taken the same church meeting he had depicted in *Enthusiasm Delineated* and changed it so that it now had one unmistakable central target: the Methodist church.

The same harlequin-suited preacher is shown in mid-sermon with the congregation going into fits of ecstasy at his words. According to a careful analysis of this picture, the preacher is a parody of George Whitefield, a highly charismatic clergyman who did much to promote the Methodist cause both in England and North America.[10] The figure of Samuel Johnson from *Enthusiasm Delineated* has been replaced by another caricature of Whitefield. Hogarth has even given Whitefield a miniature pair of angels' wings – apparently a reference to a rumour about the preacher's premature death that had circulated the capital the year before.

Other recognisable figures include John Wesley, located in the congregation lecturing a shocked-looking man whose hair is standing on end, and Mary Tofts, a woman who, in 1726, claimed to have given birth to a litter of rabbits. Like the Cock Lane ghost, Tofts's story was widely believed to be true and was the subject of an earlier print by Hogarth, which he cheekily called *Cunicularri* – a pun on the Latin for a tunneller (*cunicularri*), a rabbit (*cuniculus*) and woman's private parts (*cunnus*). To Mary's right sits the Bilson Boy, another strange character who, in 1620, claimed to vomit up pins, straw, rags and other debris. Both Tofts and the Bilson Boy were later discovered to be frauds.[11]

Dotted about the picture are quotes from Whitefield's sermons and other Methodist-related memorabilia such as books concerning the supernatural (for example, King James's *Demonology*) and, hanging from the ceiling, a map of Hell.

However, Hogarth's main inspiration for the print can be seen all about it. The most obvious example is shown at the top of a thermometer that Hogarth has drawn to measure the mood inside a Methodist's brain. (The moods range from 'suicide' at the bottom, to 'madness' and 'raving' at the top.) Above the thermometer there is an illustration of the Cock Lane ghost, dressed in its shroud and floating next to a large four-poster bed containing a sleeping Betty Parsons. The ghost holds a mallet in its right hand and is using it to thump the bedpost. In its left hand is a comblike object that it is using to scratch at the wall.

This image of the Cock Lane ghost is just one of six to be found in the print. Effigies of it can be found in the hands of several of the congregation. It can also be seen rising from the bottle held by the pin-spewing Bilson Boy. Most controversially of all, a Cock Lane effigy can be seen to be used as a sexual stimulant by an embracing couple who are standing prominently beneath the preacher. Interestingly, nobody has ever ventured a name for this embracing couple. In *Enthusiasm Delineated* they are represented by an elderly man and his younger mistress, and yet in the newer print Hogarth has taken care to replace them with a younger more clean-cut and earnest-looking couple. Could it be that this young couple are in fact a representation of William Kent and Frances Lynes? There is no way to be certain, but their youth, middle-class dress and apparent desire for one another suggest that it is at least a possibility. William's unfortunate sexual history with the two Lynes sisters had led to his being portrayed publicly as something of a lothario; maybe the depiction of him thrusting a model of the Cock Lane ghost down the woman's bust is meant to reflect this.

Hogarth clearly delighted in the Cock Lane ghost and used it to maximum effect in his bid to make mischief for the Methodist community. As if to underscore all that is happening in the picture, Hogarth signs it off with a biblical quote from the first epistle of St John that seems to apply directly to all that had passed in Cock Lane: 'Believe not every spirit, but try the spirits whether they are of God: because many false prophets are gone out into the world' (1 John 4: 1).

Unlike its unpublished predecessor, *Credulity, Superstition, and Fanaticism* judged the public's mood perfectly and was well received by most who saw it. Horace Walpole, who possessed a notable dislike of Methodism, believed that the print 'surpassed all' and 'would immortalize Hogarth's unequalled talents'.

Others were not so complimentary. Shortly after its publication, Bishop William Warburton wrote to a friend of his saying: 'I have seen Hogarth's print of the Ghost. It is a horrid composition of lewd obscenity and blasphemous profaneness for which I detest the artist and have lost all esteem for the man. The best is, that the worst parts of it have a good chance of not being understood by the people.'[12]

The Bishop was wrong; although the print has many hidden depths, the blatant anti-Methodism could be perfectly understood by anybody. *Credulity, Superstition, and Fanaticism* was popular, and it was soon joined by a number of other pictures, poems and plays about the Cock Lane ghost, all mocking the affair, or some of the characters involved in it.[13] However, Hogarth was not to enjoy the fruits of his mischief for long. A year after its publication he suffered a stroke from which he managed to recover, but his health remained shaky and in October 1764 he died.

In his memoirs, written just prior to his death, Hogarth commented that he was often 'severely treated' for his anti-religious thoughts, but that even so he 'could not help uttering blasphemous expression'.[14] Had it not been for the Cock Lane ghost, his most blasphemous work might never have seen the light of day at all.

Thus, in the hands of London's playwrights, poets and artists, the ghost, and especially the Revd Moore, had gone from being an object of fascination to a figure of fun. The English were (and are) ever ready to poke fun at the seemingly ridiculous, and the Cock Lane ghost had given them free licence so to do.

The comic interludes may have lightened the former seriousness of the affair, but it did little to bring it to a resolution and that, above all else, was what William Kent desired. He had not given up on the ghost and was determined to bring its creators in front of a judge. The final battle over the Cock Lane ghost was fast approaching.

MR MISSITER'S DETERMINATION

The Aldrich Committee's work on the night of 1 February split the opinion of Londoners. On one side were the middle and upper classes, who were now convinced (if they had ever had any doubts) that the ghost was a forgery concocted by Richard Parsons and his family. They, however, were in the minority, for the rest of London was still very much inclined to believe both in the reality of Miss Fanny's ghost and in the guilt of William Kent.

With so many stories and rumours flying about, it was clear to Aldrich, William and the other committee members that their attempt at putting an end to speculation about the ghost had failed. More importantly, William still lacked the hard evidence he needed in order to obtain the arrest of Richard Parsons, John Moore and the other central figures in the case. It was agreed by Aldrich and William that Betty Parsons would have to undergo a lengthy period of examination in the hope that she might slip up and be caught out. Given the crowds that followed Betty wherever she went, Aldrich had no desire to have her housed at his property, the address of which was well known. Finding an alternative host for the girl did not prove easy, and in the end it took Aldrich several days to make the new arrangements for Betty's examination.

Richard Parsons was deeply unhappy at the prospect of his daughter being taken away from him and subjected to a lengthy examination, but the Lord Mayor had insisted that Betty be examined, leaving him with little say in the matter. Duly, on the evening of Sunday 7 February, Betty was taken from Cock Lane to the house of John Bray in Hosier Lane. It was Aldrich's plan that she remain there for as many nights as it would take for the ghost to appear and for her examiners to uncover the mechanism behind the fraud or, better still, to obtain a confession from the girl. On Betty's first night in Hosier Lane only the house-owner, his daughter Anne and the servants were present, but she was nonetheless searched by two maids and put to bed. No untoward noises were heard either that night or the following morning.

The next evening Aldrich had arranged for a second committee of gentlemen to examine the girl. The composition of this committee is regrettably unknown, but it would appear to have been different from the original selection. Certainly Dr Johnson and Lord Dartmouth were not present, and nor was William, but whether or not Dr Douglas, Dr Macaulay, Mrs Oakes and the fiery Captain Wilkinson were there is unknown. All we know is that the examiners were 'gentlemen and ladies of virtue'.

The new committee met in the early evening and, after Betty had been examined for devices and put to bed, waited in her room for the noises to start. Silence ensued, and at midnight the guests grew tired and left. Betty's bed was moved into the same room as John Bray and his wife, and, at seven o'clock the next morning, the knocking and scratching noises were heard.

On being woken by the sounds, John Bray rang for a servant to bring a lighted candle, which he immediately took over to Betty's bed. The girl appeared to be in a deep sleep, but, as Bray turned away from her, a strange whispering sound filled the room, which his wife at first assumed was being made by her husband talking to the servant.

'What are you whispering about?' she enquired.

'Neither I nor the maid is whispering,' replied Bray. At this his wife became scared and wanted to leave the room. Bray took the light over to Betty, only to find her lying motionless, apparently asleep. The encounter had been unnerving, especially for Mrs Bray, their daughter Anne and the family's servants, all of whom were inclined to believe in the ghost.

The new committee re-formed that evening and once more sat around Betty's bed anticipating the ghost's arrival. They waited until midnight and, on hearing no noises, abandoned the house again. This time, and at the request of Mrs Bray, Betty was left in a guest room for the night. Early the next morning the house was woken by a terrible commotion as knocking and scratching noises resounded from Betty's room. By the time the servants arrived the commotion had ceased, but it had had the desired effect. Mrs Bray became hysterical, telling her husband in no uncertain terms that Betty had brought a ghost into their house and that there was every chance that it might not leave again. She told him that the girl had to go and could not be persuaded to change her mind. In this she was backed up by her daughter Anne and the servants, all of whom were terrified of Betty. Anne Bray was in doubt as to what was causing the noises, as she later explained in court:

'We have often heard the noises,' she said, 'but could never tell from whence they proceeded. I have heard the knockings and scratchings when the girl has been asleep in bed and the sound seemed to come from the wainscot and other parts of the room and not from the bed. I do not think the noise was made by the girl, but by a ghost or some other preternatural noise.'[1]

Faced with a family in revolt, John Bray had little choice. He contacted Aldrich and asked that his committee cease their investigation and that they take the girl elsewhere. Aldrich was disappointed but agreed to stop using Bray's house. He did ask that Betty be allowed to stay there for a couple more days, as it would take time to find a new house, and he did not want the girl to be returned to Richard Parsons in the meantime.

John Bray reluctantly agreed, and so for two days Betty had the run of his house, where she spent hours playing with the toys in the upstairs nursery. Only one further bout of knocking was heard, this time in the parlour, which happened to be beneath the room where Betty was then at play.

On Friday 12 February Aldrich came to Hosier Lane and collected Betty, much to the relief of all at the Bray household. Aldrich had persuaded another friend of his, Daniel Missiter, to host Betty and her nightly examiners at his Covent Garden home.[2] Missiter ran a local business manufacturing saddles, spurs, bits and reins for horses, and, like Aldrich, he was a firm sceptic. Furthermore, Missiter wanted the kudos of exposing the ghost for himself, even if that meant resorting to threats and trickery.

After saying farewell to the Brays, Betty was taken across town to Mr Missiter's house. She was allowed to settle in for a couple of days before the examinations began. Even so, a maid was ordered to sleep in the same room as her and was given strict instructions to watch the girl closely should any strange noises occur. For the first two nights nothing happened, but early on the Monday morning the knockings arrived. On hearing them the maid threw herself across Betty's legs and grabbed her hands. According to one press report, 'the knockings and scratchings continued', although Daniel Missiter's own record of Betty's time in the house does not mention this.

That night two members of Aldrich's examining committee arrived at the house. Betty was examined and put to bed in a large room, but, rather than wait up all night for the noises to occur, a tactic that had not yet worked, the two gentlemen went to bed in the same room as Betty. The noises came in the early hours of the morning, and, for the first time in two weeks, several questions were asked of the ghost, to which prompt replies were received.

The gentlemen remained in bed throughout the experience, but they claimed that the noises seemed close by and at one time were within 'six inches of their ears', and yet they could not detect its origin. The mystery was no nearer to being solved, but Missiter was a patient man, and the law decreed that he could take as long as he needed with Betty Parsons.

The next night saw a repeat of the previous night except that this time the witnesses were a man and his wife who remained in bed while the noises echoed about the bedroom.

On Wednesday night Daniel Missiter himself, with a friend, decided to sleep in the room. The noises began early in the morning, at which point Missiter left his bed and placed himself in a chair directly facing Betty, who, he observed, seemed to be sound asleep. He could not see any movement under the covers and for a while thought that the noises were emerging from a far wall that contained a large mirror.

Missiter woke Betty and insisted that she place her hands outside the covers. From that moment on silence followed. Missiter left the room momentarily, and in his absence the noises started up again. On returning, Missiter noticed that one of Betty's hands had moved under the covers once more. He immediately accused her of knocking out the messages on the bed's frame, something she flatly denied. Missiter decided it was time to get firm with the mischievous young girl.

The following night Betty was put to bed with her hands tied together inside a sling. In the early hours of the morning the knockings began, but Missiter was prepared for them. He leapt from his bed and whipped the covers from Betty's bed. Sure enough, one of her hands was free, and, as a lit candle was brought nearer, Betty could be seen frantically trying to return it to the sling.

At last she had been caught out! Betty was closely questioned for some time and pressed hard to confess to the fraud, but she would not. This was unfortunate, because both Missiter and Aldrich (when he was informed) knew that, while the freed arm was compelling evidence of a fraud, it was still not proof positive. She must be caught in the act.

Missiter was by now exasperated and so resorted to more extreme means. That night a hammock was erected in the bedroom and Betty made to lie in it. Then her hands were tied together and her feet 'extended as wide as they could without injury'. It must have been exceedingly uncomfortable for Betty, but Missiter reasoned that, if the noises still occurred when she was suspended a yard and half above the floor, with her hands tied and no solid objects within reach, then they must be supernatural in origin. Needless to say, the noises did not occur that night, and the next morning Betty was released from the hammock, her muscles no doubt aching from being immobilised for so long.

Missiter gave Betty the day to recover before he and another gentleman interviewed her. They pressed for a confession, but Betty was adamant that the ghost of Miss Fanny was real. She even described her previous encounters with her glowing white ghost, but Missiter could not be convinced.

'If the noises do not come again,' he told her, 'then you, your father and your mother will be arrested and placed in Newgate prison. I will give you half an hour to consider this.' He then left the room but gave instructions to one of his servants to watch the girl secretly, using a hole in the wall.

On Missiter's return Betty asked that she be given one more chance at conjuring Fanny. She was duly trussed up in the hammock and watched all night, but the house remained silent. The next day Missiter confronted Betty for the final time.

'This is your last chance,' he warned her. 'If no noise is heard tonight, then we shall assume the matter to be a fraud and you and your family will be arrested for such in the morning. The approaching night will be the only one allowed for a trial. I shall return in half an hour for your answer.'

After delivering this message, Missiter left the room but asked a maid to observe Betty through the spy hole in the wall. A few minutes later the maid watched open-mouthed as Betty crept from her bed and crossed the room to the large fireplace. She hunted around for a moment and then removed a small wooden board on which a kettle was resting, hid it beneath her clothes and then returned to bed. The maid ran off to find her master, informing him of Betty's actions. Missiter was delighted but asked his servant to keep quiet about what she had seen for a short while longer.

He returned to Betty, who now informed him that Miss Fanny would appear at six o'clock the next morning. Missiter was delighted and, together with another man and a maid, bedded down for the night in the room. Missiter did not want the wooden board to be discovered prematurely and so had given orders that Betty was to be given only a cursory search that night. She was then allowed to go into a normal bed, rather than the restrictive hammock.

At six the next morning the noises began as promised. Missiter let them continue for a short while before ordering lights to be brought to the room. He confronted Betty and accused her of being a fraud: she denied this.

'You were seen taking a board to bed with you.'

'No, sir, I didn't!' protested Betty.

Missiter was adamant and, to the surprise of the other witnesses, ordered his maid to search her. She did so, and, in front of everyone, the wooden chimney board was discovered hidden among the bedclothes. Betty burst into tears.

Missiter declared to the room that the Cock Lane ghost had been exposed! His relief was palpable to all present. Despite the early hour, a message was sent directly to Stephen Aldrich, who was delighted that the affair was at last settled. A heavy snow had fallen during the night, but Aldrich did not care; he took a carriage directly to William Kent's house. Together the two men made their way to Missiter's house, where a conference was held. Missiter confessed to Aldrich that, while Betty had been caught out, in his opinion: 'The noises that the girl had made that morning had not the least likeness to the former noises.'

Aldrich decided that this was probably because she had been unable to use her usual method of making the noises by thumping on the bedpost and so had been forced to use the board. Either way, he said, a fraud had been detected and it was enough to end the reign of the Cock Lane ghost once and for all.[3]

Betty, who was still in some distress, was taken home to her parents in Cock Lane. On hearing what had occurred, her father must have known that his luck had run out. After weeks of ducking and diving, he was about to receive a decisive blow from Stephen Aldrich and William Kent.

Back in Missiter's Covent Garden house, a small celebration was taking place. The Cock Lane ghost had been laid to rest! But, while Aldrich and William expressed their thanks to Missiter and his colleagues, they knew that there was much work to be done before the public would accept the truth of the affair. The party of gentlemen dissolved, still full of self-congratulation. Aldrich and William entered the cold London air and made their way back to Clerkenwell. Now at last they could start to clear the name of William Kent.

22

THE ARRESTS

The exposure of Betty Parsons in the early hours of 21 February set a number of events into motion. Aldrich and William returned to Clerkenwell by carriage, which had to pick its way carefully through the semi-liquid snow and slush that coated London's streets. On the way they must have weighed up their options, trying to decide whether they had enough evidence to proceed with a prosecution against William's persecutors. William believed that they had, and, much to his relief, Aldrich agreed with him. Since first being made aware of the allegation of murder against him, William had been anxious to resort to the law to get satisfaction against Richard Parsons, but the ghost's tenacious ability to remain undiscovered had nearly defeated him. The reluctance of the Lord Mayor to involve himself in the affair had not helped either. The onus to discover the truth behind the ghost had always been on William and Aldrich's shoulders, and, while the authorities dithered, still troubled by memories of Elizabeth Canning, the London mob and the newspapers had had a field day.

Nonetheless, since 1 February, the night of the Aldrich Committee's examination of Betty, there had been a growing certainty in William's mind that the tide of events was turning in his favour. The newspapers had calmed down (some had even come out in support of him), and the Mayor had agreed that the girl could be examined until a satisfactory conclusion had been reached.

Those examinations had begun on 7 February, and, from that date on, William had started to gather the solid evidence he needed to clear his name. The next day he had called upon Dr Thomas Cooper at his Northumberland Street practice and asked him to provide a signed statement outlining his involvement with Fanny Lynes up to the time of her death. He agreed at once and later in the day travelled to see James Jones, his apothecary friend. Between them they produced a highly detailed testimony that completely cleared William of any blame in Fanny's death and dealt specifically with some of the allegations made by the ghost, such as the idea that Fanny had told Carrots about her being poisoned. Both signed it and sent it round to William's Bartlett Court house. William was pleased with what he received, even though the vivid description of Fanny's death did not make for happy memories.

> For near fifty hours before she died [wrote Cooper and Jones] she hardly swallowed a pint of any fluid whatever, and that only, when myself, or the apothecary were present to administer it to her. The last morning of her life we found her extremely low, her eyes sunk, her speech failing, and her intellects very imperfect; we told Mr Kent she could not then live twelve hours. Accordingly, a short time after we left her, her speech was wholly taken from her, she became senseless, a little convulsed, and expired in the evening.[1]

This may have made unpleasant reading, but it would be needed if the case were ever to go to court. William then spent several restless days until the exposure of Betty, the day after which he and Aldrich visited the Lord Mayor with the evidence gathered at Missiter's house. This time the Mayor was receptive and agreed to order the arrest of the ghost's principal protagonists.

The Mayor had asked William for a list of those whom he suspected of accusing him of murder; he did so with pleasure. Within hours men were being despatched to various London addresses to take the creators and promoters of the Cock Lane ghost into custody. The list of arrests was a long one, as William sought to chastise all those who had been connected to the affair.

In Cock Lane, Elizabeth and Richard Parsons were apprehended. They had expected as much and had already made arrangements for their two daughters to go and live with friends in the country. One road along, in Hosier Lane, Mary Fraser, the ghost's communicator-in-chief for much of the time, was taken away. Then the list moved onto those who had tried to publish against William: Richard James, the businessman, was taken from his sumptuous Giltspur Street house, while a few streets further south Charles Say, the *Daily Gazetteer*'s printer, and Robert Browne, of Amen Corner, were also taken away.

The final arrest was that of the Revd John Moore, taken from his St Sepulchre's residence. His arrest was by far the most controversial, and it was with some reluctance that William had added his name to the list of the accused. In William's eyes, Moore was a sad and misguided figure whose enthusiasm for the supernatural had led him to be tricked by Richard Parsons. Aldrich, however, counselled William against letting Moore go. 'His arrest will ease the minds of the people,' he had advised. On the Mayor's instructions, those arrested were sent to separate jails so that they could not communicate with one another before the trial to agree on a story.[2]

Noticeably absent from the list were any of Fanny Lynes's brothers or sisters. There is no doubt that William also partially laid the blame for this mess at their door and did not think it a coincidence that the ghost appeared shortly after John Lynes's lawsuit against him had begun. (He believed that the ghost could only serve to 'strengthen their case'.) However, the Lynes had kept a sufficient distance between themselves and the ghost to prevent William from prosecuting them. Only Robert Browne, a distant relation of theirs, was arrested.

After his visit to the Lord Mayor, William made a further journey, this time to see the author Oliver Goldsmith, with whom he had been collaborating for some time.

At the beginning of February Goldsmith had been approached by William Bristow, the bookseller and publisher from St Paul's churchyard who had earlier aided Parsons with his initial dealings with the newspapers. Bristow had long taken an interest in the Cock Lane ghost and had witnessed some of the early séances, although his involvement appears to have ceased in late January after the Lord Mayor's office had become involved in the affair. Three years earlier Bristow had made a good deal of money publishing a pamphlet on the trial of Eugene Aram for the murder of Daniel Clarke. This work went through many editions and was still in print in the 1880s.[3]

Perhaps mindful of the success of this book Bristow wanted to publish a similar pamphlet on the Cock Lane ghost, and the person that he approached to write it was Oliver Goldsmith, a brilliant, rather controversial writer.

It so happened that at this time Goldsmith was at odds with Dr Samuel Johnson, who, like many in London, considered the Irishman gifted, if somewhat misguided. Boswell paraphrases Johnson's opinion of Goldsmith at this time:

> His mind resembled a fertile, but thin soil. There was a quick, but not a strong vegetation, of whatever chanced to be thrown upon it. No deep root could be struck. The oak of the forest did not grow there; but the elegant shrubbery and the fragrant parterre appeared in gay succession. It has been generally circulated and believed that he was a mere fool in conversation but, in truth, this has been greatly exaggerated. He had, no doubt, a more than common share of that hurry of ideas which we often find in his countrymen, and which sometimes produces a laughable confusion in expressing them. From vanity and an eager desire of being conspicuous wherever he was, he frequently talked carelessly without knowledge of the subject, or even without thought. His person was short, his countenance coarse and vulgar, his deportment that of a scholar awkwardly affecting the easy gentleman. Those who were in any way distinguished, excited envy in him to so ridiculous an excess,

that the instances of it are hardly credible. When accompanying two beautiful young ladies with their mother on a tour in France, he was seriously angry that more attention was paid to them than to him; and once at the exhibition of the *Fantoccini* in London, when those who sat next him observed with what dexterity a puppet was made to toss a pike, he could not bear that it should have such praise, and exclaimed with some warmth, 'Tshaw! I can do it better myself'.[4]

Given that Dr Johnson had involved himself in the affair of the Cock Lane ghost, much to the merriment of many of his detractors, Goldsmith may have desired to make his own attempt at unmasking the ghost. Perhaps, therefore, to spite Johnson, he accepted Bristow's offer of three guineas for the work. However, if Bristow hoped for a sensationalised version of the affair, he would be disappointed, for Goldsmith had other plans.

Dr Johnson was being ridiculed by the public, who believed that he had gone to St John the Baptist's church crypt in the hope that he would witness a ghost; Goldsmith did not want to make the same mistake. He would try to succeed where Johnson had failed – namely, to convince the public that William Kent was an innocent man and that the Cock Lane ghost was a fraud.[5]

Goldsmith approached William with his plan to write a pamphlet that would right his reputation and place grave doubts on the ghost's veracity. William was only too happy to oblige, and provided Goldsmith with a detailed history of the entire affair, including the testimony by Thomas Cooper and James Jones. However, William asked Goldsmith to delay the publication for a short while, as he believed that an arrest was imminent. Goldsmith agreed and busied himself writing the pamphlet, waiting for the nod from William. The go-ahead to publish was given by William on the same day as the arrest of Parsons and his co-conspirators, and later that morning Goldsmith advised Bristow that he could at last roll his presses.[6]

As before, news of the Cock Lane arrests soon reached the London newspapers. Those that had been sceptical of the ghost, such as the *London Chronicle*, felt that their stance had been vindicated. The *Chronicle* wrote: 'Mr K.'s connection with Miss L. and his behaviour to her, which have been grossly misrepresented, are set in their true light; the aspersions thrown at Mr K.'s character in some public papers, are wiped off.'[7]

Horace Walpole agreed, writing that 'our foolish ghost, though at last detected, lasted longer than it was in fashion; the girl made the noises herself; and the Methodists were glad to have such a key to the credulity of the mob. Our bishops, who do not discountenance an imposture, even in the sub-divisions of their religion, looked mighty wise, and only took care not to say anything silly about it, which, I assure you, considering the capacities of most of them, was a good deal.'[8]

However, those newspapers that had supported the ghost were more reluctant to conclude that the affair had been settled in a fair and equitable manner. The *Public Advertiser* falsely claimed that it was Richard Parsons who had been the inspiration behind the continued examination of his daughter, because he thought the methods used by Aldrich to be 'too inaccurate'. It stressed that, prior to her being caught with the wooden board, Betty had produced noises that could not be explained.[9]

The *London Magazine* (which possibly cribbed its articles from the *Public Ledger*) was even more adamant. Its lengthy description of the examinations were at pains to point out that between 7 and 19 February Betty was at the centre of knocking and scratching noises whose origin could not be determined. As for Betty being caught out, the newspaper's implication was that she had 'been frightened into this attempt by the threats which had been made the two preceding nights'.[10]

It was evident that, even with the arrest of Richard Parsons and others, clearing William's name was going to be an uphill struggle. He was, however, greatly aided when, on 23 February, Goldsmith's pamphlet hit the streets. Entitled *The Mystery Revealed*, the text was a resounding demolition of the Cock Lane ghost. Its opening line set the sceptical tone. 'It is somewhat remarkable,' wrote Goldsmith, 'that the reformation, which in other countries banished superstition, in England seemed to increase the credulity of the vulgar.'

There then followed a full description of William's involvement with Elizabeth and Fanny Lynes, told entirely from his point of view, vindicating his decisions and lessening the impact of some of the events. William and Elizabeth enjoyed 'all the happiness a married state could bestow', and he could be considered 'entirely blameless' for his eloping with Fanny. The account, while detailed, was not altogether true. A safe gap of eleven months was placed between Elizabeth and William's wedding and the birth of their child (as opposed to the true figure of six months) and William was said to have been in charge of a post office at Stoke Ferry, a more professional-sounding position than that of a publican. Clearly William had been keen to disguise a few truths about his former life. The sceptical Goldsmith was only too willing to oblige him.

Next came the sorry tale of the couple's stay at the Parsons' house and the subsequent death of Fanny, followed by a summary of the activities of the ghost up until the night of the Aldrich Committee's examination. The testimony provided by Dr Thomas Cooper was printed in full, as were excerpts from some of the more libellous newspaper articles. Goldsmith finished with a vociferous demolition not just of the supernatural nature of the ghost, but also of the people associated with its creation. As far as he was concerned, the agents behind William's troubles were obvious:

> Mr Kent has many who owe him an ill will. His landlord at one house, whom he arrested for money lent him, had cause of resentment; his landlord in Cock Lane, the father of the child, whom he was obliged to sue from similar motives, was, it is supposed, willing enough to retaliate the supposed injury. But

above all, Mrs Lynes' relations, who had filed a bill in chancery against him, just two months before this infernal agent appeared to strengthen their plea.[11]

Goldsmith's *The Mystery Revealed* did not become a best-seller, and for many years all copies of it were thought to have been lost or destroyed. This led one of Goldsmith's biographers to comment that, 'whether with Johnson, Goldsmith thought the impudent imposture worth grave enquiry or, with Hogarth, turned it to wise purposes of satire, or only laughed at it, as Churchill did; the pamphlet has not survived to inform us'.[12]

In fact, Goldsmith's work did survive, not just in the original pamphlet, a battered copy of which was discovered on a market stall by Edward Rimbault in 1865 and bought for a few shillings, but also in the many verbatim reprints of it that appeared in the London newspapers in the days and weeks following its official publication on 23 February. Thanks to the newspapers, the text of *The Mystery Revealed* was read by many more people than actually bought the pamphlet, and so, as William had hoped, it did go some way to restoring his reputation. In time Goldsmith's work became the official source of information on the Cock Lane ghost, and its text was still being repeated, word for word, in publications about the ghost a century later. Those who read it could not have doubted that the ghost was a folly. In this respect Goldsmith probably did more to help William than his literary rival Dr Johnson.

At the time of *The Mystery Revealed*'s publication, a number of unpublished rumours concerning the ghost were circulating through London. The most persistent of these was that Fanny Lynes's body had been removed from its coffin and disposed of by Aldrich and his colleagues. It was for this reason, went the rumour, that the ghost could no longer knock and Betty had been forced to resort to trickery. As part of his campaign to clear his name, William decided that it was necessary to quell this myth.

On the afternoon of 25 February William travelled to St John the Baptist's church, where he met with Aldrich, the church clerk, the sexton and the undertaker. Together the five men solemnly made their way down into the vault, where they located Fanny's coffin, it being the only one without a nameplate or inscription. In the half light provided by their candles, the undertaker was asked to open the coffin so that the others might check that Fanny's body was still in place.

The lid was pried off and the coffin's contents revealed. The men were horrified at the sight that greeted them. Fanny's body was there, but it was in an advanced state of decay, for, as one newspaper reported, it was 'a most awful and shocking sight; and must have been more severely felt, when we consider the tender and unalterable attachment that subsisted between Mr Kent and the distressing, putrid object before him'.[13]

The descent into the vault was well timed, for later the same day William was to receive a further boost to his campaign. From his prison cell the Revd Moore had undergone a change of heart and released a public statement that, he hoped, would act as a means of getting him released from prison. It read:

In justice to the person whose reputation has been attacked in a most gross manner, by the pretended ghost in Cock Lane; to check the credulity of the weak; to defend the attempts of the malicious, and to prevent further imposition, on account of this absurd phenomenon, I do hereby certify, that though, from the several attendances on this occasion, I have not been able to point out, how, and in what manner, those knockings and scratchings, of the supposed ghost, were contrived, performed, and continued; yet, that I am convinced, that those knockings and scratchings were the effects of some artful, wicked contrivance; and that I was, in a more especial manner, convinced of its being such, on the first of this month, when I attended with several persons of rank and character, who assembled at the Reverend Mr Aldrich's,

Clerkenwell, in order to examine into this iniquitous imposition upon the public.

Since which time I have not seen the child, nor heard the noises; and I think myself in duty bound to add, that the injured person (when present to hear himself accused by the pretended ghost) has not, by his behaviour, given the least ground for suspicion, but has preserved that becoming steadfastness, which nothing, I am persuaded, but innocence could inspire.[14]

Moore hoped that this last-minute public statement would secure his freedom and result in the dropping of all charges against him. Had he released it a month earlier, as William had requested, then this might have been the case, but now it was too late. William intended to see this affair through to the courts, and as Moore was one of the central protagonists, his conviction was needed. The ghost's principal supporter had recanted, which meant that the successful prosecution of the Parsons and their co-conspirators was now all but guaranteed.

By the end of the week a date was set for the trial, 10 July, but until then Moore and the others were remanded in jail. Their arrest had put a direct halt to the activities of the Cock Lane ghost, but the public was not finished with the affair. The gossip might have been dying down, but the satirists were only just beginning to get their hooks into the scandal.

23

THE ORATORS

The Revd Moore suffered greatly at the hands of the newspapers, but he was not alone. Samuel Johnson was also mocked after it was revealed that he had been a member of Aldrich's committee of gentlemen. Johnson was such a pompous and forthright character that many took the opportunity to portray him as a believer in the ghost. The fact that he had stood in a crypt at midnight waiting for Miss Fanny to bang on her coffin lid caused further mirth.

The poet Charles Churchill did not get along with Johnson and, after witnessing one of the ghost's performances for himself, dashed off a new work entitled 'The Ghost'. In this the role of Johnson was given to a character entitled Pomposo who was, among other insults, an 'insolent and loud, vain idol of a scribbling crowd'. The poem ends with Pomposo and two friends descending into a vault to meet the ghost. As with Aldrich's committee, the ghost fails to materialise:

> Silent all three went in, about
> All three turn'd silent, and came out

Johnson himself shrugged off the attack: 'I called the fellow a blockhead at first, and I will call him a blockhead still.'[1] He, however, remained sensitive on the subject of the Cock Lane ghost and twice rebuffed his biographer, James Boswell, for asking him about it. Some of the mud did stick, for Boswell, writing after Johnson's death, opined that 'many of my readers, I am convinced, are to this hour under an impression that Johnson was thus foolishly deceived. It will therefore surprise them a good deal when they are informed upon undoubted authority, that Johnson was one of those by whom the imposture was detected.'[2]

It was not just Churchill the poet who sought to mock Johnson over his involvement with the ghost. The scurrilous playwright and mischief-maker Samuel Foote was also keen to have a go. It was to be a decision that would cost him dear.

The relationship between Dr Samuel Johnson and Samuel Foote had always been a tempestuous one. In October 1769 James Boswell touched upon the subject with Johnson.

'[Has not] Foote a great deal of humour?' asked Boswell. Johnson agreed that indeed he had.

'He has a singular talent of mimicry,' added Boswell, but this observation touched a raw nerve with Johnson.

'It is not a talent,' said Johnson angrily; 'it is a vice. It is what others abstain from. It is not comedy which exhibits the character of a species, as that of a miser gathered from many misers: it is a farce, which exhibits individuals.'

Boswell was used to Johnson's outbursts and dared to pursue the matter further: 'Did Foote not think of exhibiting you?' he asked.

'Sir, fear restrained him; he knew I would have broken his bones. He is an infidel as a dog is an infidel. That is to say, he has never thought upon the subject.'[3]

This reaction may seem extreme, but Johnson's attitude towards Samuel Foote was uneven. On another occasion Johnson described Foote as having comic powers 'superior to all'.[4]

Samuel Foote often engendered such two-faced reactions. To most people he was a lovable rogue whose vicious mimicry was thought funny so long as the person being mimicked was somebody other than themselves. He was, and always had been, one of the eighteenth century's most controversial and theatrical characters.[5]

Foote first came to Dr Johnson's attention in October 1760 in inauspicious circumstances. A month earlier a journalist friend of Foote's,

Arthur Murphy, told him that he was short of writing ideas. Foote advised Murphy to steal a particular article from a French magazine, translate it into English and then publish it under his own name in the *Gray's-Inn Journal*. Murphy did so, only to find that the French article was itself the translation of a piece that Dr Johnson had written for the *Rambler* magazine. A horrified Murphy contacted Johnson, blaming the mess on Samuel Foote. As a consequence, Johnson met Murphy, and the two became lifelong friends. Johnson's relationship with Foote turned out to be less enduring and far from stable.

A short while after their introduction, Dr Johnson and Arthur Murphy found themselves, with several others, at a Christmas lunch hosted by Foote's friend, and sometime whipping boy, the actor David Garrick. It so happened that at that time all three men had cause to be upset with Samuel Foote. Johnson was still miffed at Foote's involvement in the plagiarism of his *Rambler* article, Murphy was annoyed because Foote had stolen the plot to one of his plays and David Garrick was permanently upset with Foote because his teasing and abuse were ungrateful, unrelenting and merciless. With a line-up like this, it was inevitable that the dinner-table conversation would turn to Foote.

It was Murphy who remarked, with some joy, that Foote had recently received a horsewhipping from a Dublin apothecary who had taken offence at the playwright's impersonation of him. Garrick, who was inclined to defend Foote, despite his often atrocious behaviour, thought that the horsewhipping was an extreme reaction. He added that people should not take offence at Foote, as he had a reputation for doing such things. 'Nobody in London ever thought it worthwhile to quarrel with him,' he said.

As ever, on hearing this, Johnson produced a reply that was quick-witted and instantaneous. 'I am glad', said he, 'to find that the man is rising in the world.'[6]

The joke went down well with his dining companions but, as is often the case, what was meant to be a private comment soon found its way into the public domain.

Some weeks later the story went into the *Public Advertiser*, causing further mirth among its readership. As a consequence Foote got to hear of Johnson's comic quip and, despite the many upsets that he had wrought with his characterisations, was furious that somebody should have a laugh at his expense. Johnson had vexed Foote and so found himself high on the playwright's list of targets. Foote wanted revenge on Johnson, but it would be some months before he had the opportunity to do so – not until Johnson was himself to fall foul of the unfolding scandal occurring in Cock Lane.

The seeds of Foote's revenge on Johnson were sown on the stormy night of 12 January 1762. That night, as the Cock Lane ghost was being witnessed for the first time by William Kent, Samuel Foote's new play *The Liar* opened to packed houses in London's Covent Garden. The play's success was in part due to its mimicry of several well-known figures, and it awakened a desire in Foote to write a farce whose central characters were all mimicries. Thus he had begun work on a new and, he hoped, controversial play that would eventually be known as *The Orators*.

The first incarnation of the play was a direct attack on Thomas Sheridan, an author and campaigner for the standardisation of English spelling and pronunciation. Foote saw Sheridan's popular lectures on elocution as a target for ridicule and so on 1 May 1762 his new play, entitled *A Course of Comic Lectures on English Oratory*, opened at the Haymarket theatre.[7] It was a one-act play in which Foote, on stage as himself, encounters several orators and, in a series of discussions, makes their thoughts and theories on aspects of the English language look pedantic and illogical. Sheridan was heavily ridiculed, as were several other figures.

However, no sooner had the play opened than Foote withdrew it. He announced that it had been postponed 'in order to prepare the pupils for an exhibition in some particular branches of oratory not yet touched upon'. The truth was that Foote had been enthused by a recent event that he felt needed his attention and that could be incorporated into his *Course of Comic Lectures*: Foote had decided to satirise the Cock Lane ghost.[8]

Foote himself had seen the Cock Lane ghost in action during the week or so prior to Aldrich's first examination of Betty Parsons, but, although he had a general interest in the affair, it was Johnson's involvement in the scandal that had grabbed his attention.[9] (The anti-Methodist sentiment that the scandal had raised was an added bonus. Wesley's followers had made life difficult for Foote in 1760 because of his anti-Methodist play *The Minor*.)

Dr Johnson had probably long since forgotten that he had slighted Foote. However, the comic playwright was not one to forget a disrespectful comment, and he certainly knew how to hold a grudge. Foote now made Dr Johnson the central character in his *Course of Comic Lectures* and intended to write a scene that mimicked an incident that had taken place at a playhouse in Lichfield. Here Johnson had momentarily vacated a seat specially placed for him between the side-scenes. On returning he found that another gentleman had taken his seat; when asked to vacate it, he rudely abused Johnson. Grabbing the chair, Johnson tossed it and the gentleman into the pit below.

An incident like this was ideal fodder for Foote, but, typically, he was unable to keep his mouth shut about his intentions. Before long he was boasting to all and sundry about how he was going to get even with Johnson. It did not take long for the news to filter back to the venerable Doctor.

Johnson was dining at a bookseller's house when one of the guests informed him of Foote's plans. Johnson turned to his host and asked him, 'What is the common price of an oak stick?'

'About six pence,' came the reply.

'Why then, Sir,' said Johnson, 'give me leave to send your servant to purchase me a shilling one. I'll have double the quantity, for I am told Foote means to take me off, as he calls it, and I am determined the fellow shall not do it with impunity.'[10]

In the following days Johnson's bookseller host got in touch with Foote, repeating what had been said at the meal. Foote, who had been on the receiving end of violence before, took the warning seriously. With much regret the satire of Johnson was removed from the play. Boswell later commented that Foote had been wise to do so, for he suspected that, had the play gone ahead as planned, then Johnson 'would have made his corporal prowess be felt as much as his intellectual'.

With Dr Johnson now a no-go area, Foote cast around for a suitable person whom he could impersonate in place of Dr Johnson. What he needed was somebody who possessed physical and intellectual characteristics that were well known to the general public and that, in Foote's hands, could be grossly exaggerated to great comic effect. So it was that his attention came to rest on George Faulkner, a Dubliner and publisher of the *Dublin Journal*.

Foote did not hold a grudge against Faulkner. In fact, they were considered to be good friends, the two of them having spent some time together in London the previous year. However, Faulkner was a man who was notoriously arrogant, was overweight and, best of all, had only one leg. Those who knew him describe him, variously, as being 'a fat little man with large welt-powdered wig and brown clothes', 'ridiculous and farcical in every way' and 'a noisy swaggerer who boasts of his conquests in spite of every physical disadvantage'.[11]

The unkempt, hobbling, pompous figure of Faulkner would be well known to the London public and very easy for Foote to take off to good comic effect. The fact that Faulkner was a friend and sensitive to his public image barely seems to have entered Foote's mind – or if it did, then he just didn't care. Foote rewrote the second act of his *Course of Comic Lectures*, placing Faulkner at the centre of events. By the end of May 1762 the play was ready for the stage again under its new title of *The Orators*.

The opening night saw a full house that included many members of the press. The opening act still contained the dig at Thomas Sheridan, but it was the new second act that was to be the crowd-pleaser. The audience at the Haymarket theatre watched the stage curtain lift to reveal a scene set in a court room. Foote entered and made an introduction to the crowd:

> The first species of Oratory we are to demonstrate our skill in [said Foote] is that of the bar. You are to suppose this is a court of justice, furnished with proper ministers to discharge the necessary functions. But to supply these gentlemen with business, we must likewise institute an imaginary cause; and, that the whole may be ideal, let it be the prosecution of an imaginary being; I mean the phantom of Cock Lane, a phenomenon that has much puzzled the brains, and terrified the minds, of many of our fellow subjects.[12]

Foote exited and the members of the cast then filed into the court, taking the place of the judge, jury and clerks. The defendant was the Cock Lane ghost, named Fanny Phantom, whose Indictment was read out by the Clerk to the Court:

> Fanny Phantom, you are indicted, that on or before the first day of January, 1762, you the said Fanny did, in a certain house, in a certain street, called Cock Lane, in the county of Middlesex, maliciously, treacherously, wickedly, and wilfully, by certain thumpings, knockings, scratchings, and flutterings against doors, walls, wainscots, bedsteads, and bedposts, disturb, annoy, assault and terrify divers innocent, inoffensive, harmless, quiet, simple people, residing in, at, near or about the said Cock Lane, and elsewhere, in the said county Middlesex, to the great prejudice of said people in said county. How do you plead?

Fanny Phantom pleaded not guilty, and a mock legal debate followed in which the lawyers and clerks argued with one another about whether a ghost without a solid body was fit to be charged in an earthly court of law. The first witness was called, one Shadrach Bodkin, a tailor from

Norwich who had quit his trade to become a Methodist preacher. Foote had done his homework well, for Shadrach Bodkin was a thinly disguised parody of William Kent.

Bodkin appeared to the court as a well-meaning but gullible man with an overly high opinion of himself. As a Methodist, he stood in support of the ghost and told the court that he had in the past been invaded by a spirit. The court counsellor then examined Bodkin's credibility as a witness:

COUNSELLOR. I think I have heard a little of you, Master Bodkin;
    and so you quitted your business, your wife, and your children?
BODKIN. I did.
COUNSELLOR. You did – but then you communed with other men's
    wives?
BODKINS. Yea, and with widows, and with maidens.
COUNSELLOR. How came that about, Shadrach?
BODKIN. I was moved thereunto by the spirit.
COUNSELLOR. I should rather think by the flesh – I have been told,
    friend Bodkin, that twelve became pregnant . . .
BODKIN. Thou are deceived – they were but barely nine.[13]

This merciless take-off of William Kent raised much laughter from the audience. The fact that Kent was not a Methodist nor a supporter of the ghost (nor a serious womaniser) was immaterial. In the eyes of Foote he was fair game, and there was little that William could do about it. In many respects he had got off lightly in comparison to George Faulkner, whose character was next to enter the stage, in the guise of Peter Paragraph, a printer from Dublin.

Foote himself played Peter Paragraph and came on stage dressed up as a ridiculous mockery of Faulkner, hobbling about on one leg and speaking in pretentious, self-referential tones. The audience collapsed with laughter, but, just in case anybody was in any doubt about who

Foote was impersonating, Paragraph is made to answer a series of questions in which he reveals aspects of his life that firmly identify him as Faulkner.[14]

Paragraph was there to provide an alibi for Fanny Phantom, claiming that, instead of being in Cock Lane, she was all the time haunting a different house. However, Foote strayed from this to discuss Paragraph's (aka Faulkner's) alleged love affair with an heiress before embroiling him in an argument with Bodkin.

Paragraph exposed Bodkin as a fraud, claiming (rather surreally) that he bought an eighteen penny set of 'counterfeit scratchings'. Bodkin protested, but the court chose to believe Paragraph's version of events. An alibi was established for Fanny Phantom (who was urged by the judge to declare herself pregnant – a reference to Fanny's unborn child), and the court was adjourned. The remainder of the play was devoted to a lecture by Foote.

As far as reviewers were concerned, the play was a success, with the highlight being Foote's imitation of Faulkner. In the course of the act Faulkner was made to look vain, physically inept, adulterous, greedy and incompetent. He was referred to as a liar, a bastard and a scoundrel. The crowd loved it, but, if Foote thought he was going to get away with such libels, then he was sorely mistaken.

Through the years Foote had accumulated a good many enemies, one of whom was Lord Chesterfield (alias Philip Stanhope). *The Orators* had been playing to packed houses in London for about a month when Lord Chesterfield penned a letter to his dear friend George Faulkner, alerting him to the outrage:

London 1st July 1762

My Worthy Friend,

I send you no news from hence, as it appears by your *Journal*, that you are much better informed of all the passes, and of all that does not pass, than I am; but one piece of news I look upon myself in duty bound to communicate to you, as it relates singly to yourself.

Would you think of it? Mr Foote, who, if I mistake not, was one of your *Symposium* while you were in London, and if so the worse man he, takes you off, as it is vulgarly called, that is, acts you in his new farce called *The Orators*.

As the government here cannot properly take notice of it, would it be amiss that you should show some spirit upon this occasion, either by way of stricture, contempt, or by bringing an action against him? I do not mean for writing the said farce but for acting it.

The doctrine of *scribere est agere* [to write is to act] was looked upon as too hard in the case of Algernon Sidney but all the greatest men of law, do, with their usual perspicuity and precision, lay it down for law, that *agere est agere* [to act is to act]. And this is exactly Mr Foote's case with regard to you; therefore any orders that you shall think fit to send me in this affair, as to retaining counsel, filing a bill of Faulkner *versus* Foote, or bringing a common action upon the case, which I should think would be the best of all, the case itself being action, shall be punctually executed by

Your faithful friend and servant

Chesterfield[15]

Lord Chesterfield was a noted humorist, and in later decades (long after his death) it was assumed by many that this letter was written to Faulkner in jest. However, those who are aware of Foote's poor relationship with Chesterfield will know that the peer was deadly serious. He had seen an opportunity to bring the comical playwright down a peg or two and was determined to take it. Nor was he alone in being appalled at Foote's portrayal of Faulkner. Johnson, whose place in *The Orators* had been taken by Faulkner, was less than impressed.

Foote is not a good mimic [said he to Boswell]. His imitations are not like. He gives you something different from himself, but not the character which he means to assume. He goes out of himself without going into other people. He cannot take off any person unless he is strongly marked, such as George Faulkner. He is like a painter who can draw the portrait of a man who has a wen upon his face, and who therefore is easily known. If a man hops upon one leg, Foote can hop on one leg. But he has not that nice discrimination which your friend seems to possess.[16]

Faulkner, a vain man at the best of times, did indeed take offence at Foote's send-up, but he ignored Chesterfield and took no legal action, perhaps because he knew that a London jury was unlikely to take the matter seriously. In the meantime *The Orators* became an outrageous success, and for months Foote continued to limp and hobble about the stage to roars of laughter.

The success of the play was such that Foote dared to take the production to Dublin, right on Faulkner's doorstep. Here it was to open at the Smock Alley Theatre in January 1763, but Faulkner heard of the production and determined that he would fill the theatre with stooges who would be paid to disrupt the proceedings as soon as Peter Paragraph came on stage. Somehow Foote learned of Faulkner's plans and managed to turn them to his own ends. A reviewer at the opening night tells the story:

When Peter Paragraph was called for to give evidence on the mock ritual in *The Orators*, no Peter appeared – he was called again, but the second had no more effect than the first. It was then thought that George's threats had intimidated Foote from performing; and the audience (according as they were influenced by party) were ready to break out into murmurs or triumph, just as the third summons brought the *figure* before them – there was such a striking resemblance in the person, and so laughable an extravagance of the manners of Faulkner, that, before the opposers could settle themselves for an opposition, Peter got sufficient time to apologise to the court for his absence, by assuring them that he had been detained at his lawyer's, in giving instructions to bring an action against a rascally fellow, one Foote, who by a *vile* imitation of his voice and figure, had brought him on the public stage.[17]

Faulkner was furious. He had paid a crowd of street urchins a shilling each, and the promise of more the next day, to attend the play and then to hiss when Peter Paragraph entered the stage. Evidently no such disruption had occurred and so when the urchins arrived the next day for their reward, Faulkner berated them severely.

Plase yer honour [said their spokesman]. We did all we could, for the actor-man had heard of us, and did not come on at all, at all. And so we had nobody to hiss. But when we saw yer honour's own dear self come on, we did clap, indeed we did, and showed you all the respect and honour in our power. And so yer honour won't forget us because yer honour's enemy was afraid to come and left yer honour to yer own dear self.[18]

Foote's impression had been so good as to fool the street urchins, much to Faulkner's chagrin. *The Orators* became a sensation in Dublin, and it was not long before Faulkner could not leave his house without being followed by crowds of children crying out 'Peter Paragraph! Peter Paragraph!' Faced with the prospect of this unending ridicule, Faulkner at last followed Chesterfield's advice and took out a court action against Foote.

The mischievous playwright was arrested and brought before the Court of King's Bench, where the judge made it clear that he disapproved of Foote's behaviour. In the course of this the judge referred to

Faulkner as being Socrates, the respected Greek philosopher, and Foote as Aristophanes, the not-so-respected Greek playwright. Despite the insult, Foote liked the comparison and referred to himself as Aristophanes many times afterwards. Even so, Foote managed to get the case deferred for several weeks.

Foote was released on £400 bail, a sum he had to borrow from several local friends. The judge granted an injunction against Foote, decreeing that he could not perform *The Orators* until after the outcome of the trial. On hearing this Lord Chesterfield wrote to his friend saying: 'I am keen to congratulate you upon your late triumph; you have made your enemy your Foot-stool! A man of less philosophy than yourself would perhaps have chastised Mr Foote corporally, and made him feel that your wooden leg which he mimicked had an avenging arm to protect it.'[19]

Naturally, Foote ignored the court injunction and continued to perform the play, making the character of Peter Paragraph ever more outrageous. He even wrote and performed a poem about his situation and had it published in papers across the British Isles (see Appendix One). The newspapers began to speculate as to what Foote's fate would be at the hands of the law: 'From the obvious sentiments of the court before,' wrote one reporter, 'and this additional contempt thereto, it is now the general opinion that Foote will be heavily fined, and sentenced either to the pillory or public whipping. However, as he has no little interest with the great, it is thought the latter part may be mitigated to a severe reproof.'[20]

Foote had also got wind of the speculation about his fate, and so, rather than face the wrath of the law, he absconded to England, leaving his friends to pick up the bill for his broken bail bond. (It is alleged that he later paid back the money he owed.[21]) In his absence Foote was fined a great amount, which is thought have been roughly equal to the profit he had made from *The Orators'* Dublin run. However, if anyone could turn a potential defeat into a triumph, then it was Samuel Foote. In the spring of 1763 a new play opened in London. It was entitled *The Trial of Samuel*

Foote Esq. for a Libel on Peter Paragraph and was a rip-off of the Dublin court case in which not only Faulkner, but also the judge and the entire legal system, were made to look stuffy and stupid.

As ever, Foote learned nothing from the aggravation caused to him by his tryst with Johnson, Faulkner and the Cock Lane ghost. He continued to ape and insult his friends and enemies both onstage and off. However, fate had an apt punishment in mind for him. In 1766, while riding recklessly, Foote took a fall and had a leg crushed by the horse. It had to be amputated, which ended Foote's acting career (he went into stage management instead) and left him with a wooden leg. Lord Chesterfield spoke for many when he wrote to Faulkner: 'I cannot help observing, and with some satisfaction, that Heaven has avenged your cause, as well and still more severely than the courts of temporal justice in Ireland did, having punished your adversary Foote in the part offending [i.e. his leg]. The vulgar saying, that mocking is catching, is verified in his case: you may in turn mock him, without danger to your adopted leg.'[22]

Dr Johnson forgave Foote but continued to have a love/hate relationship with him, sometimes dining with him and praising his comedy, the next moment accusing him of lewd behaviour. Foote died in October 1777. His many obituaries were all at pains to recount the incident with George Faulkner, but Foote turned out to be a man only of his time. After his death his plays and poems faded quickly into obscurity, including the notorious *Orators*, whose take-off of the Cock Lane ghost cost its writer much trouble and money.

THE GHOST ON TRIAL

The final set piece of the scandal surrounding the Cock Lane ghost took place in midsummer on a fine, sunny day, the weather being in stark contrast to the stormy winter nights when the ghost had made its public displays. It was Saturday 10 July 1762, the scheduled date for the trial that would settle the matter of Frances Lynes's death once and for all.

The imminent litigation and the discovery of the fraud meant that the newspapers had not made much mention of the Cock Lane ghost for some time. However, the case had awoken a craze for supernatural tales among the public, and for months stories of knocking, clanking and shrieking phantoms had graced the letter pages.[1] Many other stories circulated through London's streets and were repeated in taverns, coffee houses, school dormitories and servants' quarters. Not that the Cock Lane ghost had been forgotten: its events were being acted out in theatres and ridiculed in cartoons and ballads. Even after a gap of over four months, the ghost was still fresh in the minds of many, guaranteeing that the trial would be well attended.

In the early morning the general public began to file into the Guildhall, anxious to get a seat in the public gallery. The case had been directed to the King's Bench, the highest court of common law in England and Wales, which held jurisdiction over criminal matters of all types from minor assault through to high treason. It was a court with ancient origins, and by the eighteenth century its procedures had become elaborate and arcane, so much so that it was rare for cases that had been referred to it actually to go through to trial. This was not the situation with William Kent, whose fame was such that his prosecution against the Cock Lane conspirators was guaranteed to be brought before the judge.

Trials were a popular spectator sport, and the more notorious the case being tried, the better attended it would be. The Cock Lane trial promised to be entertaining, ensuring that the galleries were full to overflowing with people. All human life would have been there, from street workers and prostitutes to eminent gentlemen and newspaper reporters. It is probable that the majority of people in the public galleries were supporters of the accused, convinced that Parsons and the others had been stitched up by William and his band of gentlemen friends. At nine o'clock sharp the jury, clerks, lawyers and other officials filed into court, followed a short while later by the judge. The court was now in session.

It was a mark of the Cock Lane ghost's notoriety that the presiding judge was Lord William Mansfield, a highly experienced man who had been chief justice of the King's Bench since 1754. Mansfield was noted for his impartiality, but his opinions and judgments were often unpopular with the public. Mansfield called the court to order and confirmed that John Moore, Richard James, Mary Fraser, Richard Parsons and his wife Elizabeth were before him on a charge of 'conspiracy to take away the life of William Kent by charging him with the murder of Frances Lynes by giving her poison whereof she died'.[2]

The defendants had spent the previous four and half months in prison and must have looked so much the worse for it. One can imagine that Richard James and the Revd Moore were especially badly affected by the experience, both having been used to considerably finer things in life than a filthy prison cell filled with debtors, thieves and the odd murderer. That said, those with money could lessen their plight by bribing the jailers and turnkeys into providing them with food, alcohol, bedding and even prostitutes. Nonetheless, London's privatised jails were terrible places, with, in some cases, over 300 people crammed into tiny rooms with no toilet facilities. It is little surprise that typhus (also known as jail fever) claimed the lives of many inmates.

The jury were sworn in and the trial began. The prosecution, in the guise of Mr Davies, Mr Stowe and Mr Wallis, opened the proceedings by calling William to the witness box. For many people this would have been their first glimpse of the man against whom the Cock Lane ghost had set itself. He took the stand and was sworn in.

Prompted by his lawyers, William related the long tale of his involvement with the Lynes and Parsons families and then his subsequent visits to see the Cock Lane ghost perform. He had only to provide the court with reasonable proof that the ghost had been a fabrication of Richard Parsons and the other conspirators' making, and much of the story he told was designed to do just this. Moore, Fraser and all the Parsons were fully implicated in his testimony. As the key witness for the prosecution, William was on the stand for a long period of time, possibly several hours. A court reporter used up five pages when transcribing William's words and afterwards used only another six pages for the whole of the rest of the trial.

The next witness for the prosecution was James Franzen, the nervy landlord of the Wheat Sheaf pub in Cock Lane. Franzen and Parsons had at one time been friends, but the ignominy of being used by Parsons to help bolster the ghost's credibility had led to the publican switching sides. Franzen related the story of his various encounters with the Cock Lane ghost. He vividly described the white phantom that rushed past him in January 1760, the knocking noises inside the house itself and the ghost's interrogation of William and Carrots.

Despite appearing for the prosecution, Franzen still seemed terrified at all that he had witnessed. He started at several loud noises in the court and, according to the court reporter, 'barely seemed recovered, even now'. His testimony also took up a considerable period of time, and, although he at no point claimed that the ghost was a fraud, the descriptions of the phantom in a white sheet, the comic prancing about of Mary Fraser shouting 'Fanny, do come!' and the suspicious behaviour of Richard Parsons all gave the impression of a clever charade. In co-opting Franzen to the stand, William's lawyers had made a wise choice.

The rest of the prosecution's witnesses were equally strong. There was Thomas Cooper, Fanny's doctor, and James Jones, her apothecary, both of whom adamantly denied that she could have died by poisoning. There was the faithful maid Esther Carlisle (alias Carrots), who told the court that Moore tried to threaten and then bribe her into backing the ghost's allegations. Completing the picture was Daniel Missiter, who provided details as to how young Betty Parsons had finally been caught out while in his house. A brief testimony was given by Charles Say, printer of the *Daily Gazetteer*, against Richard James. After this the prosecution rested its case.

Given the prosecution's excellent line-up of witnesses, the five defendants faced an uphill struggle. In fact, John Moore and Richard James, who hired a separate lawyer from the other three, did not contest the facts but argued that they had been as much a victim of the Parsons' scam as William. To do so they had to prove that the ghost had been so convincing that nobody could blame them for being sucked into the affair.

Not so Richard and Elizabeth Parsons and Mary Fraser. They had three lawyers working for them and were determined to fight to the last. They had but one hope: to prove that the ghost was not a fraud but in fact really the spirit of Fanny Lynes. Given that mankind had been arguing over the reality or otherwise of the spirit world since the dawn of time, this was by no means going to be an easy task.

The Parsons' witnesses took to the stand, the first being Jane Wetherall, who lived near them on Cock Lane. She testified that the ghost had first made an appearance 'before it was said to be the ghost of Mrs Kent'.[3] Next was Bateman Griffith, another neighbour and the carpenter who had taken down the Parsons' wainscoting in search of the ghost. A number of similar witnesses followed: Catherine Friend, a former lodger with the Parsons; Mr Gammon, an apothecary who had tended to Betty after one of her fits; Charles Watson, another neighbour and the man who had alerted Alderman Gosling to the case; and William Bristow, publisher of *The Mystery Revealed*. All had witnessed the ghost at close quarters but could not tell where the noises had come from. None of them gave testimonies that were convincing, and they could say only that the noises did not appear to come from Betty's direction. They certainly could not offer any proof that the ghost was supernatural in origin.

Finally came the witnesses for Moore and James. Their intent was different from that of the Parsons' witnesses; they sought only to show how convincing the whole charade had been.

First up was Ann Bray, the daughter of the house-owner in Hosier Lane who had hosted Betty in the second week of February. She testified that the experience had been so terrifying that her mother had insisted that Betty be removed from their residence. Next came two intellectual heavyweights, the Revds Broughton and Ross, both of whom admitted to having been taken in by the hoax themselves. Unfortunately, both were also Methodists and so probably only reinforced the jury's prejudice concerning the gullibility of Wesley's followers.

Captain Thomas Wilkinson, a member of Aldrich's committee, then gave a vivid description of his plan to fire a pistol at the ghost and then to beat his way out of the room. He finished by recounting the midnight visit to the Clerkenwell church vault made by himself and the rest of the committee. In retrospect, Wilkinson was probably not an inspired choice of witness, for not only did he come across as demented but he also seemed to help out William's cause by telling the court that Kent had not wanted to prosecute Moore but had been persuaded to do so by others. Alderman Francis Gosling finished off the proceedings.

A number of eminent people (among them three doctors of divinity) spoke in favour of Moore's and James's good character and behaviour. Things did not go so well for Richard Parsons: 'Those that spoke to the character of Parsons', recorded the court reporter, 'acknowledged him to be a very drunken man.'

At around half past seven in the evening Lord Mansfield began his summing-up. Unfortunately his words have not been preserved, but he managed to speak for an hour and half. It must be assumed that the case was relatively clear cut and that Mansfield balanced his summary in favour of William, for the jury were out for only fifteen minutes. At just after half past nine they returned to the court, and the foreman, a Mr Hall, gave their verdict: 'All guilty.'[4]

The trial had lasted over twelve hours, and all were exhausted. The jury indicated to Lord Mansfield that they wanted some form of financial reparation made to William for the trouble he had been put to and the loss of earnings that he had suffered. Mansfield agreed and remanded all the guilty back to prison, so that they might be sentenced at a later date. The guilty verdict was more than a relief to William, who at last believed that he could set about his life once more free from the suspicion of being a murderer.

The following Monday saw a less lengthy trial, when Robert Browne and Charles Say were brought before the Court of the King's Bench. They too were found guilty, but the two men had already made their peace with William by paying him £50 each and as a consequence were set free. Their part in the Cock Lane scandal was over, but not so that of Moore, the Parsons, Fraser and James, who had to wait several months before receiving their sentence.

The conspirators were not brought up before the court again until 22 November, when they were remanded back to prison so that they might be given time to raise money for William's damages. The same thing happened on 27 January 1763.

Finally, on Saturday 12 February the five by now very dishevelled prisoners were brought back before the court for sentencing. John Moore and Richard James had not enjoyed their time behind bars. They were so anxious to be freed from their sentence that they had managed to raise £300 to offer William, plus another £188 to cover his costs; this was a massive sum of money that would have kept a well-to-do family afloat for at least two years. One cannot see how Moore could have afforded this amount; much of it must surely have come from James, whose business interests had made him a very wealthy man. To their relief the payout was deemed sufficient recompense for their crime, and both were released.[5]

Richard and Elizabeth Parsons and Mary Fraser were not so lucky. The money they had raised was not enough to buy their freedom. Mr Justice Wilmot, the prosecuting judge, was harsh in his sentencing. Mary Fraser was sentenced to six months in Bridewell prison and Elizabeth Parsons to a year with hard labour at the same place, but it was Richard Parsons who was to receive the severest sentence. From the outset he had been viewed as the ringleader, and, given the fame of the ghost that he had created, the court wanted to make him an example to other. Parsons was sentenced to two years in prison, but in addition he was to stand at the pillory three times: once at Cock Lane, once at the Royal Exchange and once at Charing Cross. The pillory (or stretch-neck) was a punishment usually reserved for beggars, impostors, conmen and vagabonds and underlined Justice Wilmot's view of Richard Parsons's persona.

To finish off, the judge gave a speech that was 'most excellently adapted to the occasion, expatiated on the indignity of such an imposture'. Richard Parsons was, however, shocked at his sentence, which was far worse than he had expected. As he was taken down to the cells he began shouting at the court. 'I was never sued by Kent,' he screamed. 'He has no grounds to hate me! Many people heard the knockings beside me – if they had been made with a mallet they couldn't have been more distinct!'[6]

It was to no avail. The struggling figure of Parsons was taken down, along with his sobbing wife and his neighbour Mary Fraser. One commentator considered the sentences to be 'much too lenient when we consider the atrocious and malignant motives which instigated the framers of this artful and villainous contrivance'.[7]

Imprisonment and the whole circus surrounding the Cock Lane ghost placed Richard Parsons into a deep depression, so much so that his first trip to the pillory was postponed because he was 'out of his mind at the time'.[8] He had good reason for wanting to avoid the pillory, for a vengeful crowd had been known to kill people who had committed crimes of which they disapproved. In April 1763, for example, a man accused of sodomy was stoned to death by the mob.

It was a nervous Richard Parsons who, on 16 March, was deemed fit enough to receive his punishment and was consequently taken from his prison cell to a pillory set up at the western end of Cock Lane. It might be thought that the neighbourhood that Parsons and his family had so disrupted would have relished the chance to exact their revenge upon the man who had created the Cock Lane ghost, but they did not.

Doubtless to much swearing and abuse, Mr Parsons's head and hands were fixed into the pillory and he was left to his fate. However, not a single stone, rotten potato, dead rat or piece of horse dung was thrown at him. Instead the gathered crowd passed around a hat and took a collection of several guineas – enough money to keep him in prison food, prostitutes and gin for many weeks. It would appear that in London's working neighbourhoods Richard Parsons was viewed not as a deceitful schemer but as a folk hero and someone who had been badly treated by the authorities for standing up for what he believed in. (From this it must also be assumed that the mob also generally believed that the ghost was real.)

This sentiment was not just restricted to the Cock Lane neighbourhood. On 30 March and 8 April he stood again at the Royal Exchange and Charing Cross. On both occasions he was again furnished with money. One wonders whether Richard Parsons actually came to look forward to his visits to the pillory, but, although the money was helpful, it could not buy his freedom. He was forced to spend the next two years in the King's Bench prison living in his own filth and that of the other criminals packed in around him.[9]

Richard Parsons was finally released on 13 April 1765. Memories of the Cock Lane ghost were still strong, his release being mentioned in most of the newspapers of the day, but the whole affair had cost the Parsons family a great deal, and one suspects that, after their reunion, it was little mentioned by them again.

25

AFTER THE SCANDAL

For such a short-lived event, the affair of the Cock Lane ghost managed to make quite a splash in Hanoverian society, the ripples of which carried through into Victorian times and even later.

The ghost was much written about, discussed and parodied at the time, but, unlike some other scandals of the age (such as the Elizabeth Canning affair), the Cock Lane story also managed to enter English folklore. For generations to come the sorry tale of William's battle with a phantom would be repeated, usually in one of two distinct forms. The first version was a bedtime horror story told to frighten children into behaving themselves lest they receive a visit from the ghost of 'scratching Fanny'. The second more widespread version was a cautionary tale, designed to highlight the gullibility of the public. Eventually the term Cock Lane became a byword for a farce of gigantic proportions. It was in this vein that in the late 1790s the pamphleteer John Pasquin wrote: 'An honest man is so affected by such gross instances of gullibility and scoundrelism that he cannot avoid turning to the subscribers and asking them if their love of life is not reduced by such a naked exposition of weakness. This century has been polluted by the Bottle-Conjurer, Elizabeth Canning and the Cock Lane Ghost, and it is miserably doomed in its old age to perish by this literary *fistula in ano* [an infected anal boil].'[1]

A century after its passing, the story of the Cock Lane ghost was still going strong. In 1865 Edward Rimbault wrote: 'Almost every one of us, young and old, have heard how cunning "Fanny", with her mysterious knockings, contrived to hoax the wonder-loving Londoners, until at length the cheat was discovered.' But it was around this time that the story began to fade in popularity, with the newspaper columnist Aleph noting that in 1863 that 'the story has almost died out'.[2]

In the latter part of the nineteenth century the rise of the spiritualist movement produced many thousands of copycat ghosts that would knock out their messages at séances given by professional mediums across the western world. Although more refined than the system devised by the Parsons, the Spiritualist séances of the Victorian era had much in common with the knocking noises in Cock Lane. In these a supposed spirit would bang out answers to questions put to it by a medium in a semi-dark room. Whether the Victorian mediums took this idea from the events in Cock Lane is uncertain, although, given that the Spiritualist movement began in rural America, it seems unlikely. Like Betty Parsons, many Spiritualist mediums were caught out (the escapologist Houdini was especially fond of unmasking them) for faking their communications from the spirit world. Some even went to prison as a result.

Overwhelmed by a sea of Victorian supernaturalism, the Cock Lane ghost was gradually overtaken by better, more exciting ghost stories, and so it began a slow exit from the public's consciousness. The story's last great outing was in Andrew Lang's 1896 spiritualist book entitled *Cock Lane and Common Sense*, which lumps the Cock Lane ghost in with many of the strange phenomena then being produced as part of the Spiritualist craze. By the First World War the story was out of general circulation, although it continues to receive an occasional mention in books about ghosts or London folklore.

Memories of the ghost may have faded, but the street that played host to it still exists. Cock Lane has seen many changes over the two and half centuries since William Kent lodged there. Perhaps unsurprisingly it has mirrored the economic fortunes of the City; in prosperous times the ramshackle houses would be pulled down and new ones put up.

In economic recessions the houses would be filled with lodgers or sold to working families.

In 1869 the entire south side of the lane was demolished, leading *The Times* to comment that 'the Cock Lane ghost is in the way to be fairly laid'. However, the Parsons' house was actually on the north side of the lane and so escaped the demolition. Earlier, in 1815, a fire in a bookseller's that was apparently 'filled with oily substances' had consumed several houses on Cock Lane. Again, the Parsons' old house was spared.[3]

Shortly after the Cock Lane affair had ended the Parsons' house was sold by Nathaniel Barber to the local and wealthy King family, who already owned much property in the area. By 1830 the houses had been assigned numbers, with the Parsons' house being allocated number twenty-one. In 1837 the Kings converted 21 Cock Lane from a domestic residence into a headquarters for a gas meter manufacturer. In the 1840s Cock Lane was home to several heavy industries, including a tinman, a pewterer and a brass founder. By the 1860s most of the metal foundries had gone and in their place came small domestic businesses such as a tailor, carpenter, newsagent and spectacles-maker. The demolition of 1869, plus other clearances, meant that by 1900 the residents of Cock Lane had changed once again. The road was dominated by a large stone merchant and builders' yard, but around this were newly built offices that housed accountants, architects and rate collectors. Between 1930 and 1970 Cock Lane was home to an odd mixture of manufacturing, including several printers, an engravers and an ox tongue curer. During this time the Parsons' old house was being used by Bishop and Brooke Ltd as a shop. From the early 1980s onwards the increasing dominance of the financial sector saw the entire City of London become an economic powerhouse. Property prices rocketed and once undesirable neighbourhoods such as St Sepulchre's became swept up in a property boom that has continued into the twenty-first century.[4]

Modern-day Cock Lane still has echoes of its medieval origins. It is narrow, steep and surrounded by towering buildings that place it in almost permanent shade and give it a canyon-like effect. However, the residential housing has now completely gone, and the area is home to wealthy businesses with their glass-fronted red brick offices and floodlit exteriors. The façade of the Parsons' house, if it is still there, must lie beneath an exterior mask of Victorian and twentieth-century alterations, it owners probably unaware of the events that once captivated all London.[5]

But what of the people at the centre of the Cock Lane affair? What do we know of them? In most cases the truth is that we know frustratingly little. Many of the central protagonists seem to have vanished into the ether in the years following the scandal. Nonetheless, I have managed to gather together a few details.

Of those convicted of conspiracy against William, few fared well. The most tragic story is that of the Revd John Moore, who, after his release from prison, was fortunate enough to be allowed to return to his post as rector of St Bartholomew-the-Great. However, the stress and shame of his association with the ghost had taken its toll, and in July 1768 he died aged only 35. He left behind a wife and two young sons, both of whom were later themselves to enter the priesthood. Despite his horrendous experience at the hands of the Cock Lane ghost, Moore evidently kept in touch with some of his fellow protagonists. His will mentions that one of his properties was occupied by Robert Browne, the relative of the Lynes family who was also prosecuted by William, while an obituary published in the *Gentleman's Magazine* reads: 'Revd Mr Moore, rector of Saint Bartholomew-the-Great, well known by the friends of the Cock Lane ghost.'[6]

Others of whose fate we can be certain include Richard James, who died in 1767 leaving behind a small fortune and several manufacturing businesses; the Revd Stephen Aldrich, who died of old age in 1769; Charles Say, the printer of the *Daily Gazetteer*, who died in 1775; Dr George Macaulay, one of the Aldrich Committee, who died in 1766, and the Revd William Dodd, a witness to the ghost, who was executed in 1777 for an elaborate but bungled forgery scheme designed to clear him of his debts.[7]

The Revd Moore's two African protégés also suffered mixed fortunes. Shortly after the Cock Lane affair ended William Cudjoe suffered a mental breakdown and thereafter died in Guy's Hospital. Philip Quaque fared somewhat better, receiving Holy Orders in the Church of England in 1765 (the first African to do so) and then returning to West Africa the year after as a missionary. He married, had three children and led a long and happy life until his death in 1816 aged 75.[8]

In the years after the scandal the Lynes family left William Kent well alone. The lawsuit over Fanny's legacy was dropped by John Lynes, who was perhaps alarmed at the severity of the sentences handed out to the Parsons and others. The Lynes continued to live in Litcham and remained one of the most prominent families in the parish. Inside the local church are several large slabs set into the floor that commemorate the deaths of many of the family. From these, and the parish registers, we can see that William's enemy John Lynes married and produced several children. His wife died in 1786, while John himself carried on until 19 April 1805, when he was aged 67 years. His son John carried on the family line into the late nineteenth century, after which the family's fortune passed to Douglas Lynes. It was probably the latter who, in 1843, got into a fight with the local tax surveyor, landing several blows on his head and face. The two men were about to undertake a duel with pistols when they were arrested and bound over to keep the peace for a year. Douglas was the last of the Lynes, and, when he died in 1873, his estate was inherited by a Charles Temple of Blakeney, who took the name Temple-Lynes in the family's honour.[9]

Tracking William Kent's whereabouts has proved to be infinitely more complicated. At any one time there were many William Kents living in London, and trying to discern which, if any, of them was the man accused by the ghost is nigh on impossible. There is just one clue as to his fate. We know that William married Bathsheba Bowers in August 1761, and yet in May 1785 there was a Bathsheba Kent, widow, who married Thomas Mennals at St Anne's church, Soho. If this Bathsheba was actually William's widow, then he must have died prior to this date (probably only some months before), something that could be confirmed by his not being mentioned in his brother's 1788 will. Beyond this, we know nothing about William, although I rather fancy that he might be the same William Kent who ran a publishing business in Holborn – a business that was eventually inherited by his son William.[10]

But what of the people that lay at the heart of this scandal? What happened to the Parsons family? Here the trail is, if anything, even more problematic. Nothing definite is known about Richard and Elizabeth Parsons, but it can be assumed that after serving their prison terms they did remain together. I say this because of a brief comment made by the author John Wallis, who had met the Parsons family and who implied that after the troubles died down the family unit remained intact.[11]

It is conceivable (but unlikely) that Richard Parsons is the man of that name who in March 1766 was drinking, gambling and uttering profanities, declaring that if he lost his next game of cards then his 'flesh might rot and his eyes never shut'. He did lose and was found two days later 'his flesh being quite rotten; nor could his eyes be shut, notwithstanding all the efforts of his friends to close them'.[12]

There is a clue to the fate of young Betty Parsons, the mischievous girl at the centre of the affair given by a friend of the family. She is alleged to have married twice (the second time to a gardener) and to have died in Chiswick in around 1807. According to a friend of hers, sometime before her death Betty demonstrated 'some specimens of her art to a young man who kept her company [and] acknowledged to him that it was by the same means that she amused her credulous attendants at Cock Lane; as well as some others upon other trifling occasions'. This is the closest thing that we have to a confession by one of the ghost's creators and would seem to vindicate the lengths that Aldrich went to to expose the Parsons. It is also the only reliable information we have as to the fate of any of the Parsons family in the years following the scandal.[13]

Given this partial confession by Betty, it is probably an opportune time to say something about the nature of the ghost.

In the months and years after the scandal it was generally accepted by the newspapers and pamphleteers that the Cock Lane ghost was nothing more than a vindictive conspiracy cooked up by Richard Parsons and others (including the Lynes family) in revenge against William Kent. However, niggling doubts remained in some people's minds and in particular about the manner in which Betty Parsons was unmasked. Some thought that the aggressive way in which Betty had been treated by Aldrich and Missiter eventually forced her to cheat. (Incidentally, this excuse was also commonly used by Victorian mediums exposed by Harry Houdini and others.) This is a valid point, and it was commented on at the time that the noises produced by Betty knocking on the wooden board were different from those that had been heard before, the implication being that the previous knockings were supernatural in origin. However, having studied the Cock Lane case intensely for some years I am as sure as I can be that the ghost was manufactured by Richard Parsons and his family.

It is my suspicion that the original performances were a team effort. When one examines the reports, it is often remarked that the séances took place in crowded rooms that were poorly lit and where it is said that the noises could be heard to be coming from different directions. Many of the people speaking in favour of the Parsons at the trial commented that they could not determine the exact origin of the noises. This is probably because they were being made by more than one person.

If Mary Fraser, Elizabeth, Betty and Richard Parsons were all in different parts of the room, it would be easy for each of them to make the noises come from different directions by taking their turn at knocking on the walls. In the half light there was no chance of their being caught, and it is little surprise that the ghost would disappear when lit candles were brought into the room.

After Betty was required to perform on her own, both by the committee of gentlemen and by Daniel Missiter, the ghost became much more shy. In fact, the noises would generally appear only in the early morning when people, weary of staying up all night, were off guard. Towards the end of the affair the ghost would come only when people were not expecting it, such as at the houses of the Brays and Mr Missiter, when it made a brief appearance while people were still sleeping but stopped again as soon as light was brought near.

There is no doubt in my mind that Betty was producing these noises herself, probably by banging on the wooden frame of her bed in the darkness. Certainly tying her hands together seemed to stop the noises in their tracks. Despite such clear-cut evidence of a fraud, the ghost even now has its supporters, most of whom cite it as a historical example of a poltergeist, a noisy and often violent species of ghost that is commonly associated with pubescent girls.[14]

A discussion of the merits or otherwise of poltergeists in general is beyond the scope of this book, but I will comment that it is not uncommon for the girls (or boys) at the centre of such cases to be caught out manufacturing the noises and other phenomena themselves. For example, the so-called Enfield poltergeist, which terrorised a family in England in 1977, was declared valid by its principal researchers. However, two other researchers called in to witness the phenomenon found nothing but trickery. Similarly, the Fox sisters, whose ability to communicate with a knocking spirit started the Spiritualist movement in 1840s America, later confessed to having manufactured the noises themselves. Defenders of poltergeist phenomena often claim that those who commit trickery (or make confessions) do so only when the real supernatural phenomena cease to operate. This excuse was also used after Betty Parsons had been caught out, but I hope that the information presented in this book is sufficient to convince the reader that the ghost was an impostor.[15]

Finally, what of the Cock Lane ghost's most famous witness, Dr Samuel Johnson? The great man endured much ribbing for his participation in the Cock Lane affair, and as a consequence he was reluctant to mention it ever again, even to his good friend Boswell. Johnson did not, however, lose his fear of death nor his desire to see proof of the afterlife. He was not to get what he considered proof until 1779, a few years before his own decease. That year saw the death of 'wicked' Lord Lyttelton. Three days before his death Lyttleton complained of having had a terrible dream the night before in which 'he had started up from a midnight sleep, on perceiving a bird flitting near the bed curtains, which vanished shortly, when a female spectre, in white raiment, presented herself, and charged him to depend on his dissolution in three days; he lamented jocosely the shortness of the warning, and observed it was too short a time for preparation after so disorderly a life.'

For the following three days Lord Lyttleton continued his life as usual and declared on the third evening that he had beaten the ghost's warning. That evening, 27 November, he climbed into bed whereupon he had a stroke and died. At that moment another friend of his dreamed that Lyttleton appeared at his bedside and said 'you see me for the last time'.

This episode, which was apparently well attested to, delighted the elderly Dr Johnson. Boswell recounts his reaction: 'It is the most extraordinary thing that has happened in my day,' said Johnson. 'I heard it with my own ears, from his uncle, Lord Westcote. I am so glad to have every evidence of the spiritual world, that I am willing to believe it.'[16] Dr Samuel Johnson was to find out about the true nature of the afterlife on 13 December 1784, when, after a short illness, he left this life. A monument was erected to him in Westminster Abbey, and, so far as I know, his spirit has not seen fit to return to Earth.

EPILOGUE

In 1844 the artist J.W. Archer found himself inside the vault of St John the Baptist's church, Clerkenwell, where he had been commissioned to make a sketch of its picturesque trefoil-headed door. He later recalled:

The place was at that time in great confusion, with coffins, remains of bodies, some of which were dried like mummies, etc. I could find no better seat than one of the coffins. The sexton's boy, who held my light, informed me that this was the coffin of Scratching Fanny, which recalled the Cock Lane ghost to my mind. I got off the lid of the coffin and saw the face of a handsome woman with an aqueline nose; this feature remaining perfect, an uncommon case for the cartilage mostly gives way. The remains had become adipocere [a waxy substance that body fat can turn into after death], and were perfectly preserved. She was said to have been poisoned by deleterious punch but this was legally disproved; and, if I remember rightly, she was otherwise declared to have died of smallpox. Of this disease there was not the least sign; but as some mineral poisons tend to render the body adipocere, here was some evidence in support of the former allegation. I made particular enquiries of Mr Bird, churchwarden, a respectable and judicious man; and he gave me good assurance that this coffin had always been looked upon as the one containing the Cock Lane woman.[1]

Appendix One

MR FOOTE'S ADDRESS TO THE PUBLIC

Hush! Let me search before I speak aloud –
Is no informer skulking in the crowd?
With art laconick noting all that's said,
Malice at heart, indictments in his head;
Prepar'd to levy all the legal war,
And ruse the clamorous legions of the bar
Is here none such? – not one? – then entre-nous
I will a tale unfold, tho' strange yet true;
The application must be made by you.
At Athens once, queen of arms and arts,
There dwelt a citizen of moderate parts;
Precise his manner, and demure his looks,
His mind unletter'd tho' dull, lov'd repartee;
And penn'd a paragraph most daintily:
He aim'd at purity in all he said,
And never once omitted eth and eh
In bath and doth was rarely known to fail,
Himself the hero of each little tale:
With wits and lords this man was much delighted,
And once (it has been said) was near being knighted,
One Aristophanes (a wicked wit
Who never heeded grace in what he writ)
Had mark'd the manner of this Grecian sage,
And, thinking him a subject for the stage,
Had, from the lumbar, cull'd with curious care,

His, voice his looks, his gesture, gait and air,
His affection, consequences and mien,
And loudly launch'd him on the comic scene;
Loud peals of plaudits thro' the circle ran,
All felt the satire, for all knew the man,
Then Peter – Petros was his classic name,
Fearing the loss of dignity and same,
To a grave lawyer in a hurry flies,
Opens his purse and begs his best advice,
The fee secur'd the lawyer strokes his hand.
The café you put I fully understand;
The thing is plain from Coco's reports,
For rules of poetry a'n't rules of court:
A libel – this I'll make the mummer know it –
A Grecian constable took up the poet;
Restrain'd the sallies of his laughing muse,
Call'd harmless humour scandalous abuse:
The bard appeal'd from this severe decree
Th' indulgent public set the pris'ner free:
Greece was to him what Dublin is to me.

Samuel Foote, January 1763
(*Gentleman's Magazine*, 33 (January 1763), 39)

Appendix Two

COCK LANE, HUMBUG

The town it has long been in pain
About the phantom in Cock Lane,
To find it out they strove in vain
Not one thing they neglected;
They searched the bed and the room complete
To see if there was any cheat,
Where little Miss that looks so sweet,
Was not the least suspected.

Then soon the knocking it begun
And then the scratching it would come
'Twas pleased to answer anyone,
And that was done by knocking;
If you was poisoned tell us true,
For yes knock one, for no knock two,
Then she'd knock I tell to you
Which needs must making it shocking.

On Friday night as many know
A noble Lord did thither go,
The ghost its knocking would not throw
Which made the guests mutter:
They being gone then one was there
Who always called it my dear,
Fanny was pleased 'twas very clear
And then began to flutter.

The ghost some gentlemen did tell,
If they would go to Clerkenwell,
Into the vault where she did dwell,
That they three knocks should hear sir;
On Monday night away they went,
The man accused he was present,
But all as deaf it was silent
The de'il a knock was there sir.

The gentlemen returned again,
And told young Missy flat and plain,
That she was the Agent of Cock Lane,
Who knocked and scratched for Fanny.
'Twas false each person did agree
Miss begged to go with her daddy
And then went into the country
To knock and scratch for Fanny.

Ballad of 1762
(The original is in the British Library)

NOTES

LMA   London Metropolitan Archives.

NRO   Norfolk Record Office, Norwich

TNA: PRO   The National Archives: Public Record Office

Chapter 1

1. Quotations from Horace Walpole, *Correspondence*, ed. W.S. Lewis (New Haven, Yale University Press, 1937–83), vol. 10, pp. 5–7; *Lloyd's Evening Post*, 1–3 February 1762.

2. The meeting between Kent and Parsons was covered by many newspapers in January 1762. See, e.g., J. Ker, *The Cock Lane Ghost: Being an Authentic Account of that Extraordinary Affair* (London, J. Dean, n.d.), pp. 5–6.

3. Walpole, *Correspondence*, vol. 10, pp. 5–7.

4. Born in 1715, Richard Parsons was the eldest of seven sisters and two brothers, all of whom continued to live in or near St Sepulchre's parish. He probably received a rudimentary education at the boys' charity school on Cock Lane and was afterwards taken on as an apprentice clerk at St Sepulchre's church. See St Sepulchre's parish registers (LMA) and J. Entick, *A New and Accurate History and Survey of London, Westminster, Southwark, and Places Adjacent* (London, E. and C. Dilly, 1766), vol. 2.

5. Anon., *London and its Environs Described* (London, R. & J. Dodsley, 1761), vol. 5, pp. 332–4. The bell may still be seen in the church.

6. See St Sepulchre's parish registers (LMA). Elizabeth was baptised on 25 January 1749; Anne on 10 June 1753. The Parsons rented their house from Nathaniel Barber, a gentleman who owned several other houses in the neighbourhood. See Land Tax Assessments, 1761 to 1763 (Guildhall Library).

7. O. Goldsmith, *The Mystery Revealed: Containing a Series of Transactions and Authentic Testimonials, Respecting the Supposed Cock-Lane Ghost which have Hitherto been Concealed from The Public*, in *Collected Works of Oliver Goldsmith*, ed. A. Friedman (Oxford, Clarendon Press, 1966), vol. 4, p. 431.

8. Elizabeth is referred to as Betty in several contemporary newspaper articles. See H.C.G. Matthew and B. Harrison, *Oxford Dictionary of National Biography* (Oxford, Oxford University Press, 2004), vol. 43, pp. 915–16.

9. For an account of William and Fanny's first few weeks at Cock Lane, Bartlett Court and Fanny's pregnancy, see Goldsmith, *Mystery*, pp. 425, 426.

10. Carrots; see 'Trial Transcript' (unpublished manuscript, Corporation of London Records Office, Small Suits Box, 9.2), fos. 6–7, 8.

11. William Kent's Norwich origins have been traced through the parish registers at Mileham and St Mary-in-the-Marsh churches and also because of Samuel Foote's parody of the Cock Lane scandal in which William's character says 'in the town of Norwich, where I was born' (S. Foote, *The Orators* (London, W. Lowndes & Co., 1763), p. 41).

12. Of all the traders in Norwich, the worsted weavers were the most affluent. According to one statistic, by the end of the seventeenth century 23 per cent of the wealthiest citizens in Norwich had made their money from worsted weaving. However, at any one time there were so many people dealing in worsted that the probability of an individual weaver becoming a rich man was actually quite small. See J.T. Evans, *Seventeenth Century Norwich* (Oxford, Oxford University Press, 1979), p. 22.

13. For Thomas's brothers, see the Norwich Poll book for 1734. Thomas Kent's weaving business had made him a wealthy man, at least by local standards, although it seems likely that this wealth may in part have been inherited from his father, also called Thomas, and also a worsted weaver. On 3 May 1715 Thomas Kent, apprenticed to Francis Bond, worsted weaver, was made a Freeman of Norwich: Norfolk Record Society, vol. 23, p. 67.

14. Thomas Kent married Elizabeth Hooper in St Mary-in-the Marsh church, Norwich, on 16th March 1717 (parish register, NRO). Little is known about Thomas's first marriage, although, tantalisingly, there was a Thomas and Mary Kent living in St Sepulchre's parish in the early 1700s. However, it is unlikely that this was the same Thomas and Mary Kent, as this couple were producing children in the late 1690s, whereas the Thomas Kent from Norwich did not marry Mary Nudd until 1703: see parish registers for St Sepulchre's (LMA) and St George Tambland, Norwich (NRO).

15. The late Thomas Kent's Norwich weaving business may well have gone to one of the (then adult) children from his first marriage or possibly to William's elder brother John, who chose to remain in Norwich, having married a local girl in 1751. In fact, William Kent was the youngest member of his family, having two

elder brothers and a sister. Only four years separated the eldest child from the youngest, but William also had four siblings who did not survive beyond their first year of life, a not uncommon occurrence in the eighteenth century. For the births and deaths of the children, see the parish register for St Mary-in-the-Marsh church, Norwich (NRO).

16. This picture of William's early life is built up from many sources but principally from descriptions given in Goldsmith, *Mystery*, 'Trial Transcript', fos 1–2, and Ker, *The Cock Lane Ghost*.

17. William mentions his having kept a public house in 'Trial Transcript', fo. 1.

18. Lynes family history is outlined in G.A. Carthew, *The Hundred of Launditch and Deanery of Brisley, in the County of Norfolk* (Norwich, Miller & Leavins, 1877), vol. 3, pp. 92, 95–8, 234. More specific information can be found in the parish registers for Litcham, Little Dunham and East Dereham (all NRO) and the wills of John Lynes (1699; NRO MF 427), Robert Lynes (1713; NRO MF 428) and John Lynes (1722; NRO MF 431).

19. The origins of William and Elizabeth's affair are obscure, but the couple's affection for one another is given in many places, including by William himself, e.g. 'Trial Transcript', fo. 1. It is possible that the Lynes and Kent families had known each other for some time. There is the marriage of a Thomas Lynes in 1713 in the parish register of St Mary-in-the-Marsh in Norwich (NRO); this is the same church used by the Kent family.

20. Elizabeth Kent gave birth around 16 September 1757 (Stoke Ferry parish register; NRO) and yet the couple married only in March. This meant that she became pregnant out of wedlock in December.

Chapter 2

1. The Marriage Act: see L. Stone, *Family, Sex and Marriage in England: 1500–1800* (London, Weidenfeld & Nicolson, 1977).

2. William and Elizabeth's marriage is recorded in Litcham parish registers (NRO).

3. William mentions that he is a publican in Frances's will and in the 'Trial Transcript', fo. 1. Goldsmith, *Mystery*, has him running a post office, but a search of the Royal Mail's archive provided no evidence of this. The dates given in Goldsmith, *Mystery*, for the wedding and other events from this time are wrong, probably to obscure Elizabeth's prenuptial pregnancy.

4. Quotations from the 'Trial Transcript', fo. 1, and Goldsmith, *Mystery*, p. 423.

5. Quotations from W. Smellie, *A Treatise on the Theory and Practice of Midwifery* (London, D. Wilson and T. Durham, 1752), pp. 448–9. If a male midwife was present, then Smellie advised him to work with any female midwives and that he should not 'openly condemn her method of practice, (even though it should be erroneous) but ought to make allowance for the weakness of the sex, and rectify what is amiss, without exposing her mistakes'.

6. These descriptions of childbirth come from Anon., *The Ladies' Dispensatory* (Oxford, Routledge, 2002; originally 1652), and E. Smith, *The Compleat Housewife* (London, Studio, 1994; originally 1758).

7. Elizabeth's burial and William's baptism on 17 September 1757 are recorded in the Stoke Ferry parish registers (NRO).

8. See Stoke Ferry parish register (NRO) and also Goldsmith, *Mystery*, p. 423.

9. For details of William and Fanny's falling in love, see 'Trial Transcript', fo. 1, and Goldsmith, *Mystery*, p. 423.

10. Elizabeth's burial is recorded in the Mileham parish register (NRO). Aside from his change in behaviour, William's sudden wealth can be seen in various references to his being well-off after his arrival in London.

11. For information on Leavy, see R.S. Kirby, *Wonderful and Eccentric Museum* (London, R.S. Kirby, 1805), vol. 3, pp. 71–2, Goldsmith, *Mystery*, pp. 423–5, and Frances Lynes's will. There seems to be a connection between Leavy and the Lynes family, although the exact nature of this link is not clear. It is possible that it was Leavy who smoothed the path for William and Elizabeth's departure from Litcham and organised for William to take his position in the public house there.

12. See 'Trial Transcript', fo. 1.

13. See *ibid*.

14. In his testimony, published in the *St James's Chronicle* (21–23 January 1762), Leavy states that Frances was brought to London in August. This contradicts the version given by William in Goldsmith, *Mystery*, p. 424, where he states that she was brought around Whitsun (3 June that year). As Fanny's will was made on 7 July, at which point she was in London, it would seem that the June date is the more correct.

15. Frances's will is preserved in TNA: PRO (PROB 11/853). Details concerning the making of the will are given in 'Trial Transcript', fos 2, 8, Goldsmith, *Mystery*, p. 424, and Leavy's testimony in *St James's Chronicle*, 21–23 January 1762.

16. William and Fanny's time in Mansion House is described in *St James's Chronicle*, 21–23 January 1762, and Goldsmith, *Mystery*, p. 424. The timing of Fanny's pregnancy can be worked out from Doctor Thomas Cooper's testimony in Goldsmith, *Mystery*, p. 426.

Chapter 3

1. Aleph, *London Scenes and London People* (London, City Press, 1863), p. 180; J. Boswell, *Life of Johnson* (Oxford, Oxford University Press, 1998; originally 1791), p. 248.
2. The Cow Lane incident comes from *Gentleman's Magazine* (May 1761). Bunyan's death from P. Ackroyd, *London: The Biography* (London, Vintage, 2001), p. 149.
3. Cock Lane history. See Anon., *A Descriptive Catalogue of Ancient Deeds in the Public Record Office, Series A* (London, HMSO, 1890), No. 1661; A.H. Thomas, *Calendar of Early Mayor's Court Rolls: 1298–1307* (Cambridge, Cambridge University Press, 1924), pp. 170–227; A.H. Thomas, *Calendar of the Plea and Memoranda Rolls of the City of London: Volume 1: 1323–1364* (Cambridge, Cambridge University Press, 1926), roll A5.
4. The list of Cock Lane residents was obtained from trade directories and land tax assessments (Guildhall Library) for 1759 to 1762, but see also J.S. Cockburn (ed.), *The Victoria History of the County of Middlesex* (Oxford, Oxford University Press, 1998), vol. 11, pp. 168–90.

Chapter 4

1. The specific mention in Fanny's will of any 'future legacies' from Thomas suggests that he may have had a long-term illness of which she was aware. In his will Thomas acknowledges himself to be 'sick in body': NRO MF 440.
2. Quite what William was doing to earn money during his time at Cock Lane is unclear. It looks suspiciously as though he may have been living off his inheritance while waiting for a business opportunity to arrive. Several contemporary references mention that William was looking to purchase himself a position in the civil service, others note that he was still keen on becoming a stockbroker; if so, then the loans that he had hitherto made displayed a remarkable lack of financial commonsense, which suggests that this would have been a bad career choice. That William still held his inn in Norfolk can be deduced from Fanny's description of him as being an innkeeper in her will, which was compiled several months after his arrival in London (TNA: PRO PROB 11/853). He also returned to Norfolk for a wedding, *London Chronicle*, 21–23 January 1762, p. 71.
3. Kirby, *Wonderful and Eccentric Museum*, vol. 3, p. 68.
4. Goldsmith, *Mystery*, p. 425; 'Trial Transcript', fo. 2.

5. During these proceedings Fanny, still believing herself to be in labour, had asked Carrots to summon a midwife, who had duly arrived with her assistant. They too believed her to be in labour until Dr Cooper put them straight. Goldsmith, *Mystery*, p. 425.

6. The fact that both William and Carrots chose to stay by her side might indicate that they had been exposed to the disease already.

7. Goldsmith, *Mystery*, pp. 426–9.

8. *St James's Chronicle*, 21–23 January 1762.

9. Quotation taken from Goldsmith, *Mystery*, p. 427; see also Cooper's testimony in the 'Trial Transcript', fo. 8.

10. The funeral and its proceedings are covered in Goldsmith, *Mystery*, pp. 429–30; *St James's Chronicle*, 21–23 January 1762. Frances's entry in the church register can be seen at LMA X102-029; it reads 'Frances Kent, buried 5th February died 2nd February'; after this somebody has scribbled, in pencil, 'Cock Lane Ghost'.

11. Robert Browne was the clerk to the Worshipful Company of Bricklayers; see John Moore's will: TNA: PRO PROB 11/941. That he is related to the Lynes family is given in Goldsmith, *Mystery*, p. 428.

12. Frances Lynes's will: TNA: PRO PROB 11/853

Chapter 5

1. Franzen's encounter with the ghost and Catherine Friend's experiences are recounted in the 'Trial Transcript', fos 5, 9.

Chapter 6

1. John Moore was born in London in 1733. His father John was a wine merchant in the parish of St Swithun's, although his children were all baptised in St Sepulchre's church, which suggests that his family had a longstanding connection with the parish. After receiving an education at Christ's Hospital, Moore went to Pembroke College, Cambridge. Moore was ordained in 1755 and for a couple of years was a master at Halstead Grammar School, Essex, before returning to London to take up his post at St Sepulchre's church. At the time of Fanny Lynes's death he had just been made the rector of St Bartholomew-the-Great church, but he also kept on the lectureship at St Sepulchre's, the two

churches being just round the corner from each other. Moore was married first to Susannah, by whom he had three surviving children, John, Nathaniel and Susannah (plus Thomas, who died an infant). Susannah died, probably in childbirth, and in 1750 he married again, this time to Sarah Bowden, by whom he had no further children. For Moore's history see: J. Venn and J.A. Venn, *Alumni Cantabrigienses: A Biographical List of All Known Students, Graduates and Holders of Office at the University of Cambridge* (Cambridge, Cambridge University Press, 1922–54), vol. 3, p. 206; G.L. Hennessy, *Novum Repertorium Ecclesiasticum Parochiale Londinense* (London, S. Sonnenschein Ltd, 1898), p. 101; St Sepulchre's parish register entries for 1742, 1744, 1745 and 1749 (LMA) and St Katherine by the Tower parish register for 1749/50 (LMA).

2. *Daily Ledger*, 31 December 1761. For a history and discussion of Africans in England, see J. Walvin, *Black and White: The Negro and English Society, 1555–1945* (London, Allen Lane, 1973).

3. In 1672 this stretch of coast had been ceded to the English 'Royal African Company' and then, in 1750, to the 'African Company of Merchants'. The Company's principal interest was in the slave trade, and by the 1750s Cape Coast Castle had become the trade's biggest administrative centre. Cabosheer is a local term for a tribal administrator. See F.L. Bartels, 'Philip Quaque, 1741–1816', *Transactions of the Gold Coast and Togoland*, 1 (1955), 153–71.

4. For details of Thompson's life, see T. Thompson, *An Account of Two Missionary Voyages* (London, SPCK, 1937).

5. C.F. Pascoe, *Two Hundred Years of the SPG* (London, Society for the Propagation of the Gospel, 1901), p. 256.

6. *Ibid.*, p. 256.

7. M.J. Sampson, *Gold Coast Men of Affairs* (London, Dawsons, 1969), p. 196; Pascoe, *Two Hundred Years*, p. 256; Bartels, 'Philip Quaque'.

8. Kirby, *Wonderful and Eccentric Museum*, vol. 3, p. 70.

9. *London Chronicle*, 19–21 January 1762.

Chapter 7

1. Moore's introduction to Methodism probably came through his friend the Revd Thomas Broughton, who was himself an early recruit to Wesley's cause. Through Broughton and through his work with the Society for the Propagation of the Gospel in Foreign Parts, Moore became a Methodist supporter.

2. For an early history of the Methodist church, see, e.g., M. Edwards, *John Wesley and the Eighteenth Century* (Canterbury, Epworth Press, 1955), and R. F. Wearmouth, *Methodism and the Common People of the Eighteenth Century* (Canterbury, Epworth Press, 1945).

3. Edited from Boswell, *Johnson*, pp. 324–5.

4. R. Porter, *English Society in the Eighteenth Century* (London, Penguin, 1990), p. 48.

5. M.J. Naylor, *The Inanity and Mischief of Vulgar Superstitions* (Cambridge, M.J. Naylor, 1795), p. 3.

6. Edited from D. Wright, *The Epworth Phenomena* (London, W. Rider & Sons, 1917), p. 82.

7. *Ibid.*, pp. 81–98.

8. Boswell, *Johnson*, p. 951.

9. V.H.H. Green, *John Wesley* (London, Nelson, 1964), p. 9.

10. *Ibid.*, p. 10.

11. Wright, *Epworth Phenonema*, p. 32.

12. Finding a cause for the Epworth phenomenon after two hundred years is problematic, but from the letters, journals and eyewitness testimonies, it is possible to suggest that one or more of the Wesley daughters (especially Emily and Hetty) was responsible for generating the knockings.

13. Transcripts of all of the Wesley family's letters, journals and other writings on the Epworth disturbances are given in Wright, *Epworth Phenonema*.

14. See, e.g., S. Tomkins, *John Wesley: A Biography* (London, Lion Publishing, 2003), p. 20.

Chapter 8

1. For details of Lynes fulfilling the bequest, see TNA: PRO C12/1489/4; for marriage, see parish register for St John Zachary, London (LMA).

2. Thomas Lynes's will: NRO MF 440.

3. In fact, the situation is far more complicated than this. The disputed land had been held as 'copyhold' by Thomas and not 'freehold' as John believed. Copyhold land has many restrictions associated with it and is thus worth less than freehold land. The mistake occurred because the title deeds to the land were initially withheld from John by another of Thomas's creditors. All this, and more, is outlined in painful detail in TNA: PRO C12/1489/4.

4. Details of the court case can be seen in TNA: PRO C12/1489/4.

5. William's view on the Lynes's persecution of him is outlined in Goldsmith, *Mystery*, p. 426.

6. The meeting between Leavy and Browne took place at the Rolls Tavern, a public house in Chancery Lane, London: *St James's Chronicle*, 21–23 January 1762.

7. Browne was a member of the Worshipful Company of Bricklayers and Tylers, a respected guild of builders based in the city of London. He would one day become secretary to this guild. See John Moore's will, TNA: PRO PROB 11/941. The Browne family had been in the building business since at least the 1620s and, like many craftsmen, had made considerable sums of money in the years following the Great Fire of 1666. After a lull around the turn of the eighteenth century, the good times had returned as London began to expand rapidly westwards, requiring the building of thousands of new houses and shops. In recent years Robert Browne's business had grown considerably, forcing him to take on a string of young apprentices to help him keep pace with demand. See C. Webb, *London Apprentices* (London, Society of Genealogists, 2003), vol. 2, pp. 1, 7, 15, 16, 22, 29, 42, 45, 54, 75, 80, 81.

8. William implicitly links the Lynes's lawsuit with the arrival of the Cock Lane ghost in Goldsmith, *Mystery*, p. 436.

Chapter 9

1. Franzen gives his own account of this in the 'Trial Transcript', fo. 6.

2. Given Moore's interaction with Whitefield's Tabernacle on Tottenham Court Road, the odds are that he had attended some of the prayer meetings there, where preachers claimed to have summoned up spirits during the service. See, e.g., *Lloyd Letters (1754–1796)*, ed. G.E. Evans (London, William Jones, 1908), p. 62.

3. This quotation, which has been edited, comes from E.D. Bond, *The Spectator* (Oxford, Oxford University Press, 1965), vol. 1, pp. 53–4.

4. For a recent discussion of Methodism and the supernatural, see O. Davies, 'Methodism, the Clergy, and the Popular Belief in Witchcraft and Magic', *History*, 82 (1997), 252–65.

5. The idea that ghosts had to return for a reason was widely promoted by many early modern philosophers. In 1681 Henry Moore recounts the tale of a maid who, on being suspected of being pregnant with her master's child, was sent away with Mark Sharp, a young man who, on the master's instructions, murdered her. The maid's ghost appeared one night to a James Graham, and told him her body was buried and who had murdered her. Graham went to a magistrate, who uncovered the body and arrested and tried the master and Sharp. See J. Glanvill, *Saducismus Triumphatus*

(Berlin, Verlag, 1978; originally 1681), pp. 3–6. See also the Drummer of Tedworth in the same volume.

6. See *London Chronicle*, 19–21 January p. 66. The description of the séance scene is based on subsequent reports.

7. Bateman Griffith. See his testimony in 'Trial Transcript', fo. 9. Mr Griffith lived a few doors up from the Parsons: Land tax assessments, 1761 (Guildhall Library). He was baptised in 1710 in St Peter-le-Poer, London (LMA) and married in 1733 in St James's church, Westminster (LMA).

8. S. Pepys, *The Diary of Samuel Pepys*, ed. H.B. Wheatley (London, George Bell, 1893), entry for 29 November 1667.

9. The belief that the ghost was Fanny's spirit (as opposed to that of Elizabeth) emerged not long after the noises restarted in late 1761. Moore's investigations into the ghost can be deduced from William's description of their first meeting. See 'Trial Transcript', fos 1, 5, 9, 10.

Chapter 10

1. H. Walpole, *Memoirs of the Reign of King George the Third* (London, Lawrence & Bullen, 1894), p. 115.

2. R. Porter, *Patients and Practitioners* (Cambridge, Cambridge University Press, 1985), pp. 145–75; see also *Gentleman's Magazine*, December 1761. The 'ghost' continued until November 1762, when it stopped as suddenly as it had begun. As with many such cases, opinion is divided as to the cause, although trickery by the children is the probable explanation.

3. The Lamb Inn ghost is the first case of which I am aware where the once for 'yes', twice for 'no' code is recorded as being used. However, similar codes may have been in use for centuries. In the case of the 1663 Demon Drummer of Tedworth, the noisy spirit was persuaded to confirm certain facts by banging on the wall thus: 'When the knocking was, many being present, a Gentleman said, Satan, If the Drummer set thee on worke, let us understand so much by giving three knockes and no more; it presently gave three knockes distinctly and audibly: then the Gentleman knockt to see where it would imitate him or no, as it had done severall times before, but it remained silent: He then further replied, For the further confirmation of this, If the Drummer set thee on work, let us have five knockes and no more; It gave five knockes, and then ceased from knocking that night any more. This was in the presence of Sir Thomas Chamberlaine of Oxfordshire (truly at present I doe not

remember whether he were the person that spake himself or no) Mr Gyles Tooker and others' (Michael Hunter, personal communication). See M. Hunter, 'New Light on the Drummer of Tedworth', *Historical Research*, 88 (August 2005).

4. For Broughton and Methodism, see Green, *John Wesley*, pp. 33, 57. For links between Moore and Broughton, see 'Trial Transcript', fo. 10.
5. The idea that it was Broughton who persuaded Moore to try a code based on the Lamb Inn case is supposition on my part, although Walpole, among others, links the two cases through the Methodist network; Walpole, *Memoirs*, p. 115.
6. The Parsons' financial benefits are mentioned in *St James's Chronicle*, 30 January–2 February 1762 and Walpole, *Memoirs*, p. 115.
7. The proceedings of this séance, including the questions, are given in 'Trial Transcript', fo. 10; *St James's Chronicle*, 17–19 January 1762; 6–9 February 1762.

Chapter 11

1. No copies of the *Public Ledger* exist from 1762; these news items were taken from editions of *St James's Chronicle* from the opening week of January 1762.
2. No copies of the *Public Ledger* survive from 1762; the wording is taken from the 'Trial Transcript', fo. 3.
3. 'Trial Transcript', fo. 3.
4. *Public Ledger*, reprinted in *London Chronicle*, 19–21 January 1762.
5. The information regarding William's reaction to the newspaper articles and his search for John Moore is given in his trial testimony; 'Trial Transcript', fo. 3.
6. It is known that William contacted Cooper and Moore and arranged for them to be present on 12 January; the conversation was paraphrased from information given in 'Trial Transcript', fo. 4. and Goldsmith, *Mystery*.
7. A description of this great storm can be found in Entick, *Survey of London*, p. 201.
8. This amusing dialogue is preserved in 'Trial Transcript', fo. 4.
9. 'Trial Transcript', fo. 4; *London Chronicle*, 19–21 January 1762; Kirby, *Wonderful and Eccentric Museum*, vol. 3, p. 74.
10. The previous notable storm was in January 1743. Neither storm was as large as that of November 1703, which is widely believed to have been the largest storm recorded in English history.
11. See Richard James's will. TNA: PRO PROB 11/927.
12. *Public Ledger*, quotation from Kirby, *Wonderful and Eccentric Museum*, vol. 3, p. 74.
13. Aldrich's history: Venn and Venn, *Alumni*, vol. 1, p. 14; Hennessy, *Novum Repertorium*, p. 245.

Chapter 12

1. 'Trial Transcript', fo. 4.
2. Land tax assessments for 1760 to 1763 (Guildhall Library). Watson was baptised in St Andrew's church, Holborn (LMA) in 1713.
3. The details of this séance, including the full list of questions, are to be found in *London Chronicle*, 19–21 January 1762; *Lloyd's Evening Post*, 20–22 January 1762; *St James's Chronicle*, 19–21 January 1762; *Daily Gazetteer*, 20 January 1762. Additional information can be found in the 'Trial Transcript', fos. 4–5. I have rephrased some of the questions.
4. Although they are not mentioned by name, the presence of 'two negroes' at the séance of 19 January is recorded by several sources; see, e.g., *St James's Chronicle*, 19–21 January 1762.
5. A. Knapp and W. Baldwin, *The Newgate Calendar* (London, Navarre Society, 1926; originally 1826), vol. 2.
6. Mr Gibson's presence is noted by Carrots ('Trial Transcript', fo. 8). I have not been able to determine who this man is.
7. The position of Alderman dates back to Anglo-Saxon times: S. Leigh, *New Picture of London* (London, W. Clowes, 1819).
8. See the 1765 will of John Hebden, TNA: PRO PROB 11/906. Gosling is commemorated in a plaque in Fleet Street for having donated the money to provide an ornate gate in West Ludgate. Later generations of the Gosling family seem to have stayed within the banking business.
9. The meeting with the Alderman: 'Trial Transcript', fo. 10.
10. Mayor Fludyer had been born and grew up in Chippenham, a prosperous town west of London. He had continued his family involvement in the cloth trade, becoming one of Chippenham's most prosperous businessmen. By his early thirties Fludyer had sought political office both in Chippenham and in London, becoming a Councillor and then Alderman of London and then, in 1753, MP for Chippenham, a post on which he is alleged to have spent £1,500 getting himself elected. For further information on Fludyer, see the archive at the Chippenham Museum and Heritage Centre. The banquet information came from G.A. Sala, *London Up to Date* (London, A.C. Black, 1895).
11. The meeting with the Mayor: 'Trial Transcript', fo. 10.
12. Canning references: see *Gentleman's Magazine*, vol. 23 (1753), pp. 7, 107–11, 144, 202, 245, 293, 347, 441; vol. 24 (1754), pp. 45, 93, 189–91, 225–7, 243, 317–21, 339. Quotation from Knapp and Baldwin, *Newgate Calendar*, vol. 2.

13. Around this time there were many omens relating to the Canning case. In November 1761 Elizabeth Canning returned to England for a visit. Even more ominously, a couple of days after Moore's meeting with the Mayor, Mary Squires the gypsy died. *Gentleman's Magazine* (November 1761, January 1762).

Chapter 13

1. Carrots's interview with Moore is given in the 'Trial Transcript', fos 7, 8. The conversation is given only in part; I have extracted the rest from the description of what happened.
2. Details of the séance are given in *St James's Chronicle*, 19–21 January 1762; 'Trial Transcript', fos 7–8, plus many secondary sources.
3. Franzen recounts this story (and his continued fear of the ghost) in 'Trial Transcript', fo. 7; *St James's Chronicle*, 19–21 January 1762.

Chapter 14

1. The information on this rivalry came from R.L. Haig, *The Gazetteer: 1735–1797* (Carbondale, Ill., Southern Illinois University Press, 1960).
2. Charles Green Say was the son of Edward and Elizabeth Say, christened 30 August 1721 in St Botolph, Bishopsgate, and died 29 June 1775 in Ave-Mary-Lane, London. For biographical information on Charles Say, see H.R. Plomer *et al.*, *A Dictionary of Printers and Booksellers who were at Work in England, Scotland and Ireland from 1726 to 1775* (Oxford, Oxford University Press, 1932), p. 222.
3. See Say's testimony: 'Trial Transcript', fo. 9.
4. See Bristow's testimony; 'Trial Transcript', fo. 10. For a brief biography of Bristow, see Plomer *et al.*, *Dictionary*, p. 34.
5. The *Public Ledger*'s version is to be found in *London Chronicle*, 19–21 January 1762, as is that of the *Daily Gazetteer*.
6. See *London Chronicle*, 21–23 January 1762; James Bruin appears as a witness in an Old Bailey trial on 22 February 1758: see *The Proceedings of the Old Bailey* (unpublished volume, Guildhall Library). Bruin was christened in 1709 in St Mary's church, Stepney (LMA).
7. The names of these three gentlemen are referred to in *St James's Chronicle*, 19–21 January 1762 as the Earl of N., the Right Hon. Mr N. and Mr C. Northumberland's

involvement is mentioned by Horace Walpole. I have not been able to determine the names of the last two, although I suspect that Mr C. is probably a Mr Chute.

8. The job offer and some of the other benefits received by the Parsons can be found in Walpole, *Correspondence*, vol. 10, p. 6.

9. The details of this séance are in *St James's Chronicle*, 28–30 January 1762. The information on Thomas Lynes and the wedding came from Little Dunham parish register (NRO MF 1395/7) and Litcham parish register (NRO MF 699/16).

10. Descriptions of the séance are to be found in *St James's Chronicle*, 19–21 January, 21–23 January 1762; *London Chronicle*, 21–23 January 1762; *Lloyd's Evening Post*, 20–22 January 1762.

11. *London Chronicle*, 21–23 January 1762.

Chapter 15

1. Leavy's testimony was widely published; see: *St James's Chronicle*, 21–23 January 1762; Kirby, *Wonderful and Eccentric Museum*, vol. 3, pp. 71–2. D. Grant, *The Cock Lane Ghost* (London, Macmillan, 1965), erroneously attributes it to John Lynes. Leavy's date of August for Fanny's coming to London is erroneous; see ch. 2, n. 14.

2. *St James's Chronicle*, 21–23 January 1762; signed R. Browne, Amen Corner, 21 January.

3. An account of this séance can be found in *St James's Chronicle*, 21–23 January 1762. The account of Anne Lynes's involvement comes from Kirby, *Wonderful and Eccentric Museum*, vol. 3, p. 78.

4. See *St James's Chronicle*, 21–23 January 1762.

5. See Kirby, *Wonderful and Eccentric Museum*, vol. 3, p. 79.

Chapter 16

1. *St James's Chronicle*, 28–30 January 1762.

2. *Ibid.*, 23–26 January 1762; Kirby, *Wonderful and Eccentric Museum*, vol. 3, pp. 80–1.

3. *St James's Chronicle*, 23–26 January 1762.

4. *Ibid.*, 23–26 January 1762; Kirby, *Wonderful and Eccentric Museum*, vol. 3, pp. 80–1; Goldsmith, *Mystery*, pp. 432–3.

5. 'Trial Transcript', fo. 10.

6. *St James's Chronicle*, 23–26 January 1762.

7. *Public Ledger*, 26 January 1762, reprinted in *Lloyd's Evening Post*, 25–27 January 1762.
8. *Lloyd's Evening Post*, 25–27 January 1762. Italics in original.
9. For Macaulay, see Matthew and Harrison, *Dictionary*, vol. 35, pp. 36–7.
10. 'Trial Transcript', fo. 10. Land tax assessment records (Guildhall Library).
11. See Douglas's 1755 anti-Methodist pamphlet *An Apology for the Clergy*.
12. Boswell, *Johnson*, pp. 163–4.

Chapter 17

1. Boswell, *Johnson*, pp. 482, 486.
2. Edited from *ibid.*, p. 167.
3. Edited from *ibid.*, p. 287.
4. Abridged from *ibid.* p. 426.
5. S. Johnson, 'Life of Roscommon', *Gentleman's Magazine*, May 1749.

Chapter 18

1. With both Moore and Aldrich absent from these séances, there are only the scantiest of details of what occurred inside the house. See, e.g., Horace Walpole's letter quoted later in this chapter.
2. *St James's Chronicle*, 28–30 January 1762.
3. Walpole, *Correspondence*, vol. 22, p. 3.
4. *Ibid.*, vol. 10, pp. 5–7. The 'rabbit woman' referred to by Walpole is Mary Tofts, who, in 1726, claimed to have given birth to a litter of rabbits. See *Medical History*, vol. 5 (1961), pp. 349–60. Walpole later went on to write *The Castle of Otranto*, a novel usually deemed to be the earliest example of gothic horror. It has been argued that this work, written in 1764, was partially influenced by Walpole's Cock Lane experience; see E.J. Clery, *The Rise of Supernatural Fiction, 1762–1800* (Cambridge, Cambridge University Press, 1999).
5. *Lloyd's Evening Post*, 27–29 January 1762.
6. *Ibid.*, 5–8 February 1762.
7. *St James's Chronicle*, 28–30 January 1762.
8. *London Chronicle*, 11–13 February 1762.
9. *St James's Chronicle*, 4–6 February 1762.

Chapter 19

1. Grant, *The Cock Lane Ghost*, p. 70.
2. *St James's Chronicle*, 6–9 February 1762.
3. The details for the night's proceedings are to be found chiefly in Johnson's account, which was reprinted widely; e.g. *Gentleman's Magazine*, February 1762, pp. 81–2, but see also *St James's Chronicle*, 6–9 February 1762; 'Trial Transcript', fos. 4, 10; Grant, *Cock Lane Ghost*, pp. 70, 77–8.

Chapter 20

1. Johnson's account was widely reproduced; this full version came from *Lloyd's Evening Post*, 1–3 February 1762.
2. Grant, *Cock Lane Ghost*, p. 80.
3. These excerpts come from Kirby, *Wonderful and Eccentric Museum*, vol. 3, pp. 87–8, and *Lloyd's Evening Post*, 12–15 February 1762. The sketch with Fanny in a beer bottle is a take-off of the so-called Bottle-Conjuror, in which a mischief-maker persuaded a London audience that he could squeeze himself into a quart bottle. Having filled a theatre, the Bottle-Conjuror ran off with the takings, leaving behind an outraged audience.
4. *London Chronicle*, 13–16 February 1762.
5. Edited from Boswell, *Johnson*, pp. 106–7.
6. 'Enthusiasm' was a word used to criticise the frenzied nature of some Methodist services.
7. J. Ireland, *Hogarth Illustrated* (London, J.E.J. Boydell,1791, 1793, 1798).
8. The identification of this figure with Johnson is given by several people. See B. Krysmanski, 'We See a Ghost: Hogarth's Satire on Methodists and Connoisseurs', *Art Bulletin* (June 1998), pp. 292–310.
9. J.T. Smith, *Nollekens and his Times* (London, Turnstile Press, 1949), p. 131.
10. For a full breakdown of this picture, see Krysmanski, 'We See a Ghost', pp. 292–310.
11. Tofts: see S.A. Seligman, 'Mary Tofts – The Rabbit Breeder', *Medical History*, vol. 5 (1961), pp. 349–60; Bilson Boy: see Richard Baddeley, *The Boy of Bilson* (London, FK, 1622).
12. D.W. Nichol, *Pope's Literary Legacy* (Oxford, Oxford University Press, 1992), pp. 147–8.

13. These are discussed in Chapters 20 and 23.
14. Krysmanski, 'We See a Ghost', p. 310.

Chapter 21

1. 'Trial Transcript', fo. 10.
2. *Ibid.*, fo. 9; see TNA: PRO PROB 11/862.
3. Details of the proceedings in Bray's and Missiter's house can be found in: 'Trial Transcript', fos. 9–10; *London Magazine* (March 1762), pp. 150–1; Ker, *The Cock Lane Ghost*, pp. 18–23; *Annual Register* (1762), pp. 145–6.

Chapter 22

1. Goldsmith, *Mystery*, pp. 426–7.
2. 'Trial Transcript', fo. 10. The arrests are given in Ker, *The Cock Lane Ghost*, p. 23.
3. W. Bristow, *The Genuine Account of the Life and Trial of Eugene Aram, for the murder of Daniel Clarke* (London, W. Bristow, 1759).
4. Boswell, *Johnson*, pp. 292–3.
5. For Goldsmith's involvement in the publication of this pamphlet, see Goldsmith, *Mystery*, pp. 417–18. *Notes and Queries*, 24 January 1852, p. 77; 13 May 1865, pp. 371–2.
6. William's cooperation with Goldsmith cannot be doubted, as much of the information in the pamphlet is to be found nowhere else and is evidently first hand. The delay in publication seems probable, given that the work was published the day after the arrests took place.
7. *London Chronicle*, 23–25 February 1762.
8. Walpole, *Correspondence*, vol. 22, pp. 8–9.
9. *Public Advertiser*, 26 February 1762.
10. *London Magazine* (March 1762), pp. 151–2.
11. Goldsmith, *Mystery*, pp. 435–6.
12. J. Forster, *The Life and Times of Oliver Goldsmith* (London, Ward Lock, 1848), p. 240.
13. *St James's Chronicle*, 25–27 February 1762; Ker, *The Cock Lane Ghost*, p. 24.
14. Grant, *Cock Lane Ghost*, pp. 78–9.

Chapter 23

1. Boswell, *Johnson*, p. 135.
2. *Ibid.*, p. 288.
3. Edited from *ibid.*, pp. 417–18.
4. *Ibid.*, p. 864.
5. Samuel Foote was born in 1720 to a wealthy Cornish family. The anarchic streak that was to rule his life was present even in his earliest years. At Winchester College, to which he had been admitted only because he was a descendant of one of its founders, Foote was noted for his idleness, insolence and lack of respect for authority. He once played a practical joke on the College's dean by creeping out at night and tying hay to the church's bell ropes. The cow in the churchyard was attracted by the hay and as she pulled on the hay, the bells rang out. According to local legend, the dean and the sexton believed the church to be under attack by vandals and ran to it. The sexton was first to arrive and seized the cow by the tail while the dean grabbed its horns. Each believed that they had got hold of a human assailant and continued to struggle with the unfortunate cow until a light was brought, at which point the mistake was realised. The local town dined out on the story for years. See P. Fitzgerald, *Samuel Foote: A Biography* (Reading, Chatto & Windus, 1910), pp. 14, 92–3.
6. *Monthly Review*, vol. 76, p. 374.
7. Sheridan was well known for his teaching of elocution, something that had become a fad among the chattering classes. But the craze for elocution was not popular with everyone and drew many side swipes. 'Attendants upon Mr Sheridan's lectures fancied a right Elocution would cure all the ills of venality in public as well as private life,' wrote one reviewer (*Lloyd's Evening Post*, vol. 10, pp. 322–3). 'One would imagine that he considers elocution as the consummation of all earthly perfection, and that even the virtues of the heart depend, in a great measure, on the utterance of the tongue and the gesticulations of the body,' wrote another (*Critical Review*, vol. 14, p. 161.)
8. M.M. Belden, *The Dramatic Work of Samuel Foote* (Oxford, Oxford University Press, 1929), p. 110.
9. Foote is certainly shown as a witness in *English Credulity*, one of the many satirical cartoons produced during the ghost's reign.
10. Boswell, *Johnson*, p. 580.
11. S.A.O. Fitzpatrick, *Dublin: A Historical and Topographical Account of the City* (Dublin, Curtis Green, 1907); Fitzgerald, *Samuel Foote*, p. 235.
12. Foote, *Orators*, p. 35.
13. *Ibid.*, p. 42.

14. For a review of the opening night, see *London Magazine* (May 1762), pp. 258–9.
15. B. Dobrée, *The Letters of Philip Dormer Stanhope, 4th Earl of Chesterfield* (London, Eyre & Spottiswoode, 1932), pp. 2394–5.
16. Fitzgerald, *Samuel Foote*, p. 95.
17. *London Magazine* (March 1763), pp. 135–6.
18. This quotation, including the dialect spelling, came from T. Sadler, *Diary, Reminiscences, and Correspondence of Henry Crabb Robinson* (London, Macmillan & Co., 1869), vol. 1, ch. 14.
19. Dobrée, *Letters*, p. 2465.
20. *Public Advertiser*, 28 January 1763; *London Magazine* (March 1763), pp. 135–6.
21. See *Gentleman's Magazine*, vol. 47, pp. 534–6.
22. Dobrée, *Letters*, p. 2737.

Chapter 24

1. For the effect that the Cock Lane ghost had on other ghost stories, see Clery, *Rise of Supernatural Fiction*.
2. In the 'Trial Transcript', Fanny's surname is consistently given as being Lisle, just one of a number of errors made by the court reporter.
3. Her name is given as Joyce Wetherall in the 'Trial Transcript', fo. 9, and Jane Wetherall in the 1762/3 land tax assessment (Guildhall Library). Given that the court reporter makes continual errors with names, I have gone for the latter.
4. A detailed transcript of the trial proceedings can be found in the 'Trial Transcript'.
5. *London Magazine* (February 1762), pp. 102–3; See their wills: TNA: PRO PROB 11/941 and 11/927.
6. Grant, *Cock Lane Ghost*, p. 114.
7. Kirby, *Wonderful and Eccentric Museum*, vol. 3, p. 86.
8. Kirby, *Wonderful and Eccentric Museum*, vol. 3, p. 86.
9. *London Magazine* (March and April 1763); Kirby, *Wonderful and Eccentric Museum*, vol. 3, p. 86.

Chapter 25

1. Quotation edited from *Notes and Queries*, 20 May 1899, p. 384.
2. *Notes and Queries*, 13 May 1865, p. 371; Aleph, *London Scenes*, p. 180.
3. *The Times*, 16 August 1869; 18 January 1815.

4. Most of this information came from Post Office and Robson's directories between the years 1830 and 1975. See also wills belonging to the King family (TNA: PRO PROB 11) and Grant, *Cock Lane Ghost*, p. 5.

5. On my visits to Cock Lane I have not been able to identify with certainty the Parsons' house, although there are many who claim that it is still standing.

6. Will: TNA:PRO PROB 11/941; *Gentleman's Magazine* (July 1768), p. 350; Venn and Venn, *Alumni Cantabrigienses*, vol. 3, p. 206.

7. Wills: TNA: PRO PROB 11/927 (James); TNA: PRO PROB 11/951 (Aldrich); Plomer *et al.*, *Dictionary of Printers*, p. 222 (Say); Knapp and Baldwin, *Newgate Calendar* (Dodd).

8. Sampson, *Gold Coast Men*, p. 196; Pascoe, *Two Hundred Years*, p. 256; *Transactions of the Gold Coast and Togoland*, vol. 1, pp. 153–71, 1955.

9. E. Puddy, *Litcham: The Short History of a Mid-Norfolk Village* (Norwich, Arthur Coleby, 1958), p. 147; Carthew, *Hundred of Launditch*, vol. 3, p. 266; W. Rye, *Norfolk Families* (Norwich, Goose and Sons, 1911), p. 511.

10. Church parish registers; Will: TNA: PRO PROB 11/1164 (Thomas Kent); *British Directory*, 1793.

11. J. Wallis, *London: Being a Complete Guide to the British Capital* (London, Sherwood, Neely, and Jones, 1811), entry for 'Cock Lane'.

12. *Berrow's Worcester Journal*, 20 March 1766.

13. *Gentleman's Magazine* (May 1811), p. 465.

14. For more information on the history and nature of poltergeists, see H. Carrington and N. Fodor, *Haunted People: Story of the Poltergeist down the Centuries*, London, Dutton, 1951. Interestingly, their entry for Cock Lane (p. 31) notes that it was 'never explained'.

15. For the Enfield poltergeist, see *Journal of the Society for Psychical Research*, vol. 1 (1980), pp. 538–41. For the Fox sisters, see H.G. Jackson, *The Spirit Rappers* (Garden City, NY, Doubleday, 1972).

16. Boswell, *Johnson*, p. 1296.

Epilogue

1. This passage was taken from C. Mackay, *Extraordinary Popular Delusions and the Madness of Crowds* (London, Wordsworth, 1995; originally 1841), p. 607. The idea of Frances having been poisoned after all is a neat twist, but the body seen by Archer is unlikely to have been hers as it was already badly decomposed ('putrid') by 25 February 1762 (*St James's Chronicle*, 25–27 February 1762; Ker, *The Cock Lane Ghost*, p. 24). St John the Baptist's vault was cleared of all its coffins in 1860.

BIBLIOGRAPHY

Ackroyd, P., *London: The Biography*, London, Vintage, 2001

Aleph, *London Scenes and London People*, London, City Press, 1863

Anon., *The Ladies' Dispensatory*, London, Routledge, 2002 (originally published in 1652)

Anon., *London and its Environs Described*, London, R. & J. Dodsley, 1761

Anon., *The Life, Travels, and Adventures, of Christopher Wagstaff, Gentleman, Grandfather to Tristram Shandy*. 2 vols, London, J. Hinxman, 1762

Anon., *A Descriptive Catalogue of Ancient Deeds in the Public Record Office, Series A*, London, HMSO, 1890

Bakewell, S., 'Scratching Fanny', *Fortean Times*, 150 (September 2001), 30–3

Barker, H., *Newspapers, Politics and Public Opinion in Late Eighteenth Century England*, Oxford, Oxford University Press, 1991

Bartels, F.L., 'Philip Quaque, 1741–1816', *Transactions of the Gold Coast and Togoland*, 1 (1955), 153–71

Belden, M.M., *The Dramatic Work of Samuel Foote*, Oxford, Oxford University Press, 1929

Black, J., *The English Press in the Eighteenth Century*, Aldershot, Gregg Revivals, 1991

Boswell, J., *Life of Johnson*, Oxford, Oxford University Press, 1998 (originally published in 1791)

Bristow, W., *The Genuine Account of the Life and Trial of Eugene Aram, for the Murder of Daniel Clarke*, London, W. Bristow, 1759

Carrington, H., and Fodor, N., *Haunted People: Story of the Poltergeist down the Centuries*, London, Dutton, 1951

Carthew, G.A., *The Hundred of Launditch and Deanery of Brisley, in the County of Norfolk*, Norwich, Miller & Leavins, 1877

Clery, E.J., *The Rise of Supernatural Fiction, 1762–1800*, Cambridge, Cambridge University Press, 1999

Davies, O., 'Methodism, the Clergy, and the Popular Belief in Witchcraft and Magic', *History*, 82 (1997), 252–65

Dobrée, B., *The Letters of Philip Dormer Stanhope, 4th Earl of Chesterfield*, London, Eyre & Spottiswoode, 1932

Edwards, M., *John Wesley and the Eighteenth Century*, Canterbury, Epworth Press, 1955

Elliott, C.W., *Mysteries or Glimpses of the Supernatural*, London, Harper & Brothers, 1852

Entick, J., *A New and Accurate History and Survey of London, Westminster, Southwark, and Places Adjacent*, 3 vols, London, E. and C. Dilly, 1766

Evans, J.T., *Seventeenth Century Norwich*, Oxford, Oxford University Press, 1979

Fitzgerald, P., *Samuel Foote: A Biography*, Reading, Chatto & Windus, 1910

Fitzpatrick, S.A.O., *Dublin: A Historical and Topographical Account of the City*, Dublin, Curtis Green, 1907

Foote, S., *The Orators*, London, W. Lowndes & Co., 1763

Forster, J., *The Life and Times of Oliver Goldsmith*, London, Ward Lock, 1848

Foster, J., *Alumni Oxoniensis*, Parker & Co., 1888

Goldsmith, O., *The Mystery Revealed; Containing a Series of Transactions and Authentic Testimonials, Respecting the Supposed Cock-Lane Ghost which have Hitherto been Concealed from the Public*, in *Collected Works of Oliver Goldsmith*, ed. A. Friedman, 5 vols, Oxford, Clarendon Press, 1966, vol. 4, pp. 419–41 (originally published in 1762)

Grant, D., *The Cock Lane Ghost*, London, Macmillan, 1965

Green, V.H.H., *John Wesley*, London, Nelson, 1964

Haig, R.L., *The Gazetteer: 1735–1797*, Carbondale, Ill., Southern Illinois University Press, 1960

Hennessy, G.L., *Novum Repertorium Ecclesiasticum Parochiale Londinense*, London, S. Sonnenschein, 1898

Highfill, P.H., Burnim, K.A., and Langhans, E.A., *A Biographical Dictionary of Actors, Actresses, Musicians, Dancers, Managers and other Stage Personnel in London, 1660 to 1800*, Carbondale, Ill., Southern Illinois University Press, 1973

Ireland, J., *Hogarth Illustrated*, 3 vols, London, J.E.J. Boydell, 1791, 1793, 1798

Jackson, H.G., *The Spirit Rappers*, Garden City, NY, Doubleday, 1972

Johnson, S., 'Life of Roscommon', *Gentleman's Magazine* (May 1749)

Ker, J., *The Cock Lane Ghost: Being an Authentic Account of that Extraordinary Affair*, London, J. Dean, n.d.

Kirby, R.S., *Wonderful and Eccentric Museum*, London, R.S. Kirby, 1805

Knapp, A., and Baldwin, W., *The Newgate Calendar*, London, Navarre Society, 1926 (originally published 1826)

Krysmanski, B., 'We See a Ghost: Hogarth's Satire on Methodists and Connoisseurs', *Art Bulletin* (June 1998), 292–310

Lang, A., *Cock Lane and Common Sense*, London, Longmans, Green & Co., 1896

Leigh, S., *New Picture of London*, London, W. Clowes, 1819

Lloyd, D., *Lloyd Letters (1754–1796)*, ed. G.E. Evans, London, William Jones, 1908

Mackay, C., *Extraordinary Popular Delusions and the Madness of Crowds*, London, Wordsworth, 1995 (originally published in 1841)

Maitland, W., *The History of London*, London, W. Maitland, 1756

Matthew, H.C.G., and Harrison, B., *Oxford Dictionary of National Biography*, Oxford, Oxford University Press, 2004

Moxon, J., *The Most Agreeable Companion*, London, J. Moxon, 1782

Naylor, M.J., *The Inanity and Mischief of Vulgar Superstitions*, Cambridge, M.J. Naylor, 1795

Nichol, D.W., *Pope's Literary Legacy*, Oxford, Oxford University Press, 1992

Parkin, C., *An Essay towards a Topographical History of the County of Norfolk*, Norwich, William Miller, 1809

Pascoe, C.F., *Two Hundred Years of the SPG*, London, Society for the Propagation of the Gospel, 1901

Pennant, T., *London, or, An Abridgement of the Celebrated M. Pennant's Description of the British Capital*, London, John Wallis, 1790

Pepys, S., *The Diary of Samuel Pepys*, ed. H.B. Wheatley, London, George Bell, 1893

Pickersgill, R., *Mirth's Magazine*, London, R. Pickersgill, 1785

Plomer, H.R., *et al., A Dictionary of Printers and Booksellers who were at Work in England, Scotland and Ireland from 1726 to 1775*, Oxford, Oxford University Press, 1932

Porter, R., *Patients and Practitioners*, Cambridge, Cambridge University Press, 1985

Porter, R., *English Society in the Eighteenth Century*, London, Penguin, 1990

Puddy, E., *Litcham: The Short History of a Mid-Norfolk Village*, Norwich, Arthur Coleby, 1958

Pyle, H., 'The Cock Lane Ghost', *Harper's New Monthly Magazine* (August 1893)

Rye, W., *Norfolk Families*, Norwich, Goose & Sons, 1911

Sadler, T., *Diary, Reminiscences, and Correspondence of Henry Crabb Robinson*, London, Macmillan & Co., 1869

Sala, G.A., *London Up to Date*, London, A.C. Black, 1895

Sampson, M.J., *Gold Coast Men of Affairs*, London, Dawsons, 1969

Seymour, R., *A Survey of London*, London, Robert Seymour, 1733 (an updated version of Stowe, 1633)

Smellie, W., *A Treatise on the Theory and Practice of Midwifery*, London, D. Wilson & T. Durham, 1752

Smith, E., *The Compleat Housewife*, London, Studio, 1994 (originally published in 1758)

Smith, J.T., *Nollekens and his Times*, London, Turnstile Press, 1949

Stone, L., *Family, Sex and Marriage in England: 1500–1800*, London, Weidenfeld & Nicolson, 1977

Stowe, J., *A Survey of the Cities of London and Westminster*, London, John Stowe, 1633

Thompson, E.P., 'The Moral Economy of the English Crowd in the Eighteenth Century', *Past and Present*, 50 (1971), 76–136

Thompson, T., *An Account of Two Missionary Voyages*, London, SPCK, 1937

Tomkins, S., *John Wesley: A Biography*, London, Lion Publishing, 2003

Venn, J., and Venn J.A., *Alumni Cantabrigienses: A Biographical List of All Known Students, Graduates and Holders of Office at the University of Cambridge*, Cambridge, Cambridge University Press, 1922–54

Wallis, J., *London: Being a Complete Guide to the British Capital*, London, Sherwood, Neely, & Jones, 1811

Walpole, H., *Memoirs of the Reign of King George the Third*, London, Lawrence & Bullen, 1894

Walpole, H., *Correspondence*, ed. W.S. Lewis, New Haven, Yale University Press, 1937–83

Walvin, J., *Black and White: The Negro and English Society, 1555–1945*, London, Allen Lane, 1973

Wearmouth, R.F., *Methodism and the Common People of the Eighteenth Century*, Canterbury, Epworth Press, 1945

Wright, D., *The Epworth Phenomena*, London, W. Rider & Sons, 1917

Young, M., 'Murder, Most Foul', *Family Tree* (July 1987)

INDEX